IMAGES
of America

GREENWOOD

ON THE COVER: BIRD'S-EYE VIEW OF GREENWOOD. This photograph offers an aerial view of Greenwood, South Carolina, as the city appeared in 1910. The Union Passenger Depot is central to the city, and offers a location for all of its cultural events. This is evident from the throngs of people and parade floats participating in one of the many annual parades held in Greenwood in the early 1900s. Due to a constant stream of railroad traffic, businesses grew in the Uptown region, and Greenwood boasted the widest Main Street in the world, stretching 316 feet across. The first railroad line came to Greenwood in 1852, and by 1914, four companies, Seaboard Air Line Railway, Southern Railway, Atlantic Coast Line Railway, and Piedmont & Northern Electric Railway ran through Uptown Greenwood. By 1930, Greenwood had more railroad lines running through the city than any other city in South Carolina.

IMAGES
of America

GREENWOOD

Stacey Thompson and Bethany Wade
The Museum and Railroad Historical Center

ARCADIA
PUBLISHING

ISBN 978-1-4671-1292-5

Published by Arcadia Publishing
Charleston, South Carolina

Printed in the United States of America

Library of Congress Control Number: 2014938371

For all general information, please contact Arcadia Publishing:
Telephone 843-853-2070
Fax 843-853-0044
E-mail sales@arcadiapublishing.com
For customer service and orders:
Toll-Free 1-888-313-2665

Visit us on the Internet at www.arcadiapublishing.com

This book is dedicated, with much gratitude, to those who believe in saving, sharing, and celebrating Greenwood's history.

Contents

Acknowledgments

This project would not have been possible without the support of the following individuals and organizations: the Museum and Railroad Historical Center board of directors, the City of Greenwood, Greenwood County, the Self Family Foundation, the Greenwood Community Foundation, the Greenwood Woman's Club, the Arts Center, the Greenwood Community Theatre, Lander University, and the Greenwood County Library System.

We would like to express our sincerest thanks to the individuals and organizations that provided photographs for this project. Unless otherwise noted, all photographs came from the Museum and Railroad Historical Center archives. Also, to those who responded to our e-mails, phone calls, and visits requesting information on Greenwood's history, we could not have completed this book without you. We would like to thank Ann Bowen, author of *Greenwood County: A History*, and the family of Jimmy Wade, author of *Greenwood County and Its Railroads: 1852–1992*. Additionally, we would like to thank Dessa Wideman, author of the Museum and Railroad Historical Center's online exhibit found at www.greenwoodhistoryproject.org. These sources, published by the museum over the past two decades, have proven to be invaluable in telling the story of Greenwood.

Lastly, we would like to honor Bill Cervenka, Betty Warner, and Jack Graves, whose tireless support of the Museum and Railroad Historical Center and their willingness to act as both sources and historical investigators allowed this book to be completed.

INTRODUCTION

What defines a community? This is the question that we at the Museum and Railroad Historical Center began to ask ourselves when presented with this book project. Certain things contribute to the growth of a community, including businesses and industry, education, community services, and cultural activities. However, from our reading and research, we have come to understand that true community goes so much deeper. It is found not in profits or production, not in maps or merchants, but in the spirit of a people and their stories.

As a nonprofit history museum, the Museum and Railroad Historical Center is a keeper of our community's stories. We are dedicated to "saving, sharing, and celebrating Greenwood's History" through our educational exhibits, programs, and now this book. Oh what stories we found while reading, researching, and compiling photographs! Some of them were familiar to us, with names and businesses already well known to many members of the community. Others were a surprise, an exciting (and sometimes shocking) look back into our past. Through it all, we became better connected to Greenwood, tracking the growth of its industries, learning about the character of its people, and studying its development.

Greenwood began as a summer home for a young couple named John McGehee and Charlotte Dozier McGehee. Natives of the community of Cambridge (now Ninety-Six), they established a lovely home on 600 acres, which Charlotte named "Green Wood," after its lush surroundings. Soon, a village sprung up around this plantation, and the name came to apply not only to the McGehee homestead, but to the town as well. When the first railroad line came through in 1852, the center of Greenwood shifted. Businesses moved to be more accessible to this modern form of transportation, forming a downtown area in the process. In fact, trains, and later textiles, were responsible for transforming Greenwood from a rural village into a bustling town. From this point on, Greenwood continued to grow, with the first mill opening in 1890 and Greenwood's county status finalized in 1897. Businesses run by the likes of Beaudrot, Aldrich, Rosenberg, Durst, and others flourished. People began to move to Greenwood from other cities, drawn by the opportunities for wealth and advancement here.

As a county, Greenwood boasted not only railroads, mills, and numerous businesses, but also great educational and cultural opportunities. There was a distinct emphasis placed on education in this area. Radical educators and progressive denominations founded schools for all children, regardless of race or gender. Furthermore, Greenwood advocated cultural experiences such as fairs, parades, and theaters. Within the mill communities, recreational activities such as Textile League baseball flourished. Despite all of these opportunities, Greenwood still faced many challenges. Wars took away members of its population. The Great Depression hit businesses hard, and natural disasters and accidents forever changed the community. With each challenge, however, Greenwood showed itself to be a community capable of overcoming.

The information mentioned above is captured in better detail in the pages that follow. However, this book is not an all-inclusive history of Greenwood. It is practically impossible to give the entire history of our community in 200 pictures and 18,000 words. We were bound by several limitations in this project. First, the lack of original photographs presented some difficulties. Many stories that we would have loved to have included simply had no photograph to go along with them, or the original was not accessible to us. Secondly, we had a limited amount of time to research and write the text. We could not investigate every business that existed in Greenwood or every school that ever served the students of its county. Lastly, we tried our best to make sure all of Greenwood's citizens were represented in this book. Before integration, Greenwoodians, like many other populations, lived separate lives. Photographs and information about African Americans in Greenwood in the early 1900s were more difficult to obtain. Segregation was a very real part of both our nation and our community, and we believed that it was important to approach this topic with honesty and intention. With the exception of businesses, we were able to tell several stories about the experience of African Americans in Greenwood before integration.

Even with these difficulties, we are still so very thankful for this project. Through research, we have come to understand more about the community the Museum and Railroad Historical Center serves. We feel more connected to the spirit of Greenwood and to the people who have gone before us, paving the way. From the very beginning, Greenwood has been a place of opportunity and a place filled with an overcoming spirit. Individuals, businesses, and organizations strived to create a better life for themselves and their neighbors. No matter the obstacles, no matter the risk, they believed in the future of Greenwood. The contents of this book are a testament to their hard work and unwavering belief. However, we do not pretend to be perfect historians. We tried our best to provide an interesting and correct account of some of the people, places, and events upon which Greenwood was built. We apologize in advance for any mistakes or exclusions.

We hope you enjoy reading this book as much as we enjoyed writing it! Flip through the pages. Enjoy the photographs. Read the captions, and allow yourself to be connected to the Greenwoodians who have gone before you. They were not so different from you. They may have dressed differently and experienced a world vastly different from the one around us, but we are connected to them by our humanity with its kindred emotions, struggles, and dreams.

We hope that by reading this book you will learn a little bit more about the community in which you live, and by learning about it, you will also learn a little bit about yourself.

One

Early Businesses

Businesses were transforming tools for the small, rural community of Greenwood. But more than the businesses themselves, it was the entrepreneurial spirit of the citizens who risked it all to set up fledgling enterprises in this community. Some were natives who had lived in this area their whole lives, and some were travelers, just passing through, who chose to make Greenwood their home. Both groups shared a deep belief in Greenwood's future. They saw so clearly the community that it could become and took steps to creatively bring this vision to pass. Present-day Greenwoodians have businesses such as C.L. Beaudrot & Son (1879), the Rosenberg Clothing & Shoe Company (1884), the Bank of Greenwood (1888), and many others to thank for this area's early economic and cultural growth. Due to their tireless efforts, Greenwoodians can both look back with pride at the early businesses and look forward with hope toward an even brighter future.

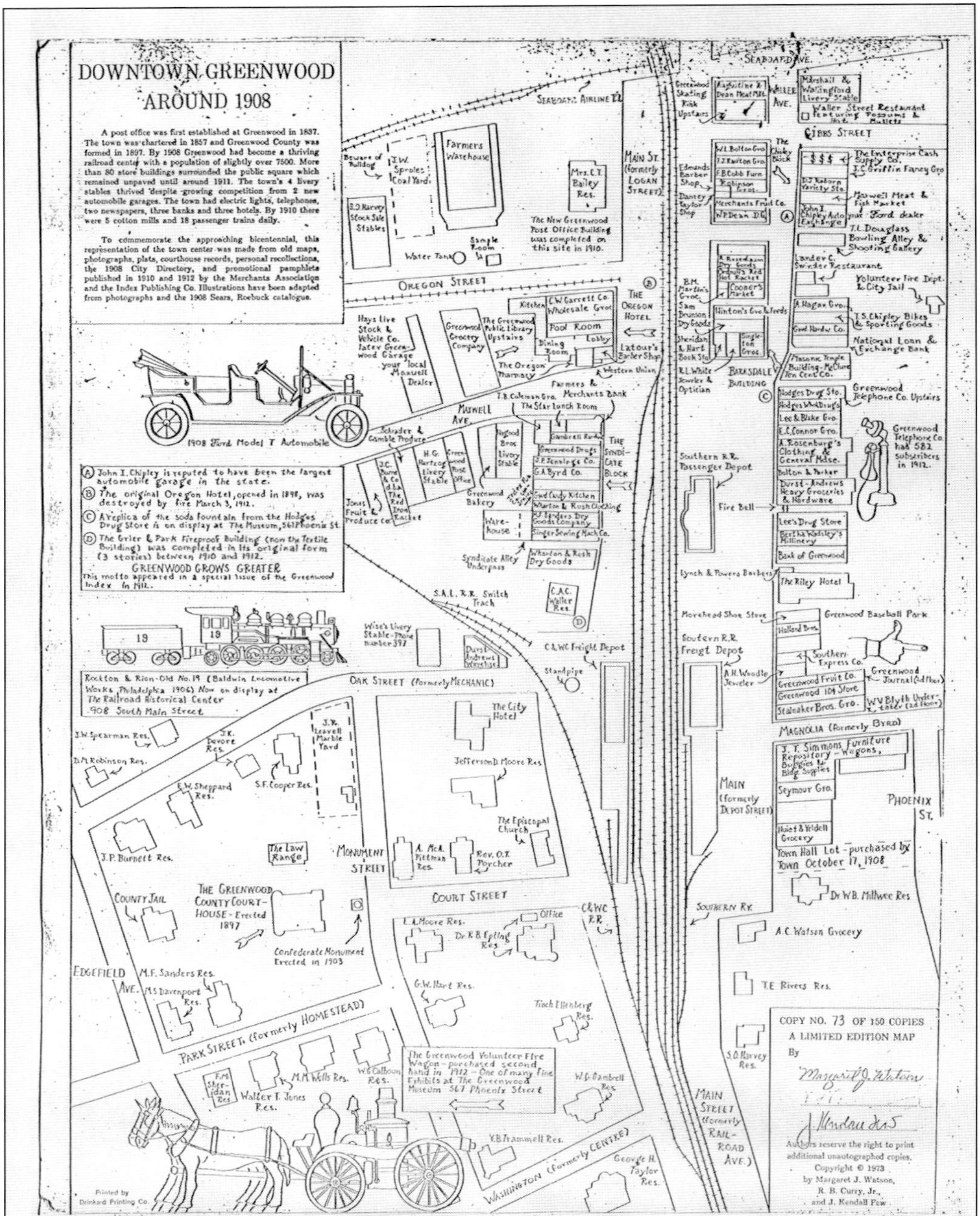

Map of Downtown Greenwood. Now referred to as Greenwood's Uptown, the area on this map shows the businesses that existed on and around Greenwood's Main Street in 1908. Many of these buildings are still in use today. This map was created by Boykin Curry, Margaret Watson, and Kendall Few.

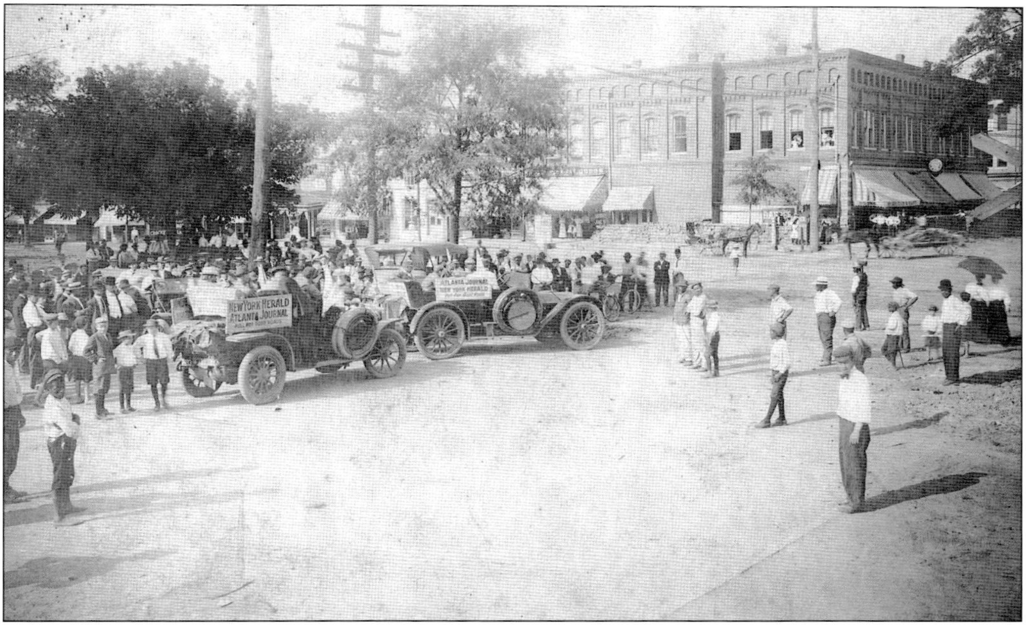

SHERIDAN AND HART BOOKSTORE. Originally started as a textbook and school supply depository by the Greenwood school superintendent F.M. Sheridan, this store eventually moved from the Syndicate Block to the southwest corner of the Barksdale Building. In 1919, around the time that this photograph was taken, Gus and Foster McCaslan took over the business. By 1931, the name of the business had changed to McCaslan's Bookstore, and it had moved to its current location.

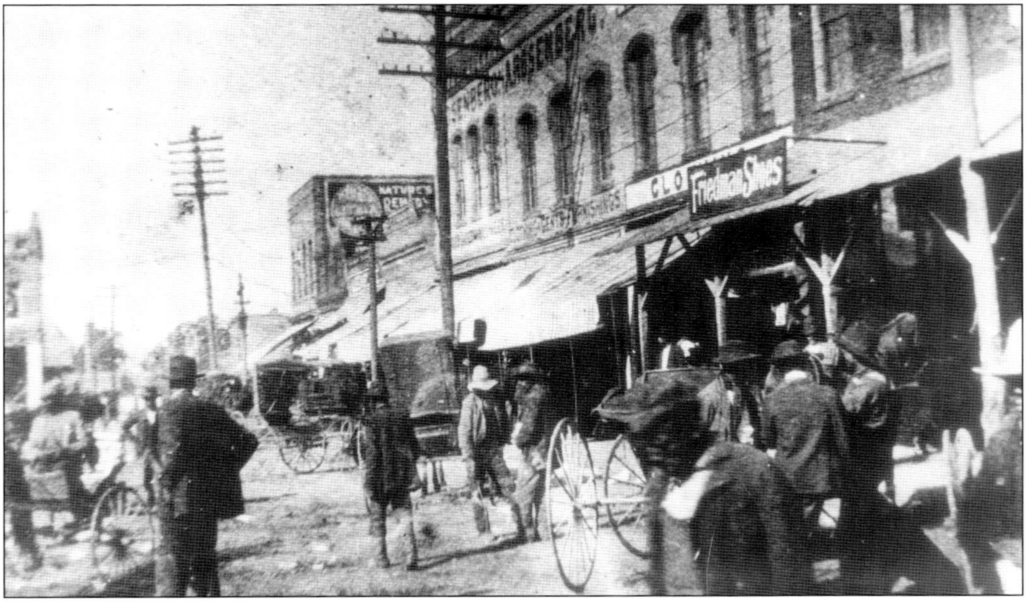

WALLER AVENUE. Waller Avenue was a bustling section of Greenwood during the early 1900s. This street is named after one of Greenwood's most famous citizens, C.A.C. Waller. It seems like there was not an area of Greenwood life that Waller was not involved in. Public servant, advocate for education, and merchant, Waller was also a forward thinker. When the square was being established, he convinced other business owners to build businesses facing the railroad tracks, which, ultimately, set into motion the growth of Greenwood's Uptown.

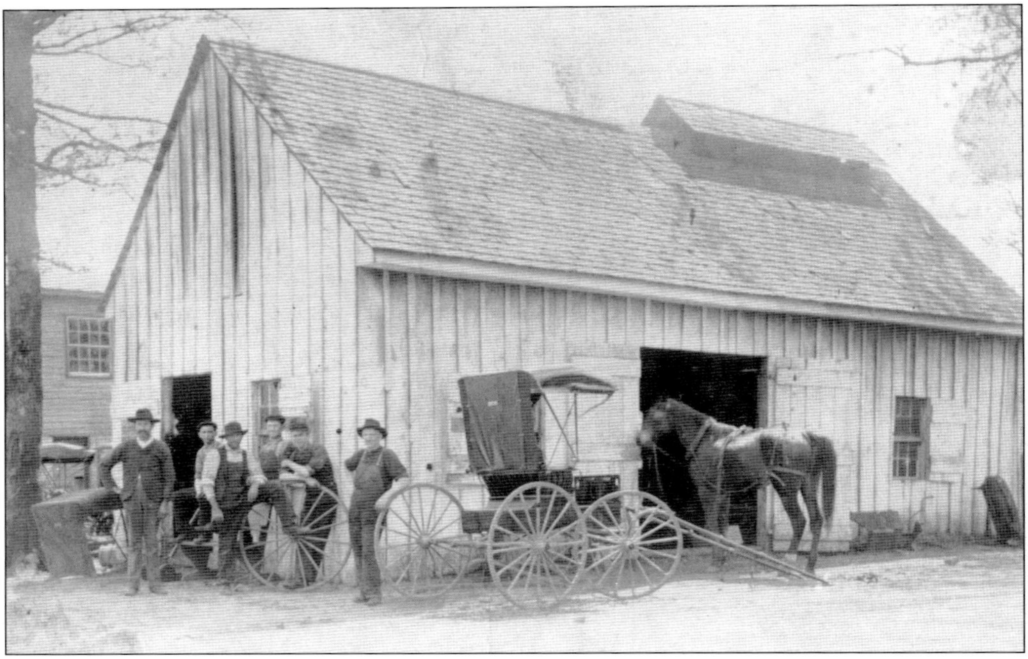

C.L. Beaudrot & Son, Blacksmith. After working as a smithy in Charleston during the Civil War, Charles Louis Beaudrot opened up his own shop in Greenwood in 1879. Considered to be the oldest continually operated business in Greenwood, it repeatedly adapted with the changing times, serving the Greenwood community in various forms of metalwork until the 1990s, when it closed after over 100 years of business. (Courtesy of the Greenwood County Library System.)

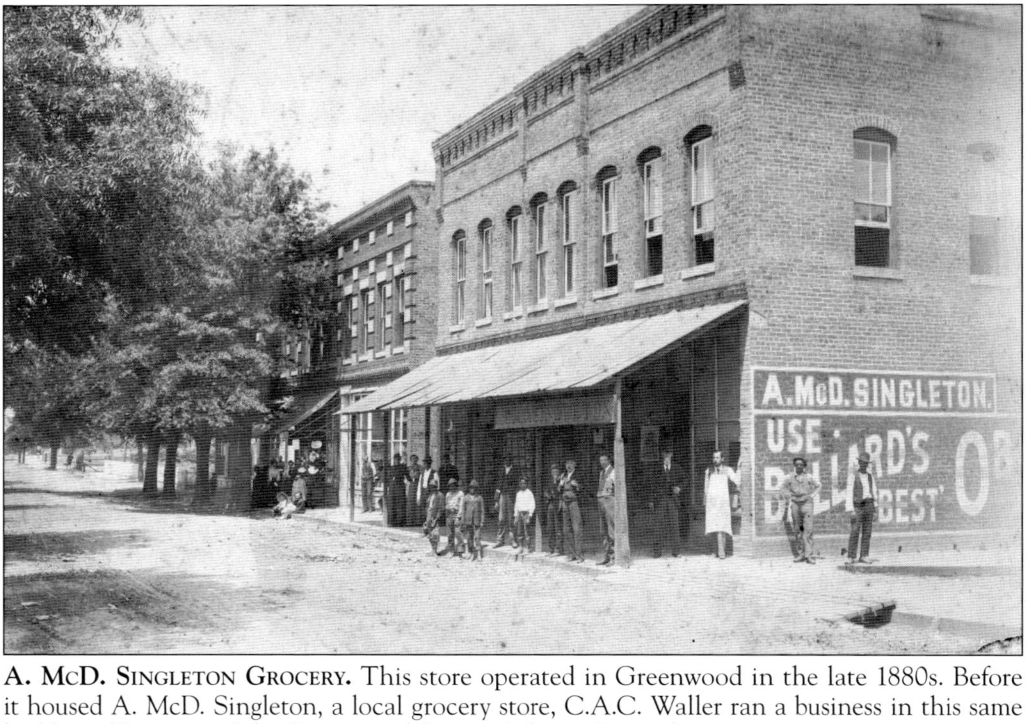

A. McD. Singleton Grocery. This store operated in Greenwood in the late 1880s. Before it housed A. McD. Singleton, a local grocery store, C.A.C. Waller ran a business in this same building. (Courtesy of the Greenwood County Library System.)

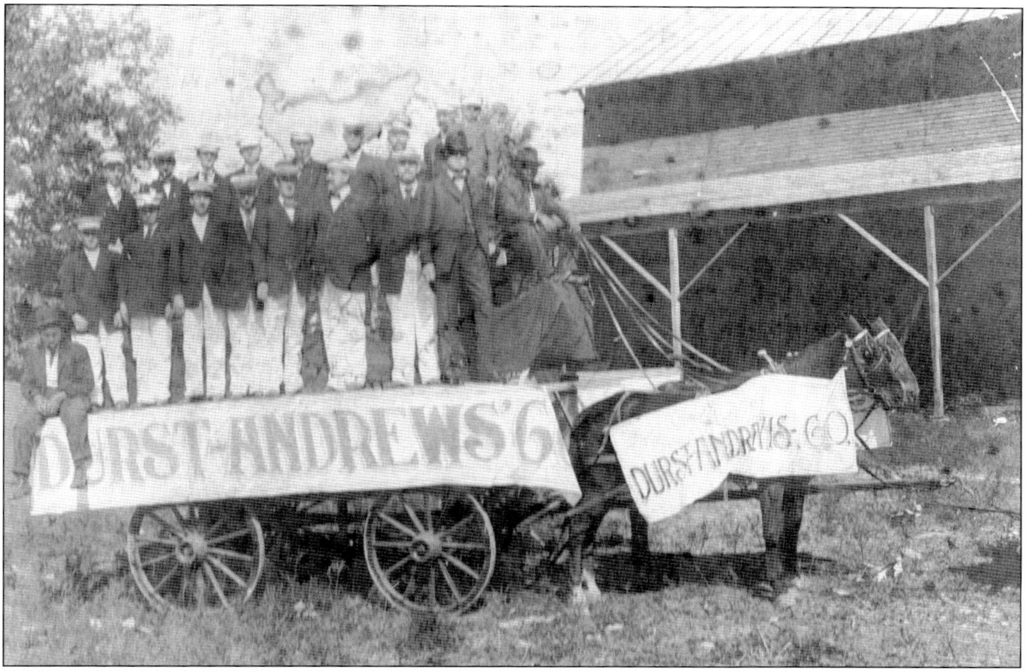

DURST-ANDREWS COMPANY. Established in Greenwood as early as the 1880s, this business was founded by John Kemp Durst. In the early 1900s, the store was considered a "heavy grocery," meaning that people could buy items in bulk. However, in 1914, The Durst-Andrews Company transitioned from selling to individuals to selling to local retail stores. They became a middleman of sorts, purchasing goods directly from manufacturers and selling it wholesale.

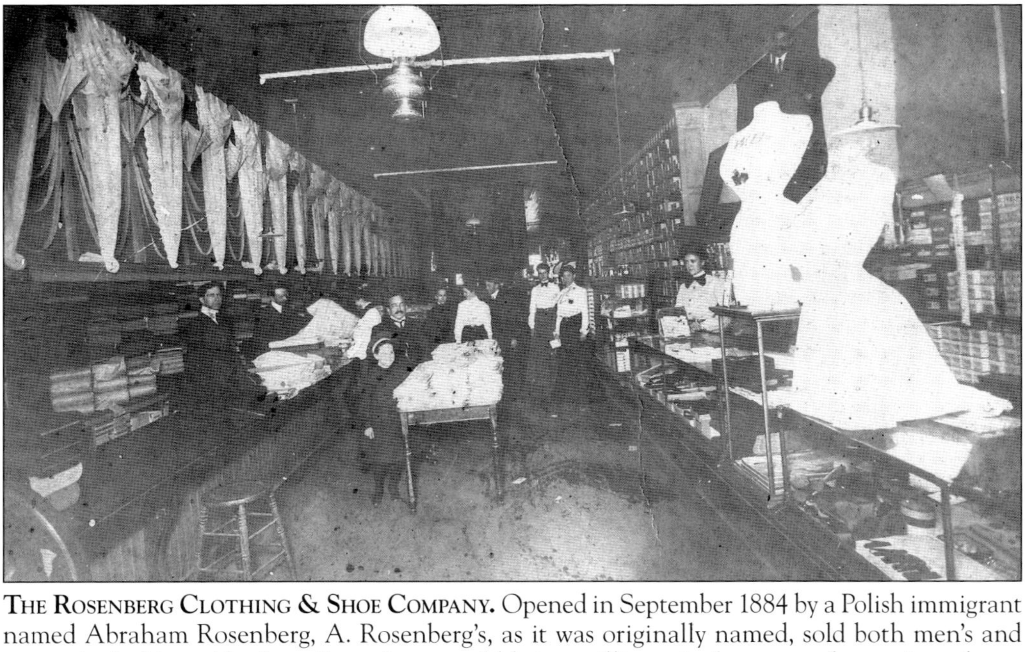

THE ROSENBERG CLOTHING & SHOE COMPANY. Opened in September 1884 by a Polish immigrant named Abraham Rosenberg, A. Rosenberg's, as it was originally named, sold both men's and women's clothing. Abraham Rosenberg would bring milliners in from out of town in order to keep Greenwood's ladies in the latest style of hats. Abraham Rosenberg was a pioneer in many ways, including being the first businessman in Greenwood to employ women.

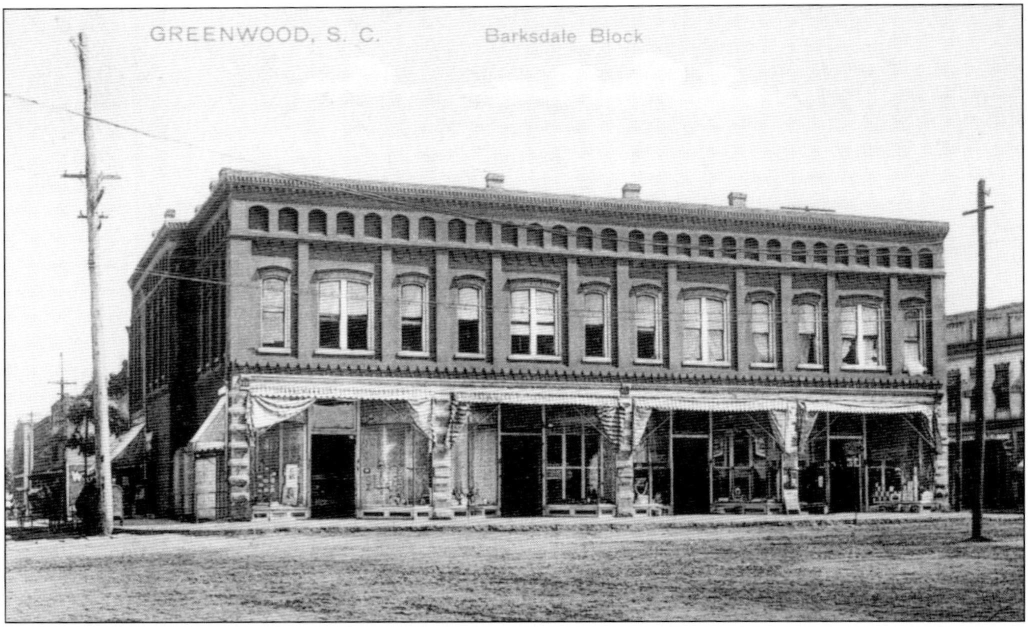

The Barksdale Block. Originally a wooden building, after 1852, the Barksdale Building was rebuilt in brick and named the Bailey-Barksdale Company. One of the first three stores to call the Barksdale Building home was Sheridan & Hart, the forerunner of McCaslan's Bookstore.

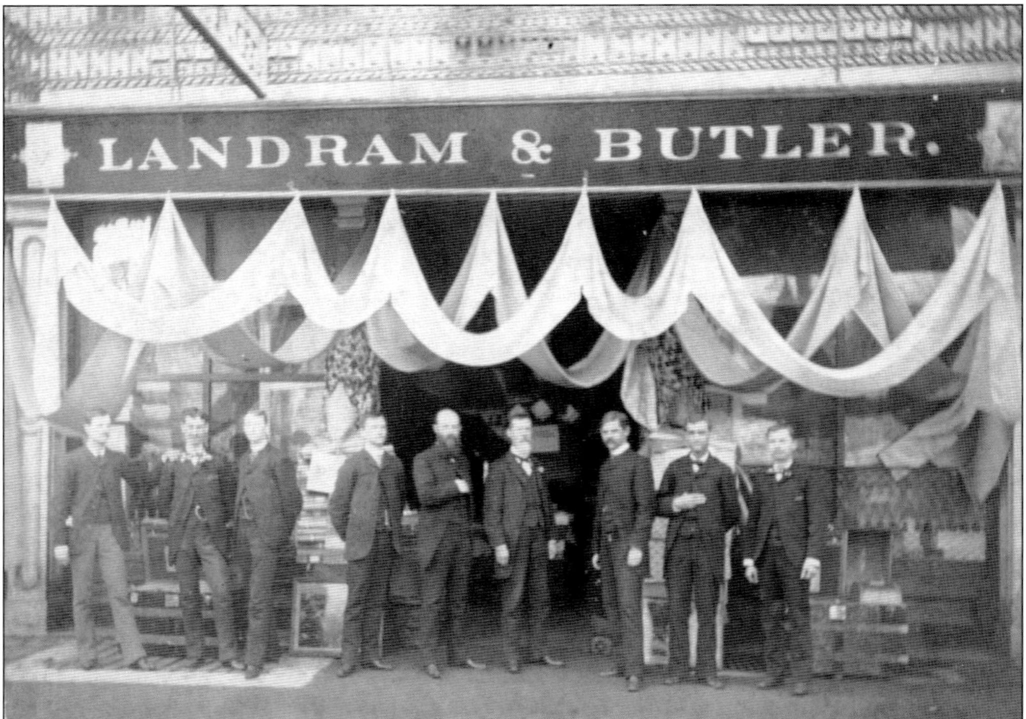

Economic Boom. Greenwood became an economic center in the early 1900s when train travel and the textile industry came together to offer a welcoming and prosperous city center. Pictured is the Landram & Butler store at the turn of the 20th century.

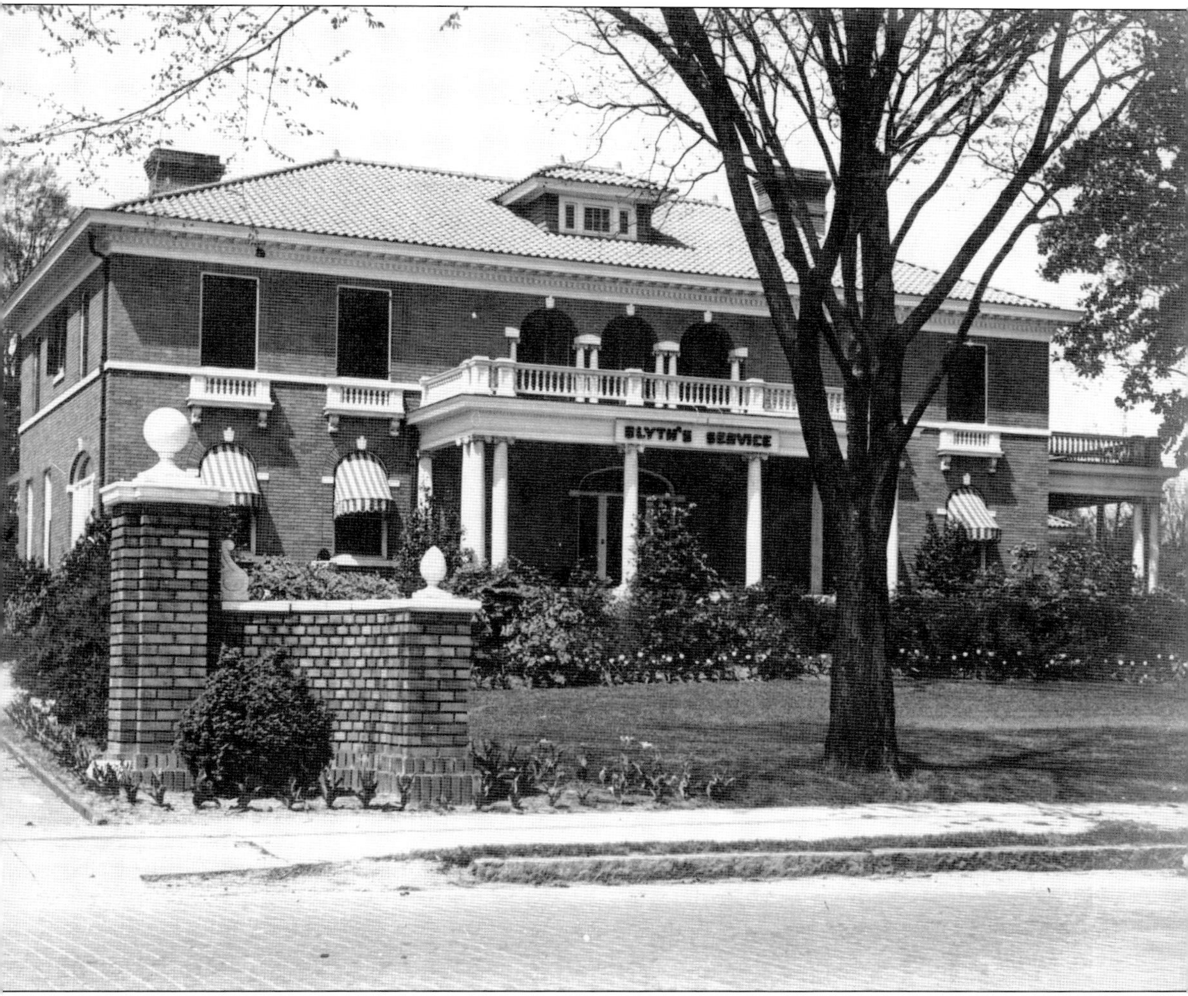

Blyth Funeral Home. Considered to be among Greenwood's oldest businesses, this funeral home was originally known as W.V. Blyth, Undertaker, established in 1884 by William V. Blyth, a Scottish immigrant. Originally a coffin, buggy, and cabinetmaking business, this business was housed at several different locations in Greenwood. W.V. Blyth became known as the first undertaker to use embalming methods in South Carolina. The business is depicted in its second location on Main Street, before it settled on Montague Avenue.

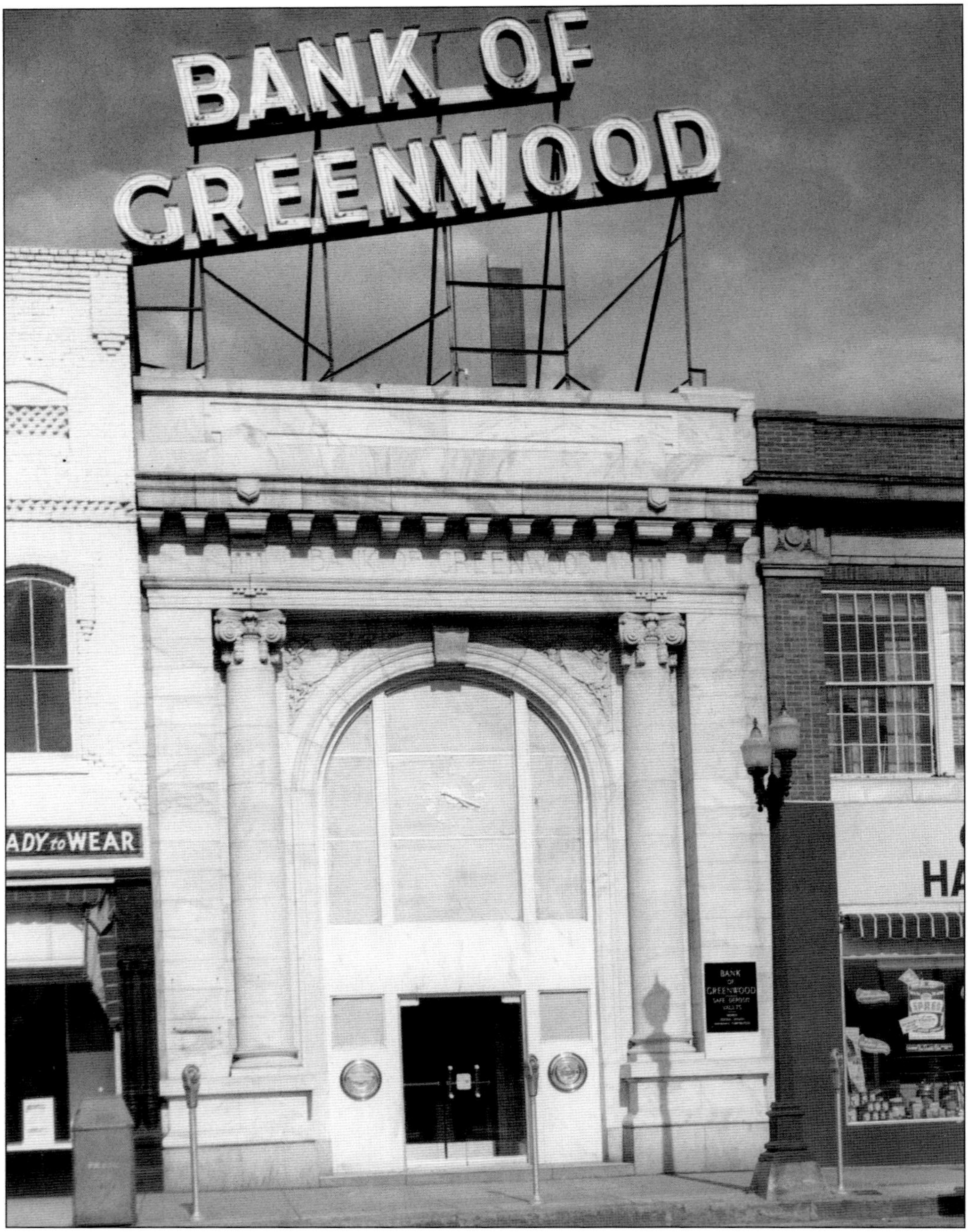

Bank of Greenwood. This Greenwood establishment opened in 1888 and was actually located in the Durst-Andrews Company heavy grocery for the first year. Under its first president, J.K. Durst, the bank started with a capital stock of only $40,000, but soon grew and moved twice before settling in its final location on Main Street in 1905. (Courtesy of Lander University.)

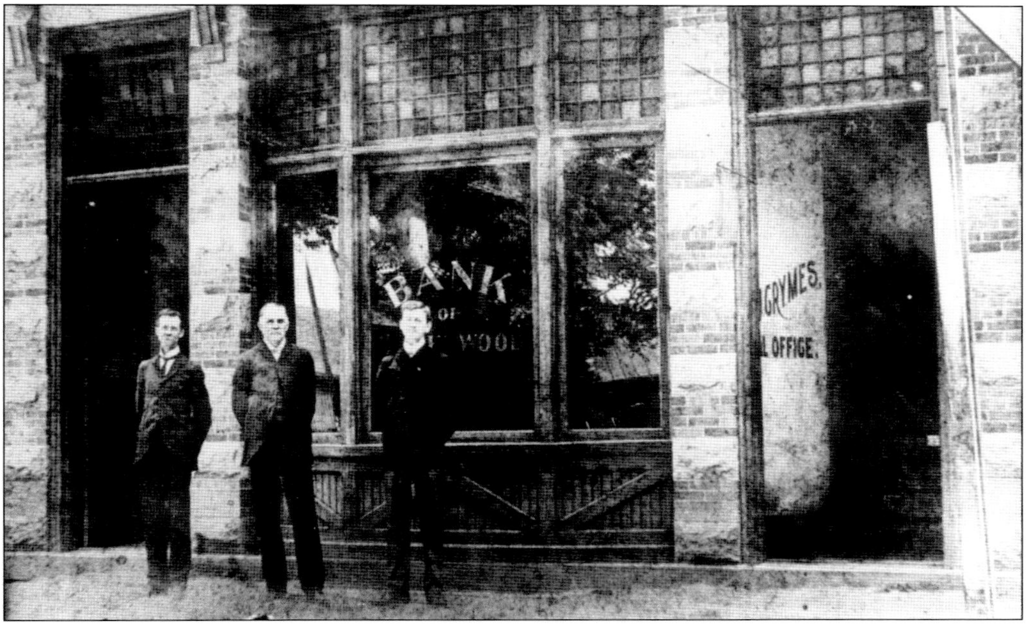

BANK OF GREENWOOD ADMINISTRATION. From left to right, J.T. Medlock, J.K. Durst, and J.C. Self Sr. are pictured in front of the Bank of Greenwood's first building. This early photograph depicts the bank prior to 1905 and shows the young J.C. Self Sr. as a cashier. In less than three years, Self would become the president of Greenwood Cotton Mill in place of the deceased W.L. Durst, brother of the bank's president.

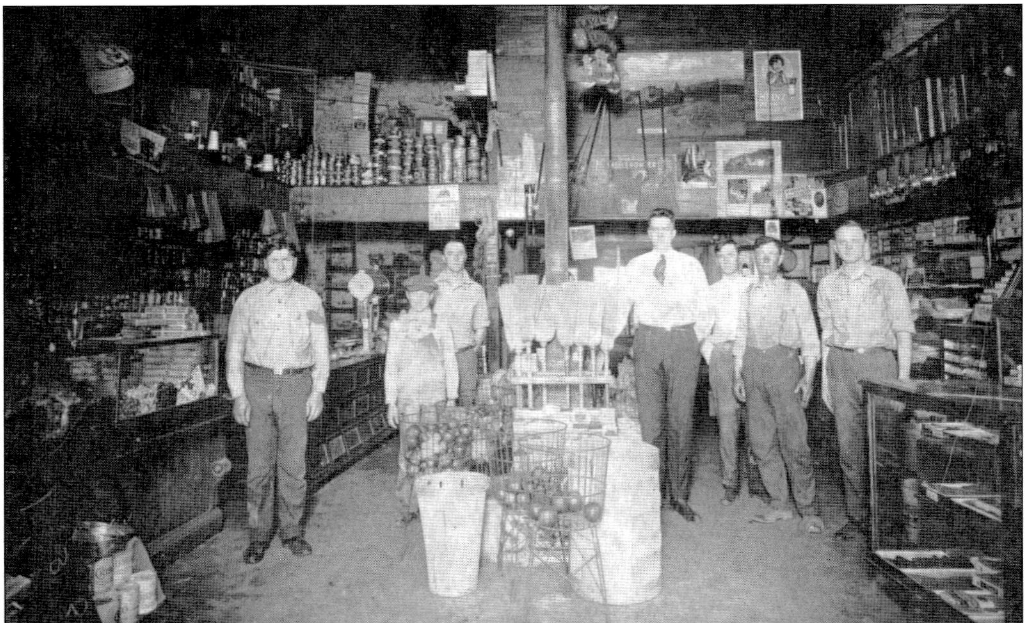

COURSEY BROTHERS GENERAL STORE. In the early 1900s, general stores were a standard sight in towns across the United States. Greenwood was no exception. General stores were known for carrying "general" merchandise, meaning a variety of products. Whatever items were not on site could be ordered by the store for a specific patron. (Courtesy of Betty Warner.)

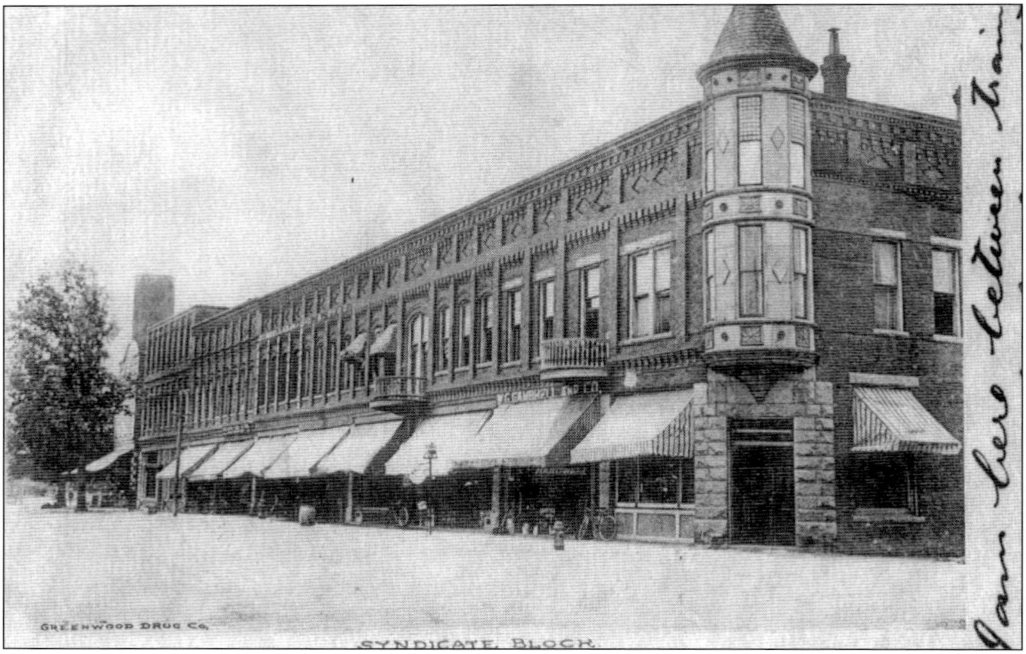

GAMBRELL HARDWARE. Located in the Syndicate Block, Gambrell Hardware was one of the first employers of James C. Self, the future textile giant. He worked as a clerk and bookkeeper for the local business until 1899. By 1920, Gambrell Hardware was considered by *The Southern Hardware and Implement Journal* to be one of the largest hardware stores in the region.

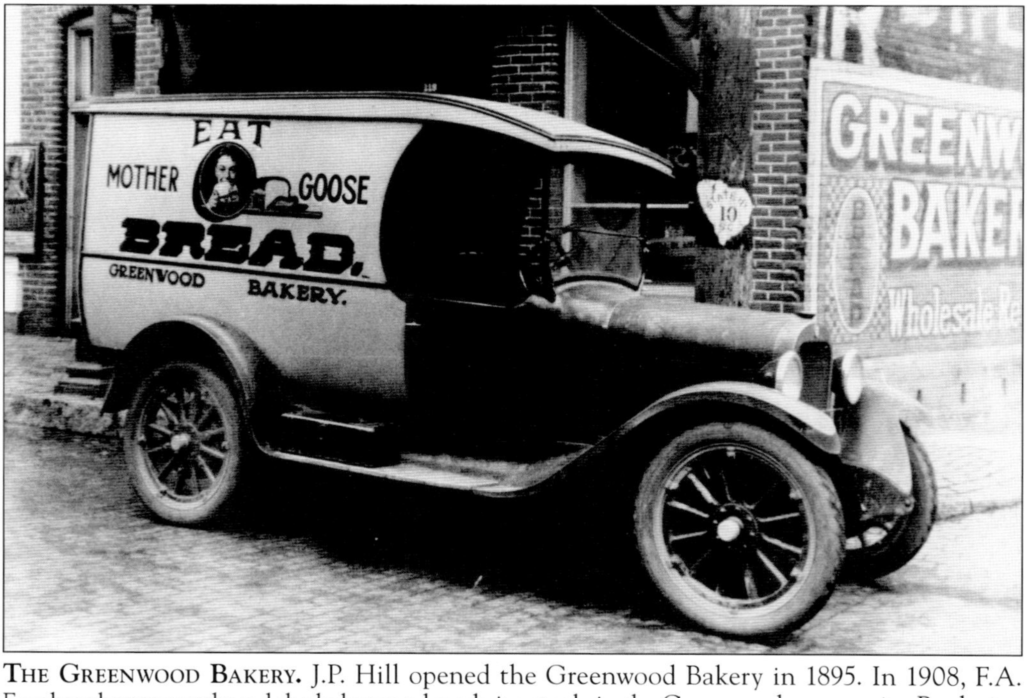

THE GREENWOOD BAKERY. J.P. Hill opened the Greenwood Bakery in 1895. In 1908, F.A. Feuchtenberger purchased the bakery and made it a staple in the Greenwood community. Producing delicious pastries and even using a delivery truck to take bread and other baked goods to local homes, the Greenwood Bakery was producing 10,000 loaves of bread each day in 1912.

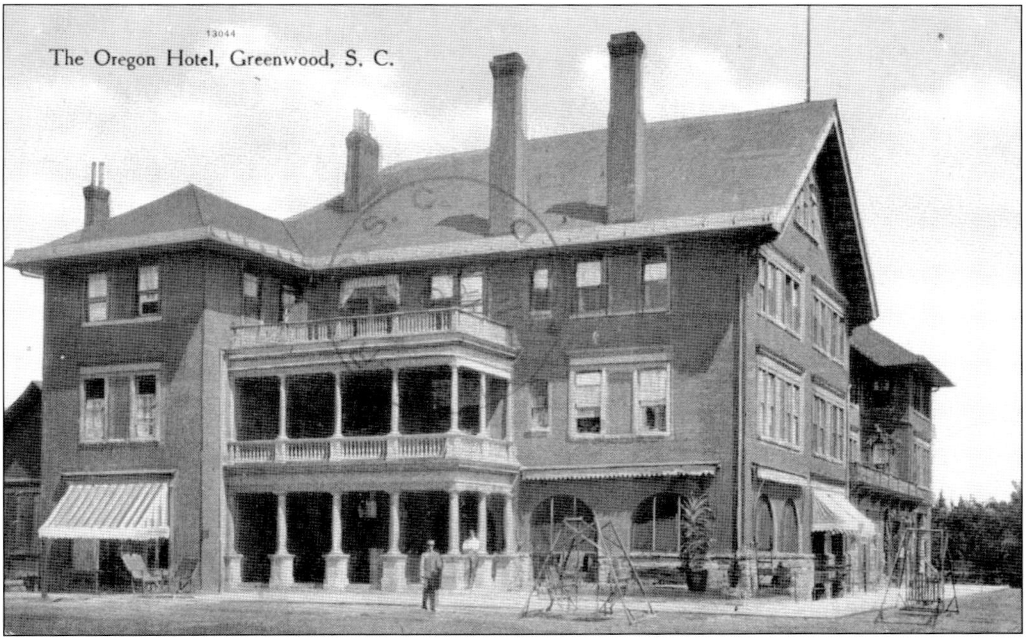

The Oregon Hotel. Named after a famous Spanish-American War battleship, the Oregon Hotel was built in 1898. It was the premiere hotel in the state, and Greenwood's claim to fame in the 1900s. Businessmen passing through Greenwood via train would often stay at this downtown establishment. Soon, the Oregon became more than just a stopover. This hotel housed conventions and became a gathering place for the socialites of Greenwood. In 1912, the Old Oregon Hotel burned to the ground but was replaced by a new, updated building in 1914, pictured below.

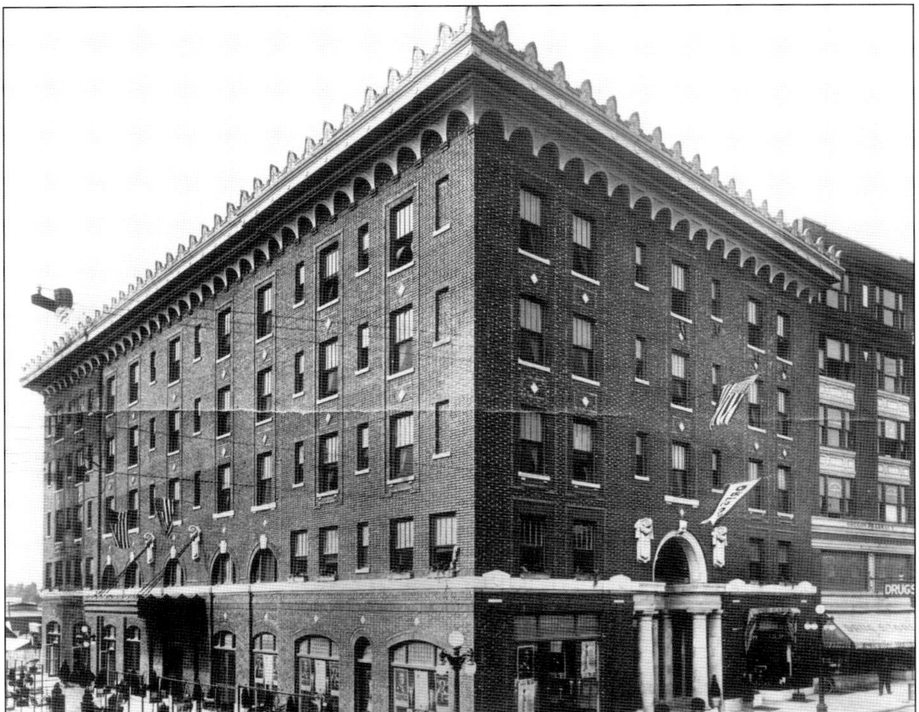

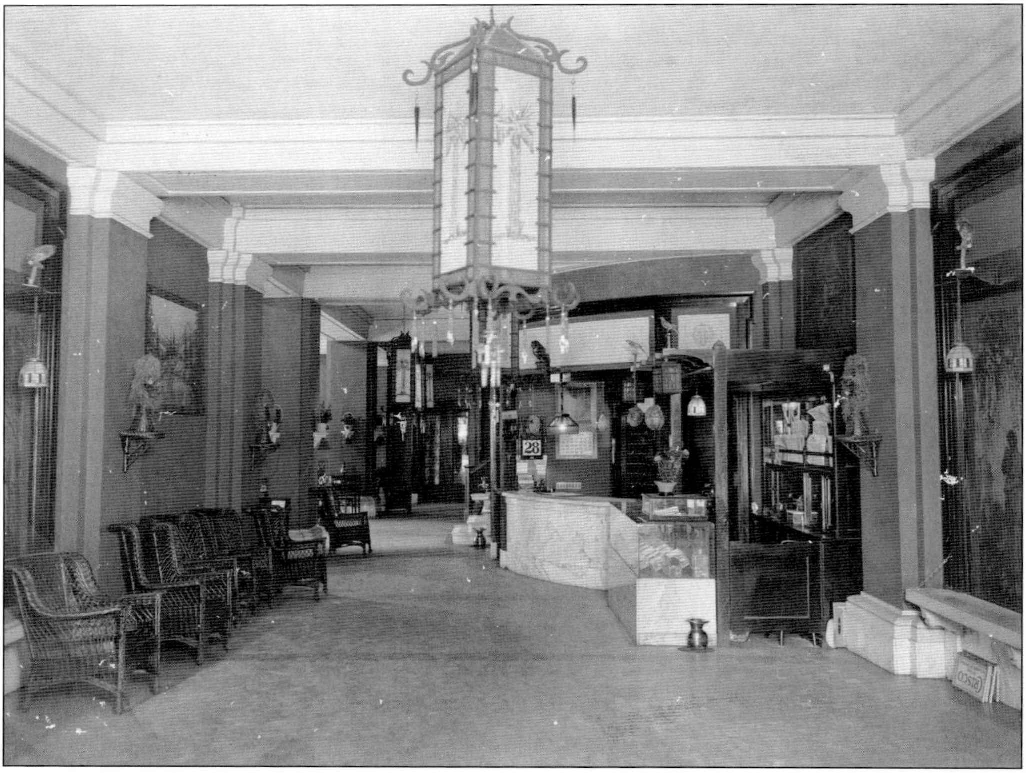

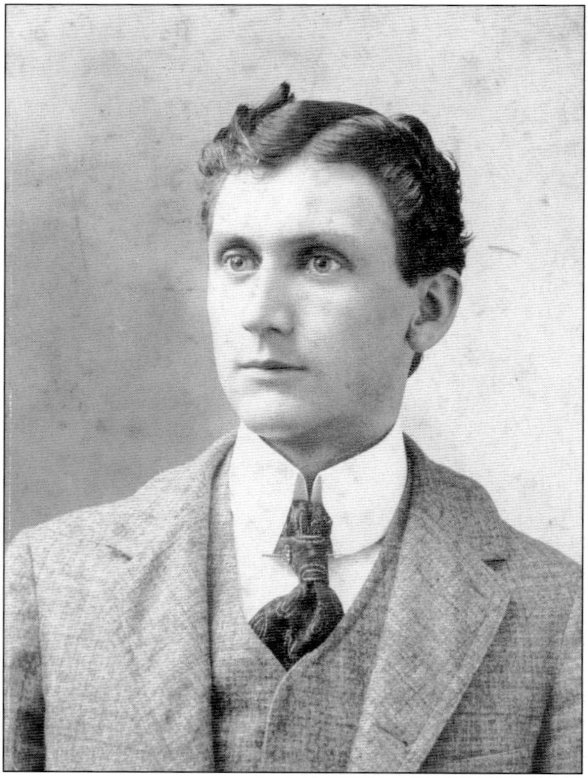

Lobby of the Oregon Hotel. At its peak, the Oregon Hotel contained its own pharmacy, grocery store, barbershop, library, and restaurant. This high-class establishment served European-inspired dishes such as *croquettes de dindon petit pois verts* and *tenderloin de boeuf aux champignons*. The china was all emblazoned with images of the battleship *Oregon*. In this photograph, one can see the splendor of the old Oregon Hotel lobby.

The Red Iron Racket. James C. Burns Sr. and his brother Lee opened the original Red Iron Racket store in 1897 in Laurens, South Carolina. Arriving in 1902, the Red Iron Racket in Greenwood operated for more than 30 years and is one of the earliest examples of a chain store. The brothers opened branches in Spartanburg, Greenville, Greer, Anderson, and Charlotte. James C. Burns is pictured soon after opening the Red Iron Racket.

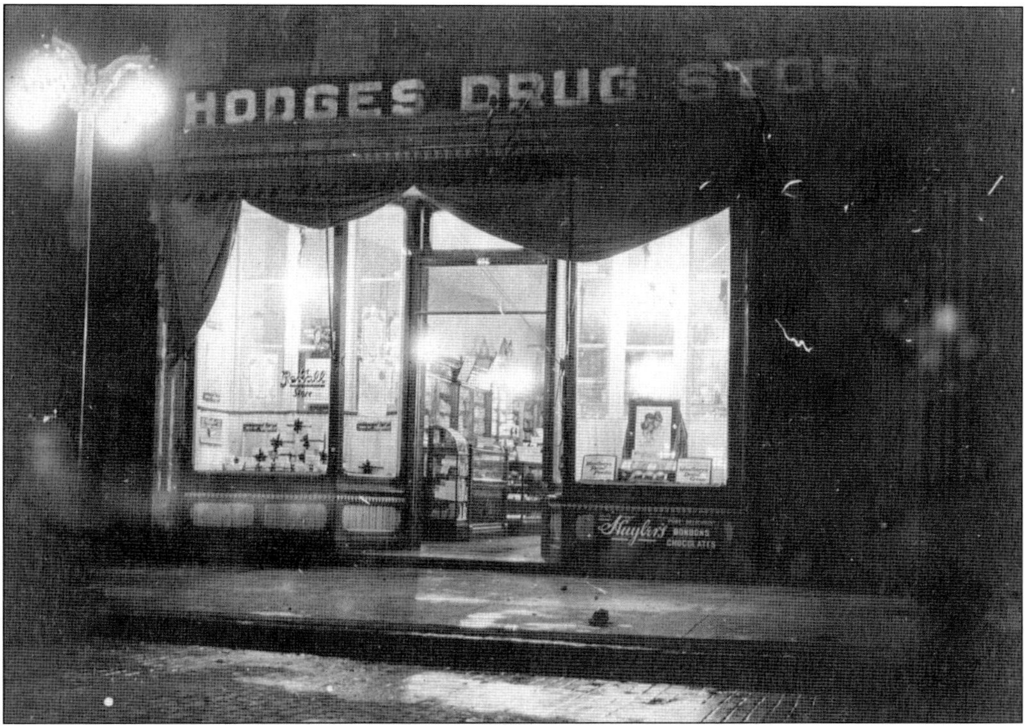

HODGES DRUGSTORE. Dr. Sam Hodges worked at his uncle's pharmacy from the age of 12. After passing his pharmaceutical examination and working as a partner in the store, he bought out his uncle's interests and opened Hodges Drugstore in 1904. His father and two brothers worked with him in this family business, which operated in Greenwood for over 50 years.

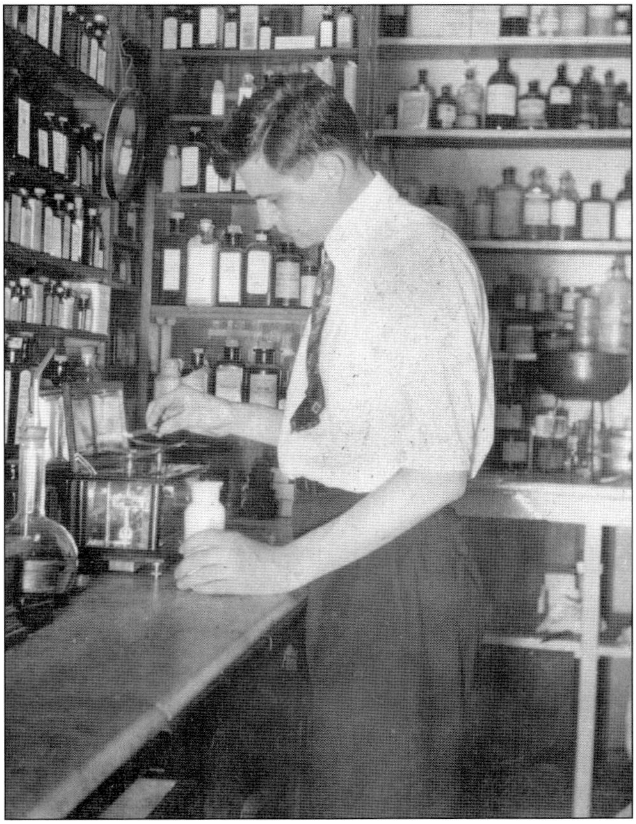

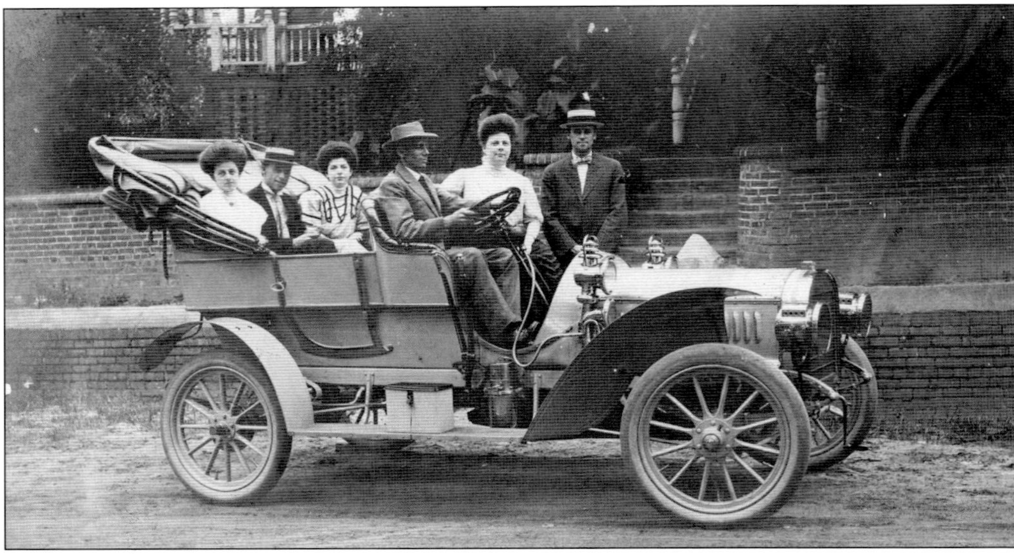

THE CHIPLEY FAMILY. John Chipley was one of the many innovative thinkers in Greenwood, and he was the first person in Greenwood to own an automobile. He purchased a Locomobile Steamer from Atlanta in 1903 for $335. Captured in this photograph are John and Lanier Chipley in the front seat, along with Cora Falker, Marvin Chipley, and Lula Falker in the back.

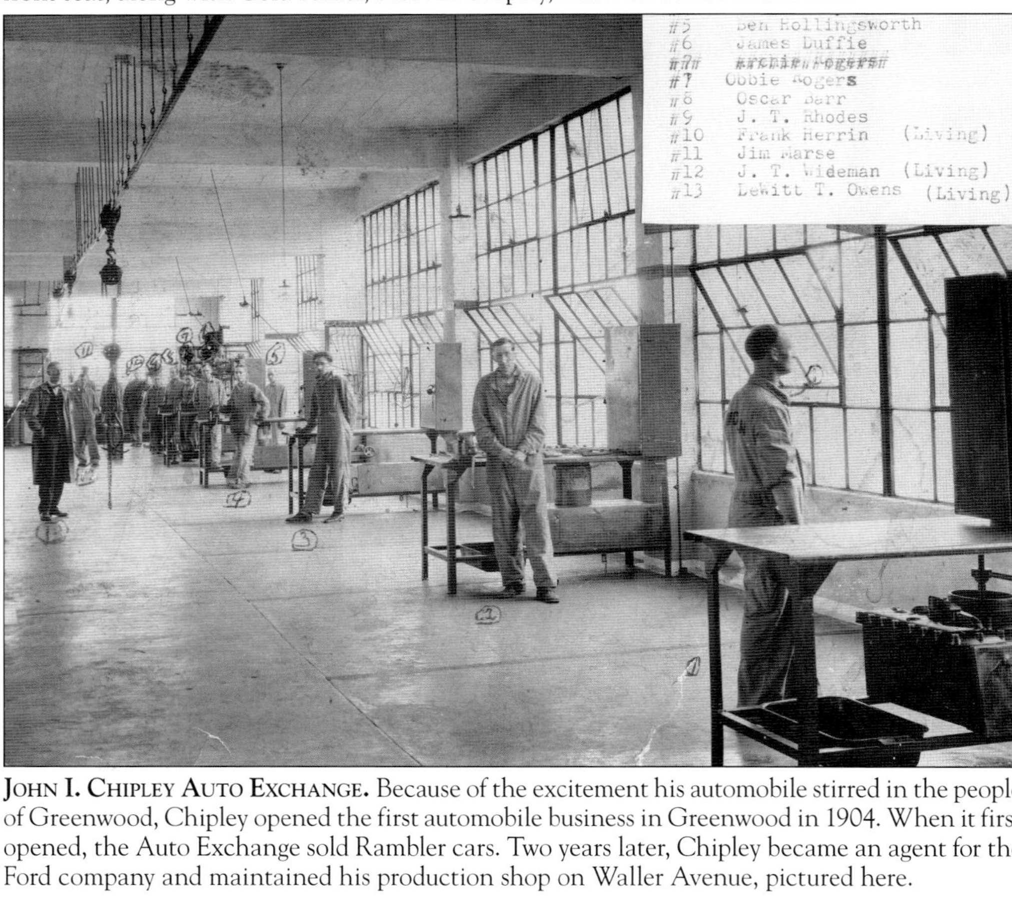

JOHN I. CHIPLEY AUTO EXCHANGE. Because of the excitement his automobile stirred in the people of Greenwood, Chipley opened the first automobile business in Greenwood in 1904. When it first opened, the Auto Exchange sold Rambler cars. Two years later, Chipley became an agent for the Ford company and maintained his production shop on Waller Avenue, pictured here.

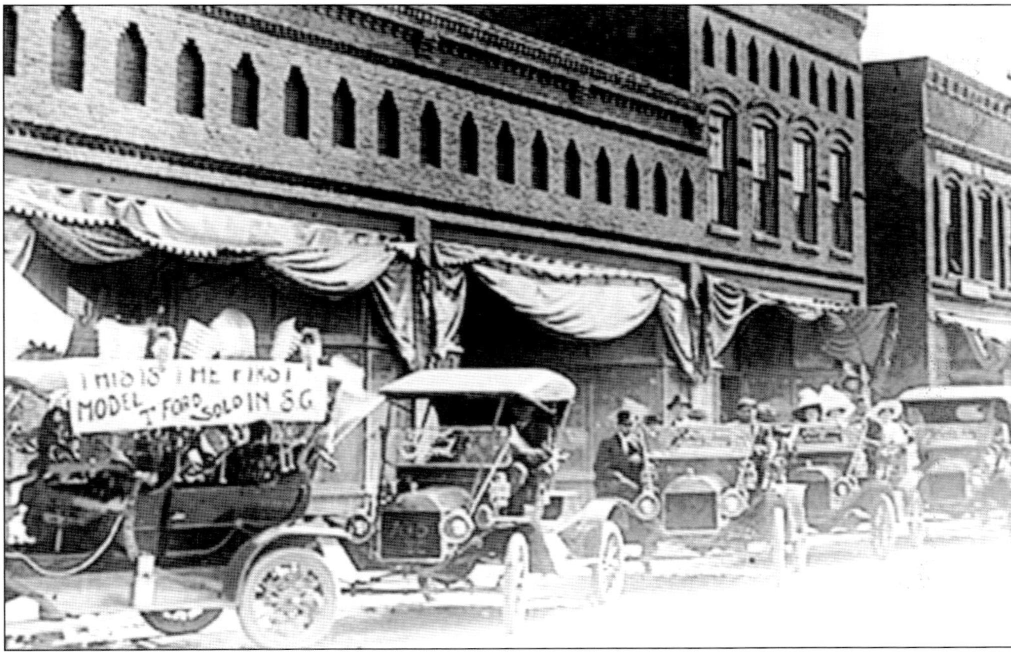

First Model T. The Chipley Auto Exchange was actually the first to sell a Ford Model T in the state of South Carolina. By 1914, Greenwoodians could buy a roadster or a touring car for up to \$550, and if they encountered any problems, they could have them serviced at Chipley's for 60¢ per hour. Pictured above is the first model T sold in South Carolina, and below are the Chipleys driving in their Model T after a parade.

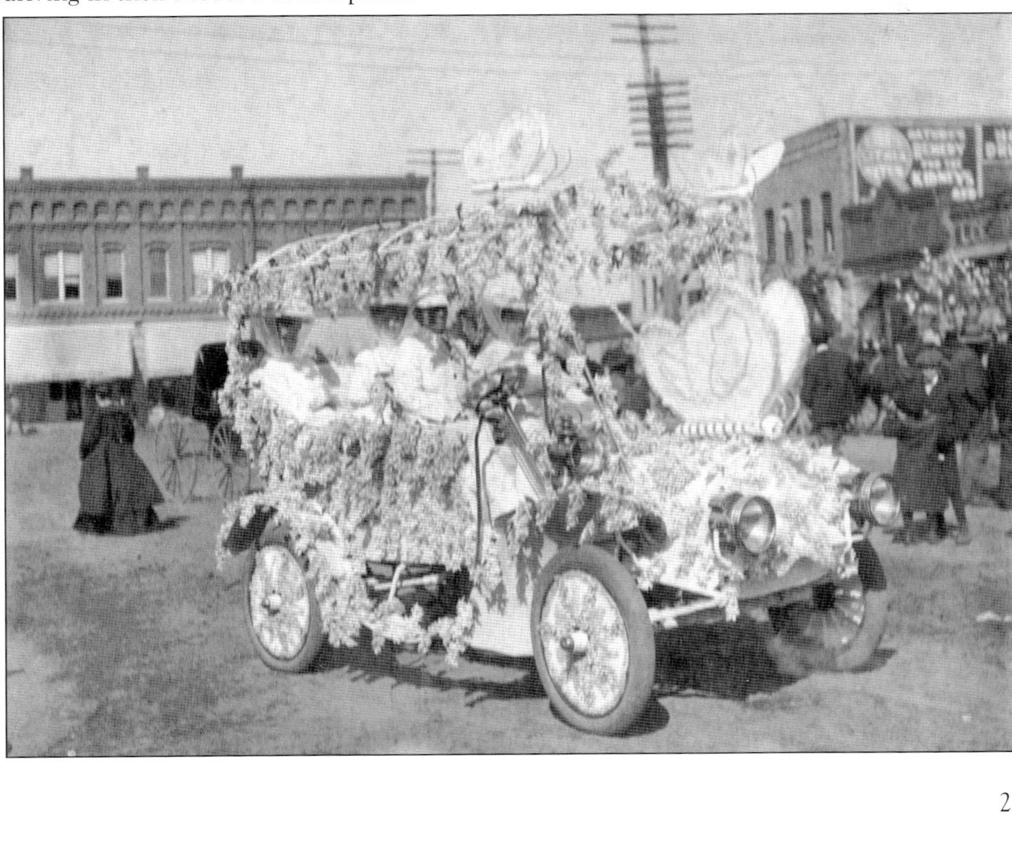

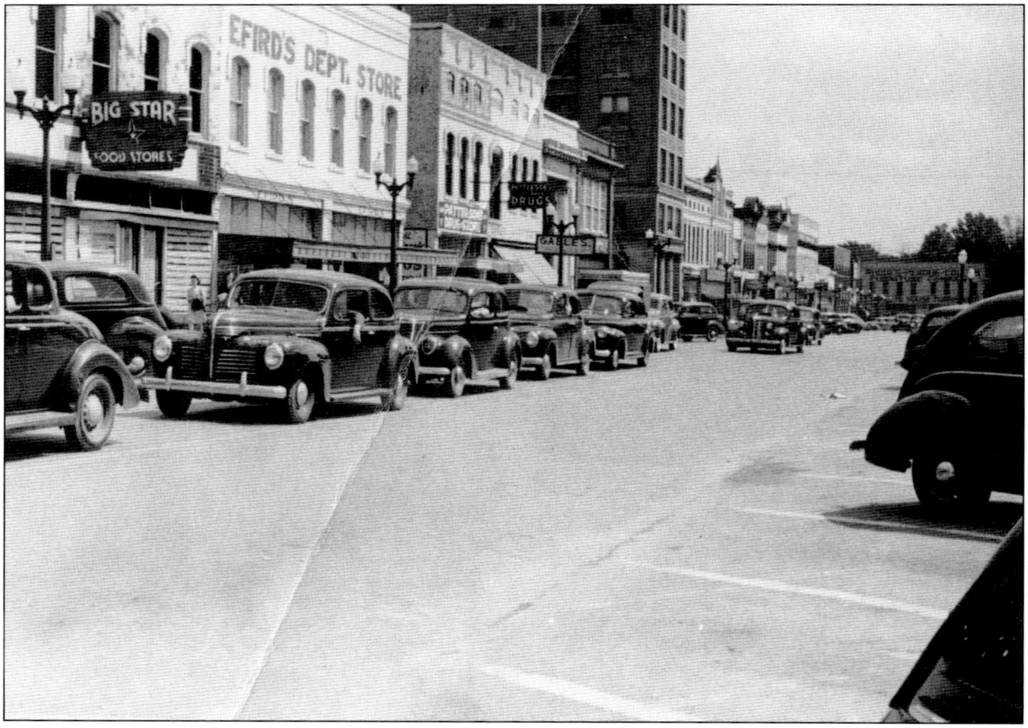

Big Star Food Stores. Big Star was a chain of grocery stores that began in 1937. Created as part of the David Pender Grocery Company, Big Star's South Carolina stores were sold to Harris Teeter in 1988. Before the advent of chain supermarkets, most shopping was done in general stores or other specialized shops.

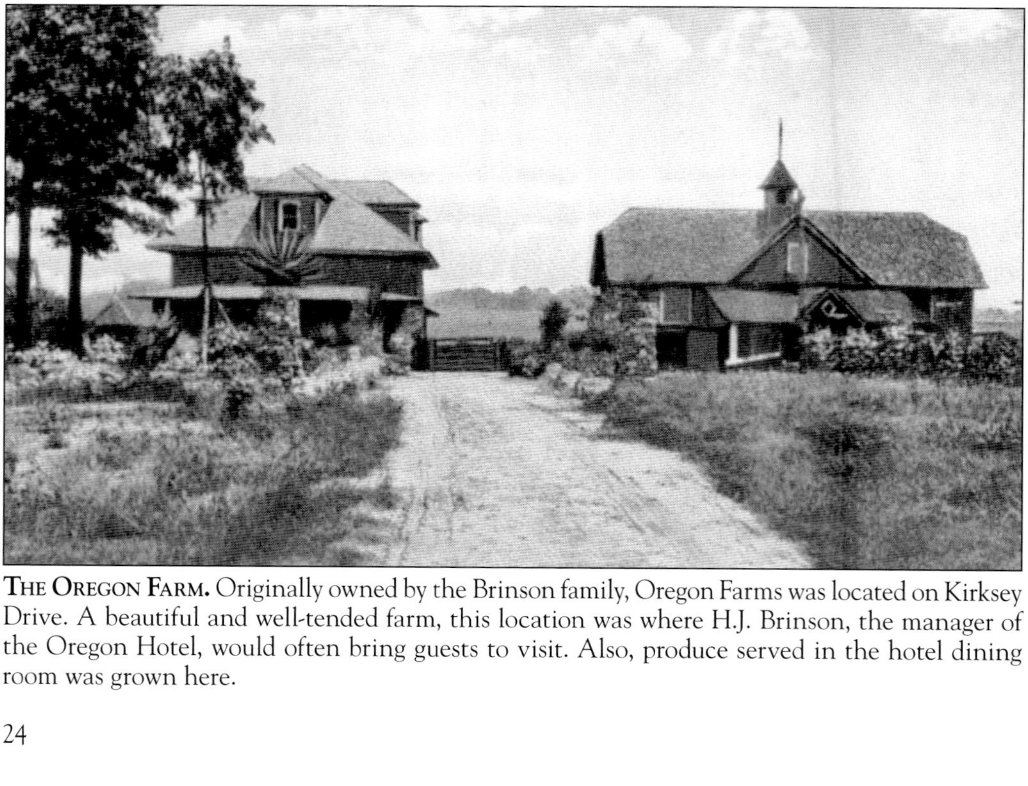

The Oregon Farm. Originally owned by the Brinson family, Oregon Farms was located on Kirksey Drive. A beautiful and well-tended farm, this location was where H.J. Brinson, the manager of the Oregon Hotel, would often bring guests to visit. Also, produce served in the hotel dining room was grown here.

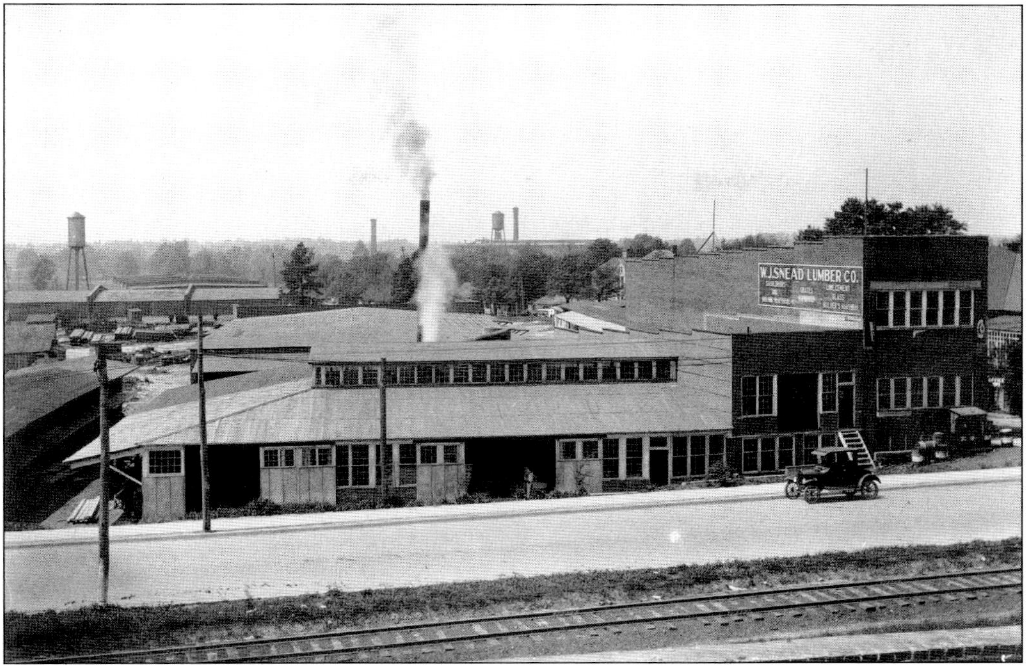

SNEAD LUMBER COMPANY. By 1910, Greenwood's enterprises were booming! Besides seven cotton mills, three bottling plants, and two marble yards, the city also boasted two lumber companies. Besides W.J. Snead Lumber Company, pictured here, there was also Greenwood Lumber and Manufacturing. (Courtesy of the Greenwood County Library System.)

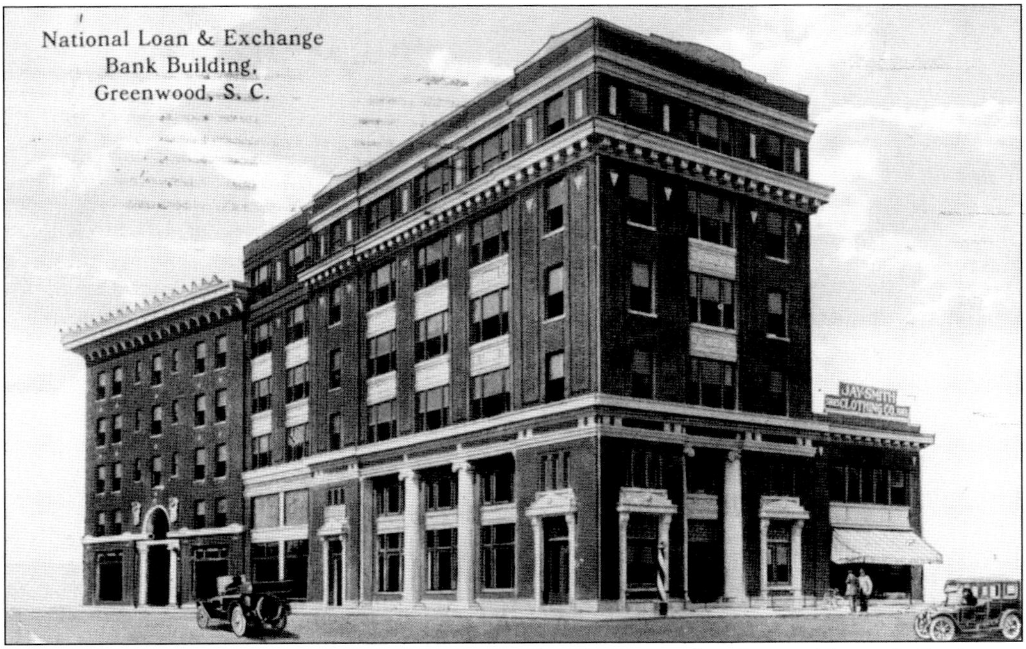

THE NATIONAL LOAN & EXCHANGE BANK. Completed in 1914, the National Loan & Exchange Bank Building not only served the financial needs of the Greenwood community, but also housed several other organizations including the chamber of commerce; the dentist office of J.M. McLees; Dr. Crosby's eye, ear, nose, and throat office; and J.R. Blake Insurance.

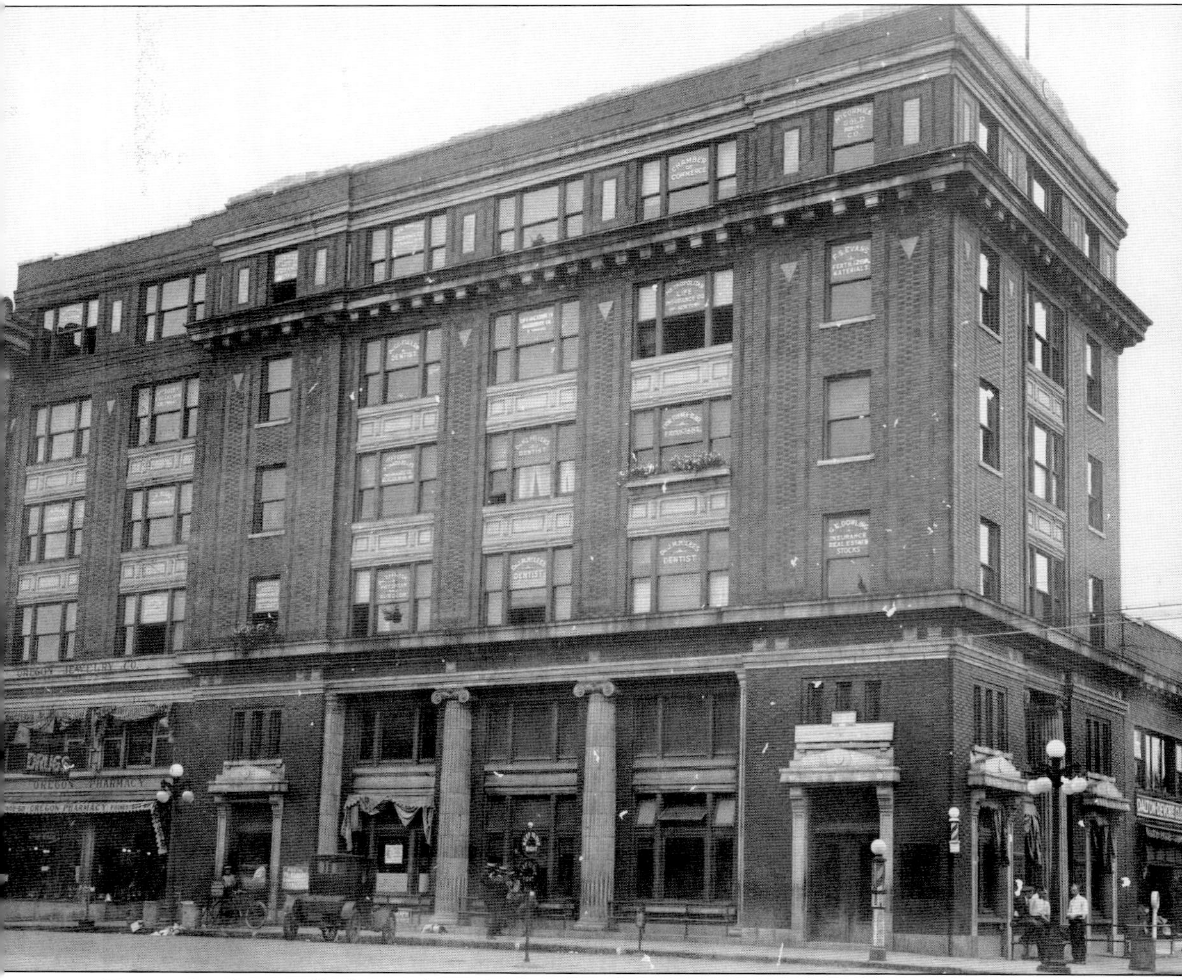

Thayer's. Originally located inside the Oregon Hotel, Thayer's, or the Oregon Pharmacy, was founded in 1911 by Henry K. Thayer. After the disastrous Oregon Hotel fire, the business moved across the street, and a gift department was added. When the hotel reopened (as pictured here), the pharmacy once again did business on the first floor. However, in 1933, it found a permanent home across the street and became known as Thayer's in 1953. Pictured is the Oregon Pharmacy, standing between the National Loan & Exchange Bank and the Oregon Hotel on Maxwell Avenue.

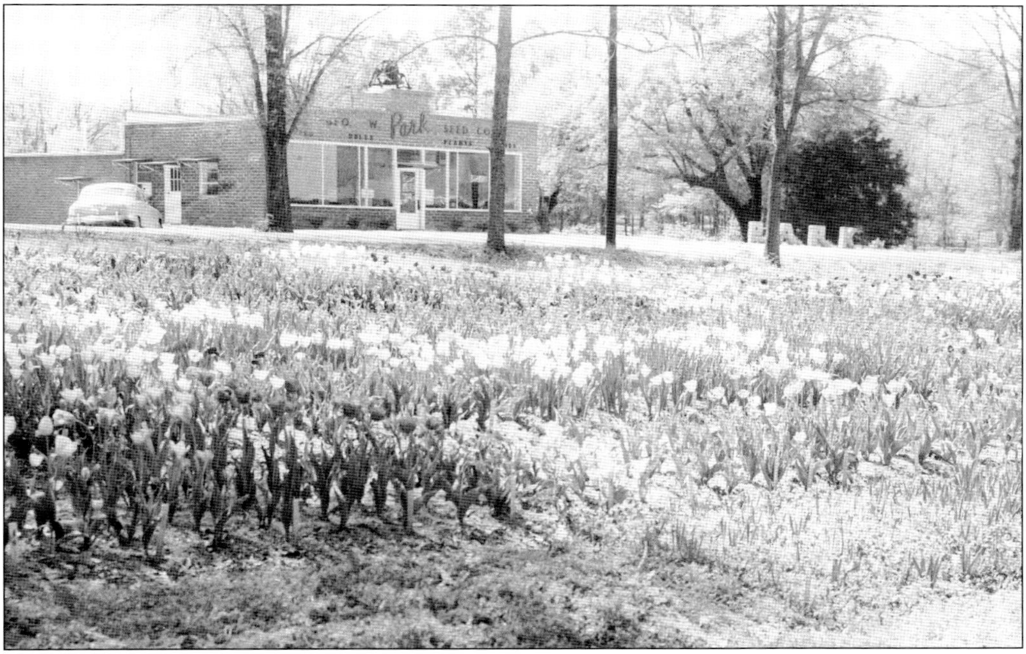

Park Seed Company. Founded by 16-year-old George Watt Park in 1868, Park Seed Company came to Greenwood in 1924. Established on 17 acres of land off of Spring Street, this company had both a seed house and a print shop where catalogs were created and mailed to subscribers nationwide. In this photograph, the Park Seed Office is seen as it appeared between 1950 and 1961.

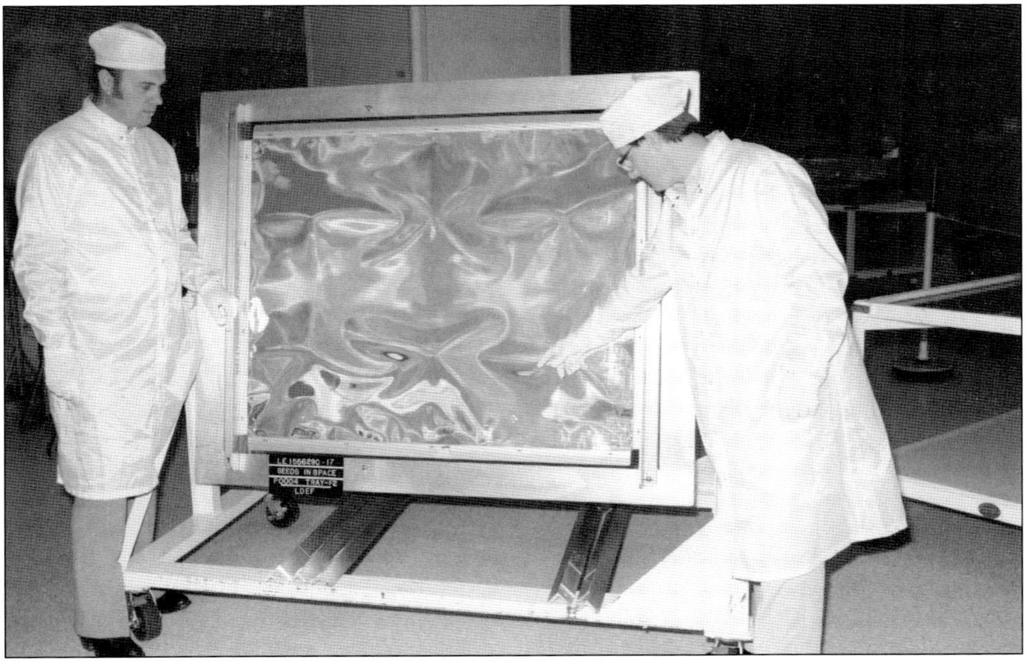

Seeds in Space. Beginning in the 1980s, Park Seed Company partnered with NASA and sent over 20 pounds of seeds into space. This experiment was meant to test the effects of long-term space travel on seeds, determining whether future space stations or settlements could rely on seeds from their home planet for food production.

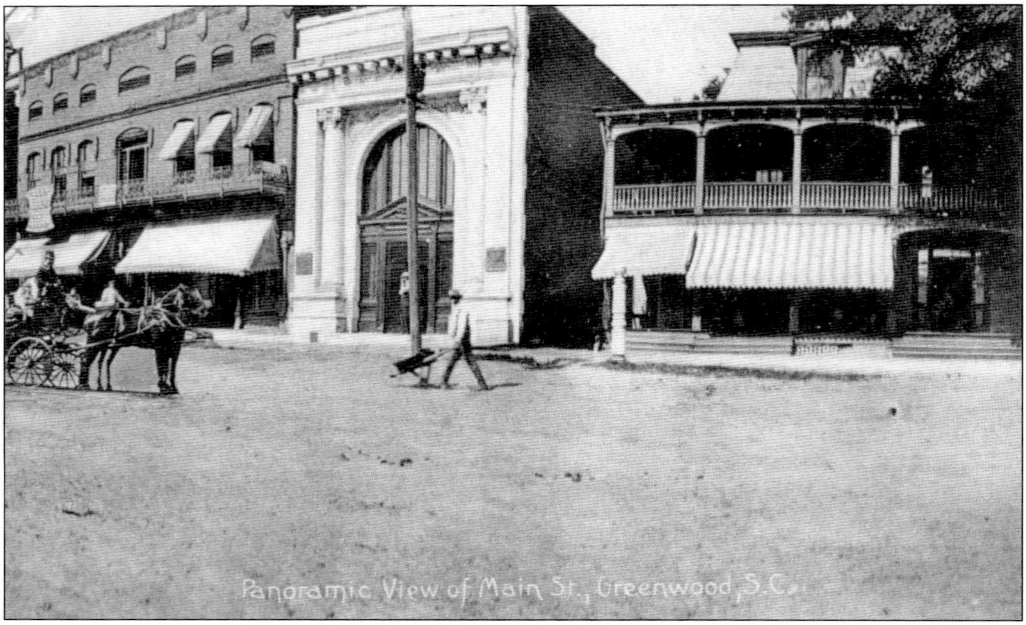

The Grier Building. In 1920, the Commercial Trust Building was constructed. It later became known as the Grier Building, in tribute to Abney Mills president F.E. Grier. The building was constructed on the site of the Riley Hotel, pictured above around 1900. In the mid-1900s, the building held a sign that read "Greenwood Grows Greater" atop its roof. Pictured below is the Grier Building standing behind the Southern Railroad Union Station.

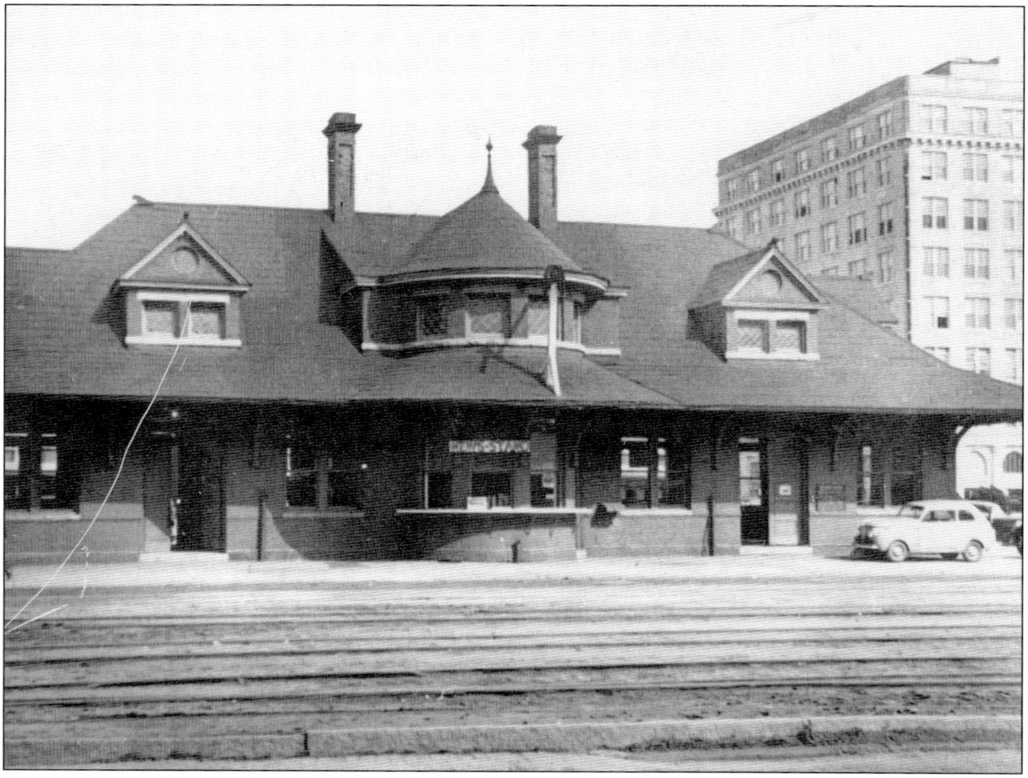

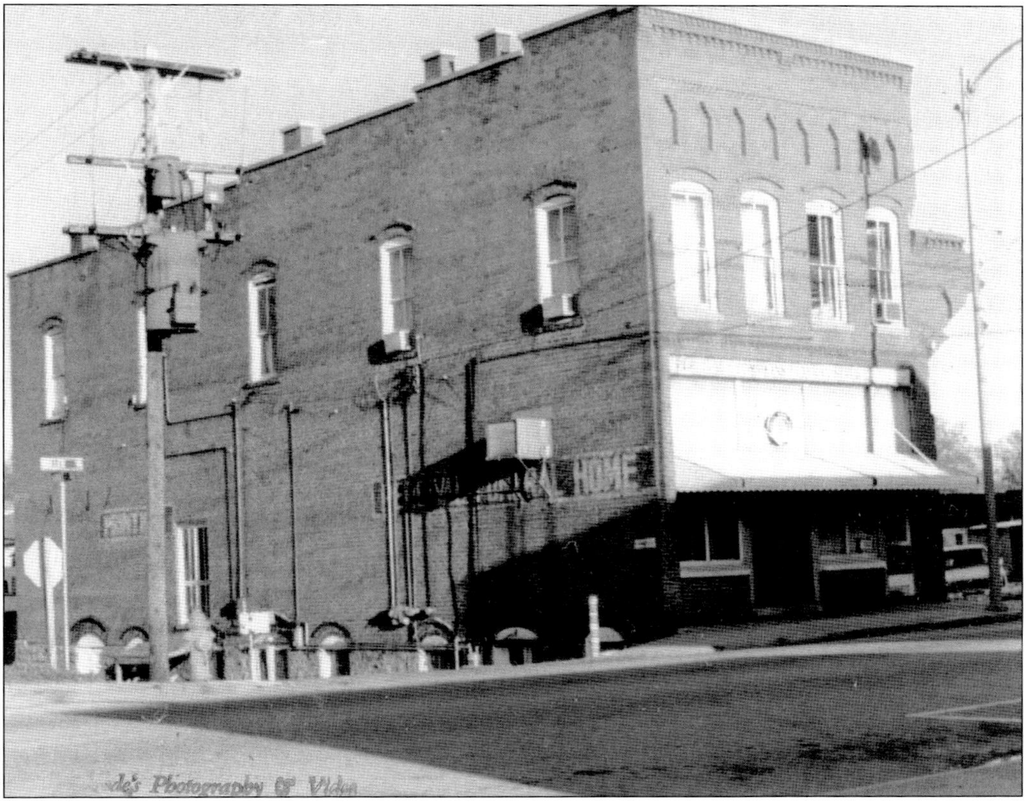

PERCIVAL-TOMPKINS FUNERAL HOME. In 1938, Robert William Tompkins acquired the Percival-Tompkins Funeral Home in Greenwood. The original building is pictured here. (Courtesy of Percival Tompkins Funeral Home.)

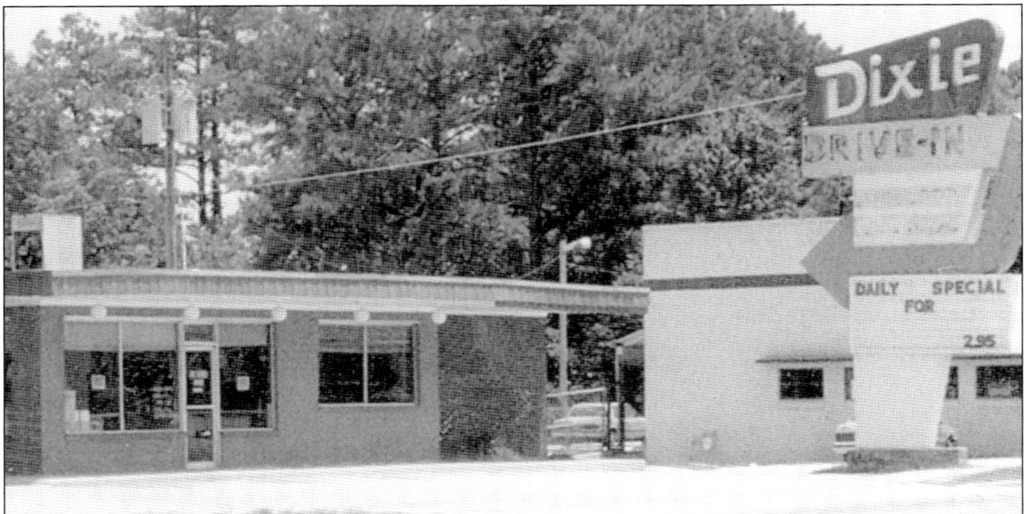

DIXIE DRIVE-IN. Opened in 1959, the Dixie Drive-In became a staple eatery for all Greenwoodians. In 1974, the Kerhoulases bought the restaurant from original owners Angelo and Dino Chatos. The Kerhoulases coined the phrase "Dixie Cheese, half and half," signifying an order of a cheeseburger with half an order of onion rings and half an order of fries.

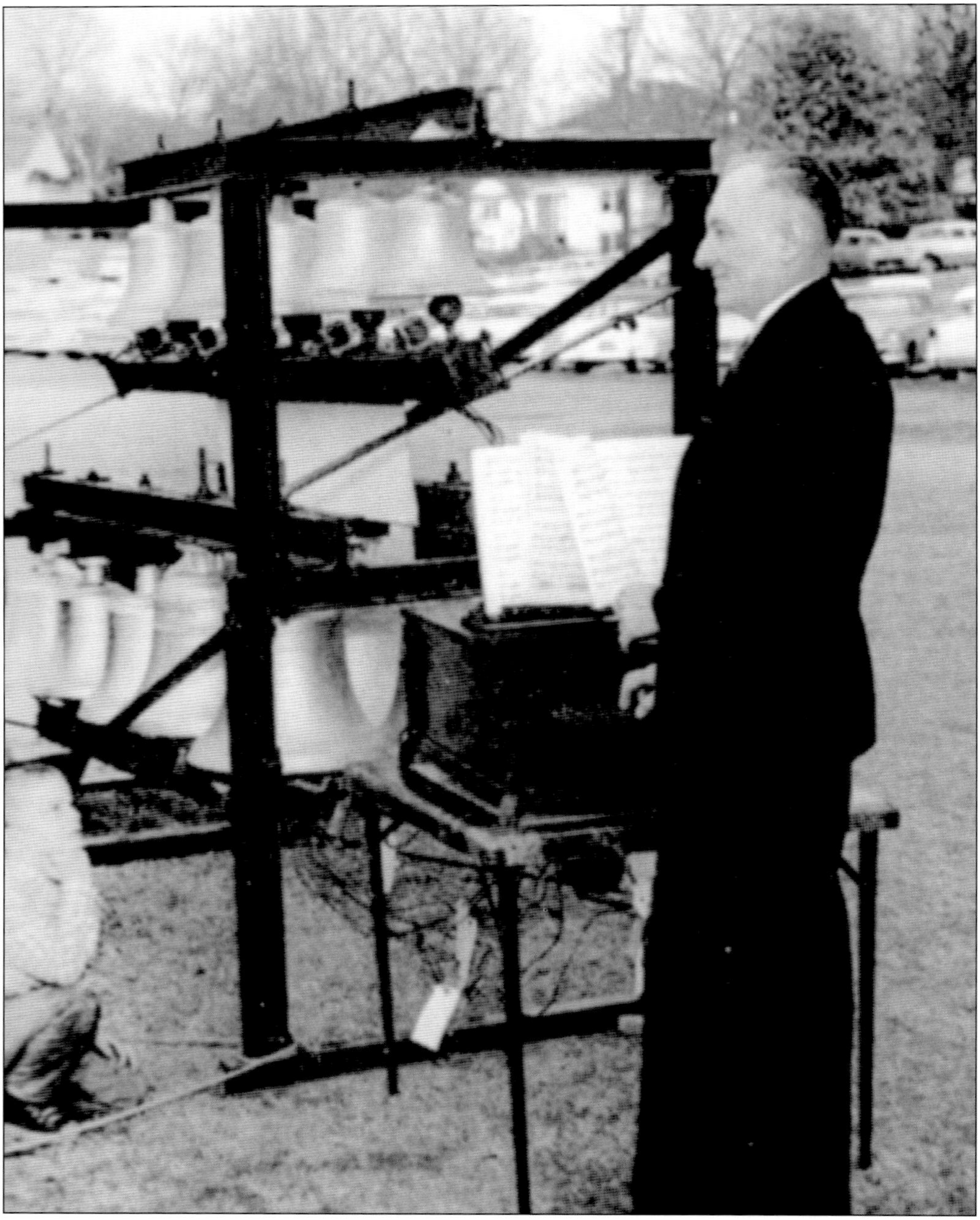

VAN BERGEN BELLFOUNDRIES INC. H.T. Van Bergen came to Greenwood at the request of J.C. Self to install carillon bells in the tower of the church Self had built to memorialize his mother. After the installation in Callie Self Memorial Baptist Church, H.T. Van Bergen stayed in Greenwood and created this enterprise, which was the only tuned bell foundry in the United States before 1980. Pictured is H.T. Van Bergen during a demonstration. (Courtesy of the First Presbyterian Church.)

Two

RAILROADS

Greenwood once boasted the widest Main Street in the world. Five different railroads laid the base for a booming economy and an influx of travelers and settlers to the city of Greenwood during the early 1900s. By 1930, Greenwood had become the center of South Carolina railroad travel, playing host to a greater number of rail lines than any other city in the state. Union Station, located in the middle of the city square, was the central location for parades, political speeches, and rallies, not to mention extensive freight and passenger travel. The very last train rumbled through the city square in 1982.

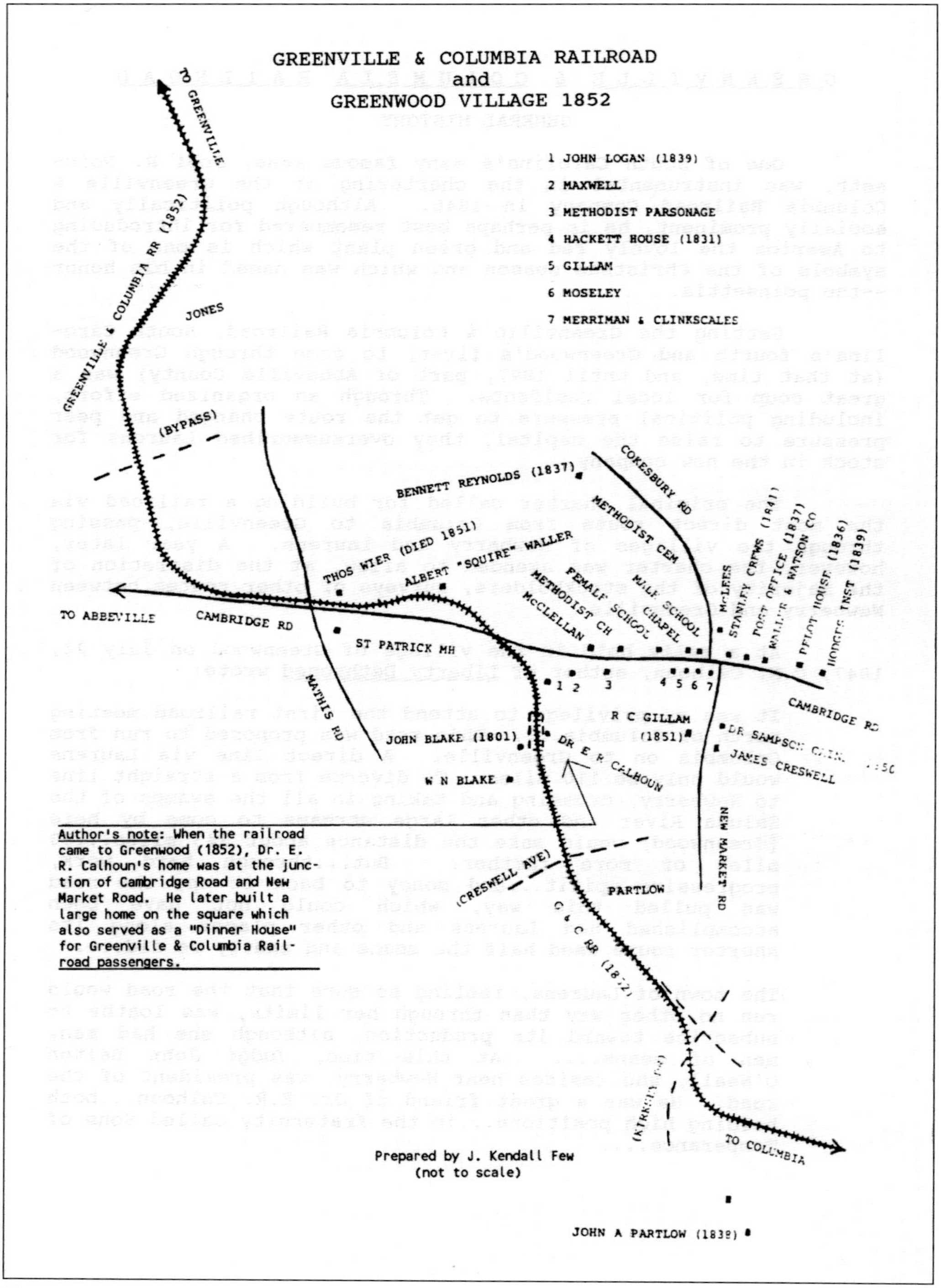

The Railroad Committee. Greenwood would not have welcomed the Greenville & Columbia Railroad if it had not been for the hard work and perseverance of Dr. E.R. Calhoun, Judge John Belton O'Neall, and many Greenwood citizens who secured money, labor, and land in order to ensure that the railroad company would lay lines through Greenwood, some 33 miles out of the way of its original path.

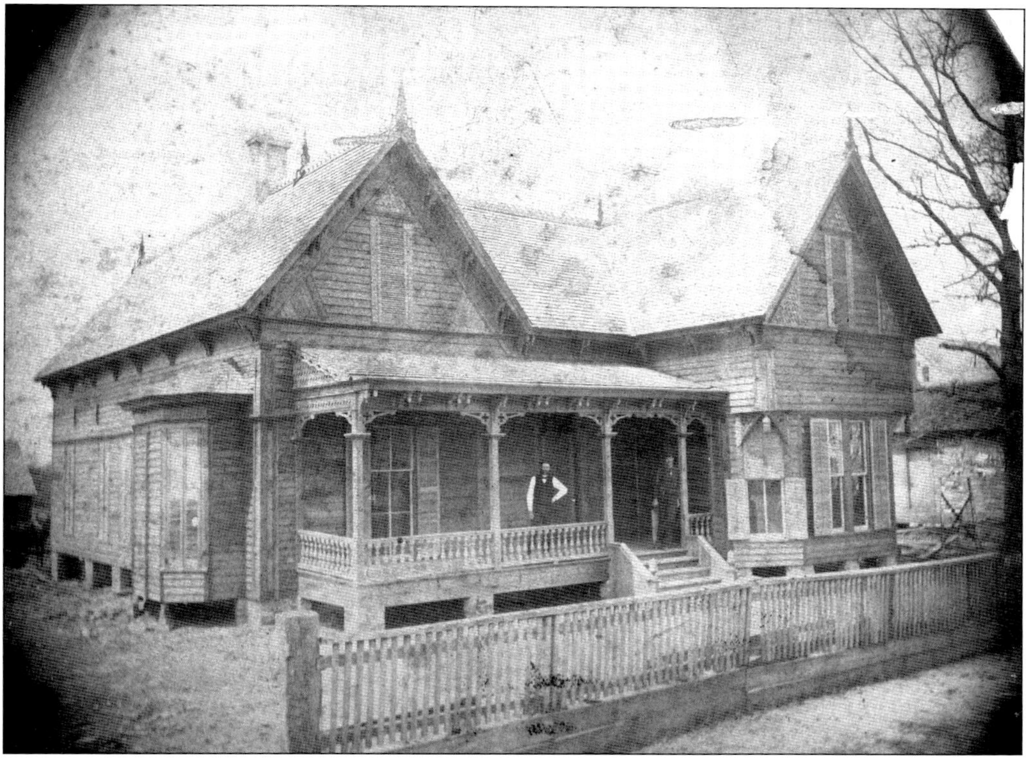

Ephraim Calhoun's Homestead. Ephraim Calhoun was a well-known leader in Greenwood during the mid- to late 1800s. He was a powerful proponent for the railways coming to Greenwood. Pictured is his house downtown, where he often hosted railroad passengers for dinner.

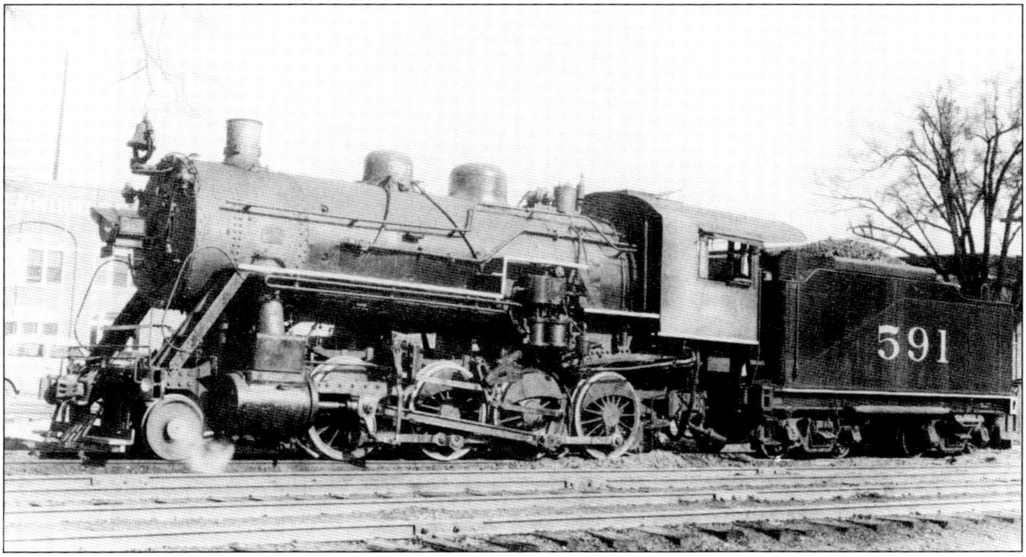

Greenville & Columbia Railroad. Train travel became a necessity in the mid-1800s when Greenwood acquired its first railroad line. The Greenville & Columbia Railroad began to operate in Greenwood in 1852, only five years before Greenwood was incorporated. In 1894, this line became part of the Southern Railway company. Pictured is Southern steam Engine No. 591, parked across from Greenwood City Hall in March 1948. (Courtesy of James H. Wade Jr.)

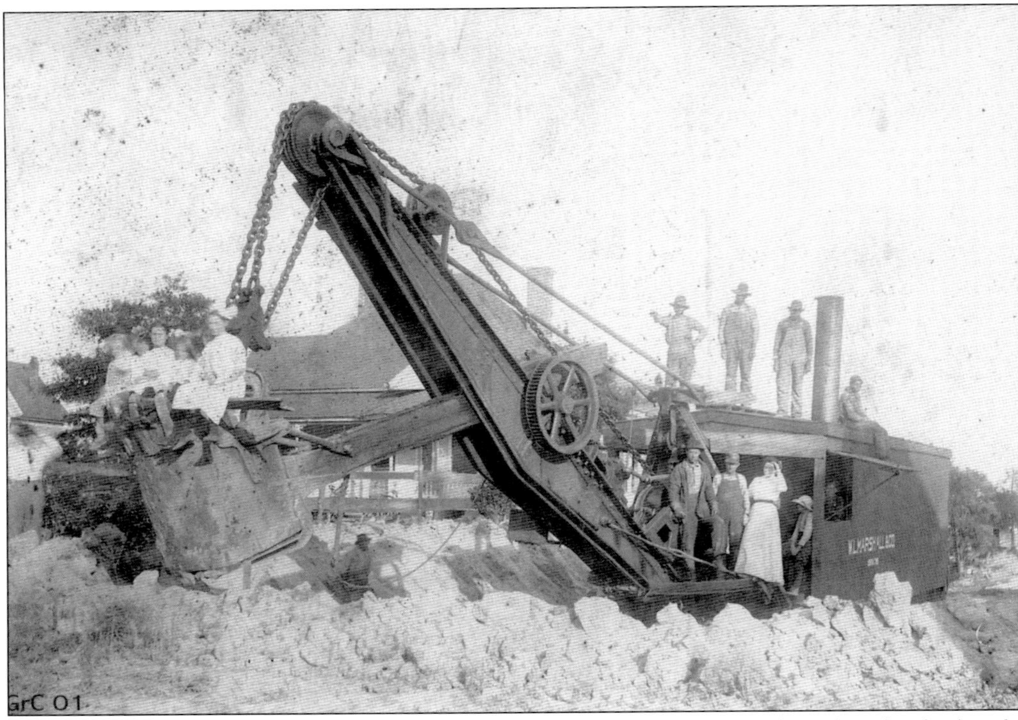

Steam Shovel. This early 1900s photograph shows a large steam shovel used to dig ditches for the railroads and other local construction projects. This shovel is representative of the earliest type of power shovel, or excavator.

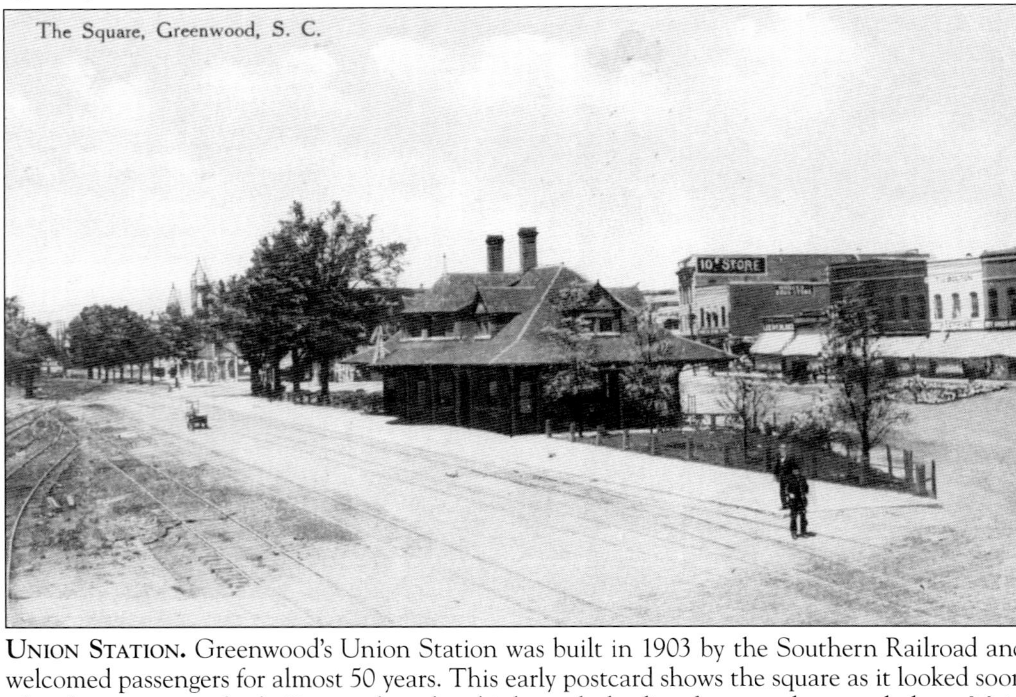

Union Station. Greenwood's Union Station was built in 1903 by the Southern Railroad and welcomed passengers for almost 50 years. This early postcard shows the square as it looked soon after the station was built. Dirt roads and multiple tracks leading from north to south down Main Street were typical of what would become known as the widest Main Street in the world.

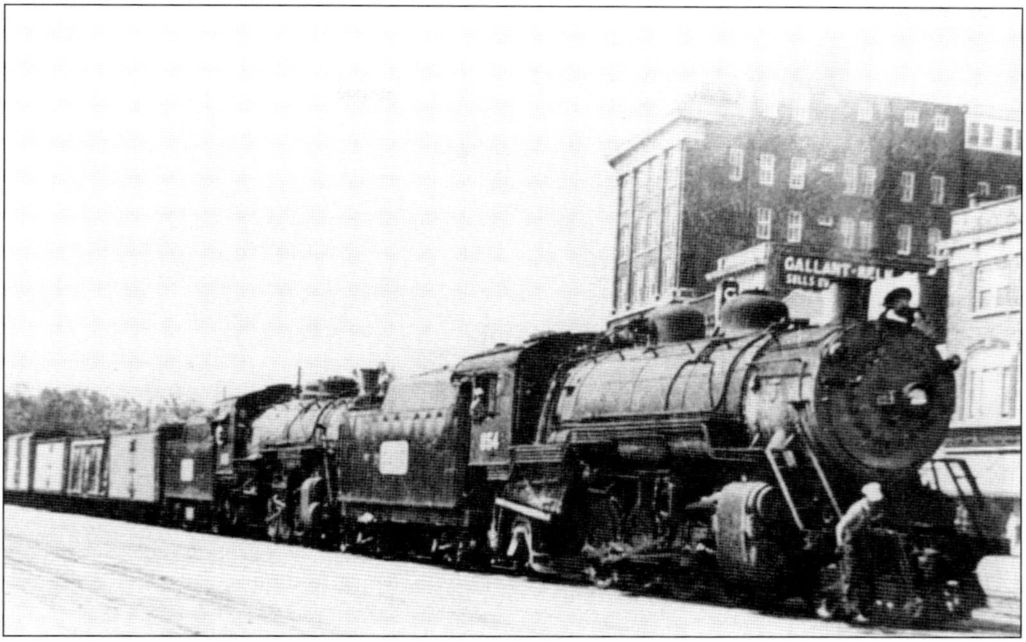

Augusta & Knoxville Railroad. The second railroad to reach Greenwood established a long-sought-after freight and passenger connection with Augusta, Georgia, on May 1, 1882. This connection provided trading opportunities that made way for new economic growth in Greenwood. A large archway was constructed at the corner of Circular Avenue and Main Street, through which the first train traveled to a large welcome ceremony. The line merged to become the Charleston & Western Carolina (C&WC) in 1896. The photograph shows steam Locomotive No. 854 on a noon trip through town in 1946. (Courtesy of Max Miller.)

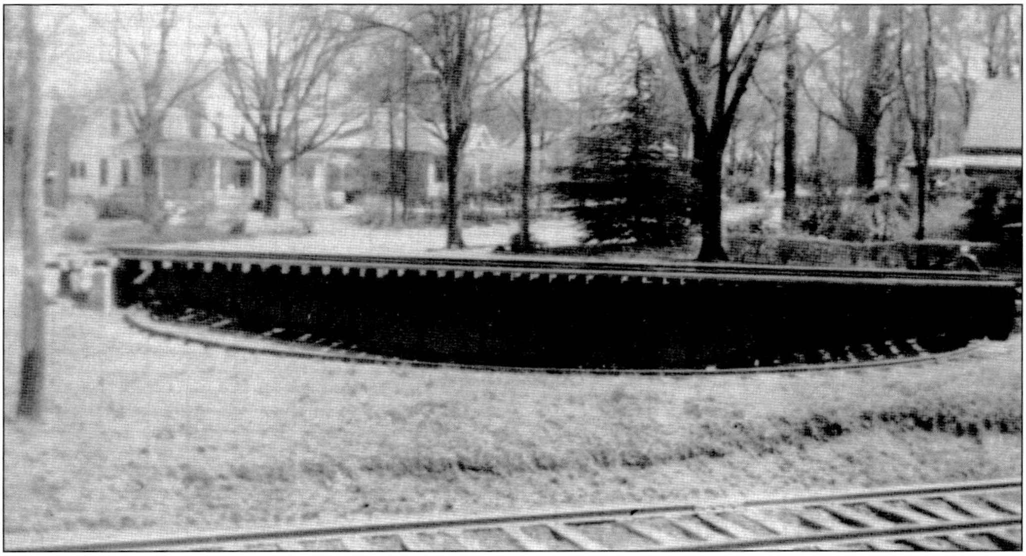

Charleston & Western Carolina Turntable. In April 1942, Greenwood High School students flocked to their classroom windows every time they heard the creaking of the C&WC's manually operated turntable across the street. Through the late 1940s, trainmen would turn engines around using the cumbersome South Main Street turntable that was located at the end of Circular Avenue. (Courtesy of James D. Sheppard.)

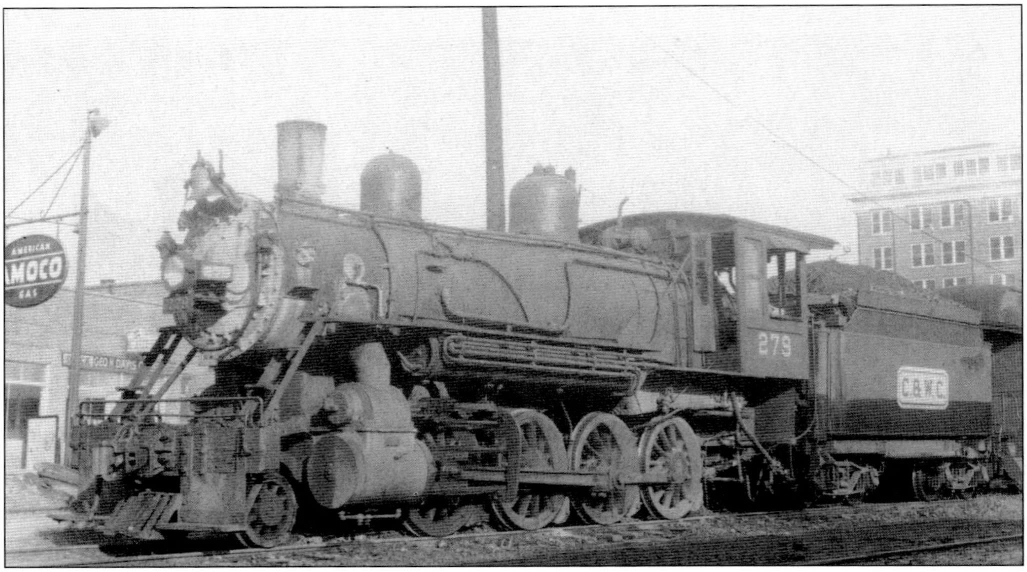

Charleston & Western Carolina Steam Locomotive. Locomotive No. 279 is heading south on Main Street toward the manual turntable, where engines were often turned for round-trip routes. The Augusta & Knoxville Railroad had merged to become the C&WC Railroad by 1948. (Courtesy of James H. Wade Jr.)

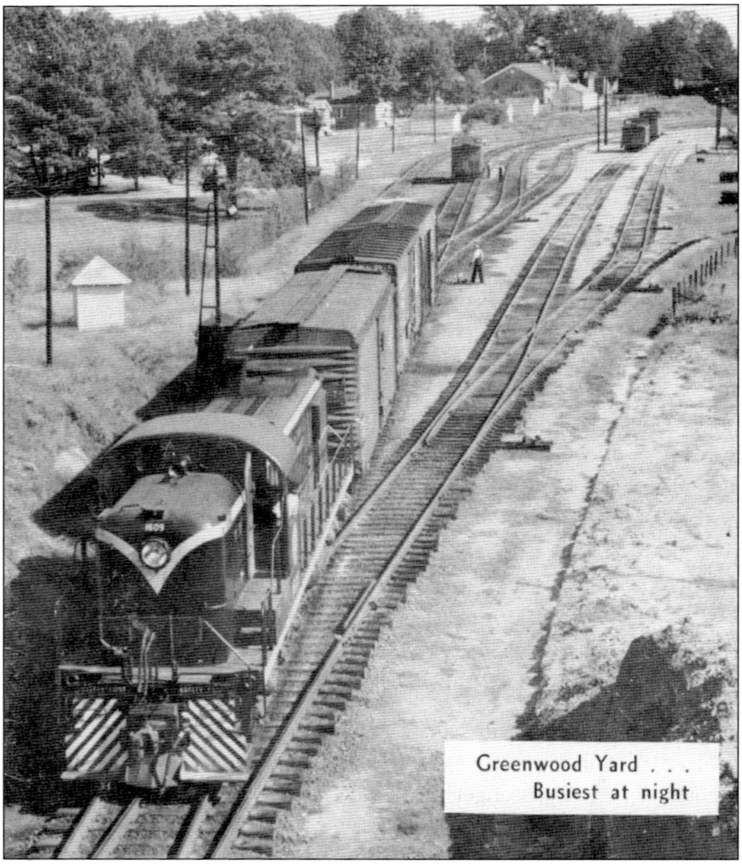

Chester, Greenwood & Abbeville Railroad. In 1891, Greenwood's third railroad line was completed. The line was supported by Greenwood citizens during construction and became one of Greenwood's busiest railroads through mergers that resulted in the Seaboard Air Line Railway in 1901. The company became well known for its high-quality passenger service through Greenwood. Pictured is Maxwell Yard, where Seaboard passenger and freight services operated, off Maxwell Avenue. (Courtesy of the Piedmont & Northern Railroad.)

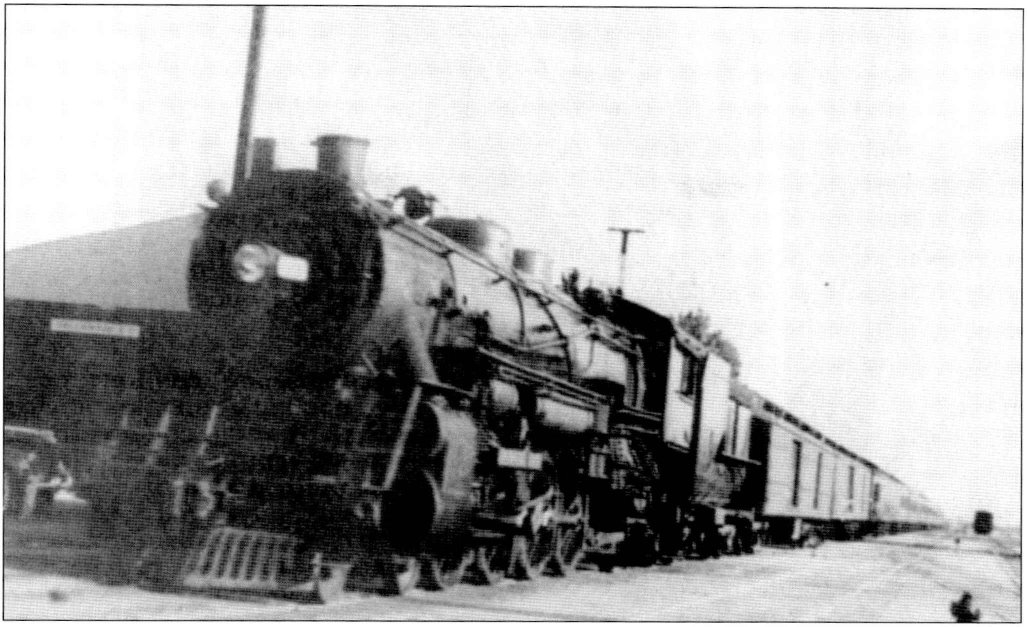

SEABOARD RAILWAY. In November 1901, local railways merged under Seaboard Railway and began a momentous service that included the *Robert E. Lee*, advertised as the finest train in the South. This locomotive could travel from Washington to Atlanta in 24.5 hours. Pictured in June 1942 is the *Robert E. Lee* in Greenwood. (Courtesy of James D. Sheppard.)

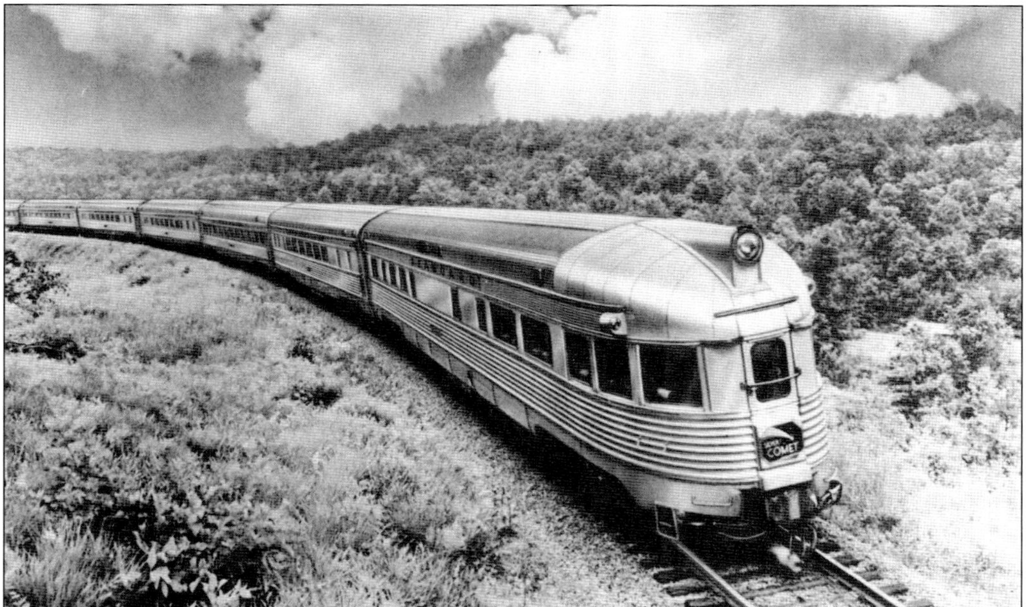

THE *SILVER COMET*. In 1912, Greenwood merchants offered to pay the fares of out-of-town shoppers visiting Greenwood. Recorded in their ledgers are 35¢ fares to Cross Hill and 40¢ fares to Abbeville. This famously posh Seaboard passenger train was the last to transport passengers through Greenwood. By October 15, 1969, the *Silver Comet* ceased to operate between Richmond and Atlanta.

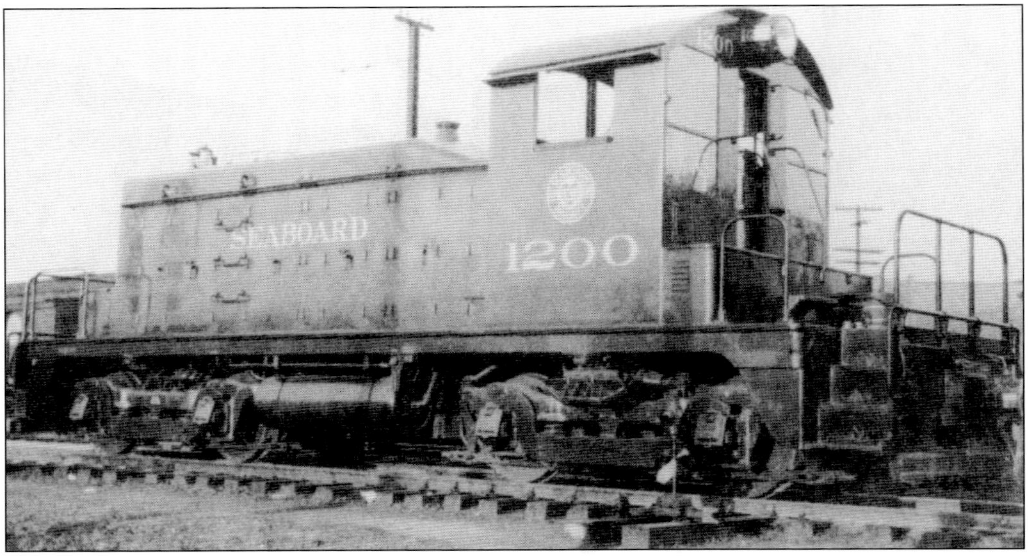

First Diesel Locomotive. Seaboard Air Line Railway Company was the first to provide a diesel locomotive for service in Greenwood. The General Motors diesel switch Engine No. 1200 is pictured in April 1940. (Courtesy of F.E. Ardrey Jr.)

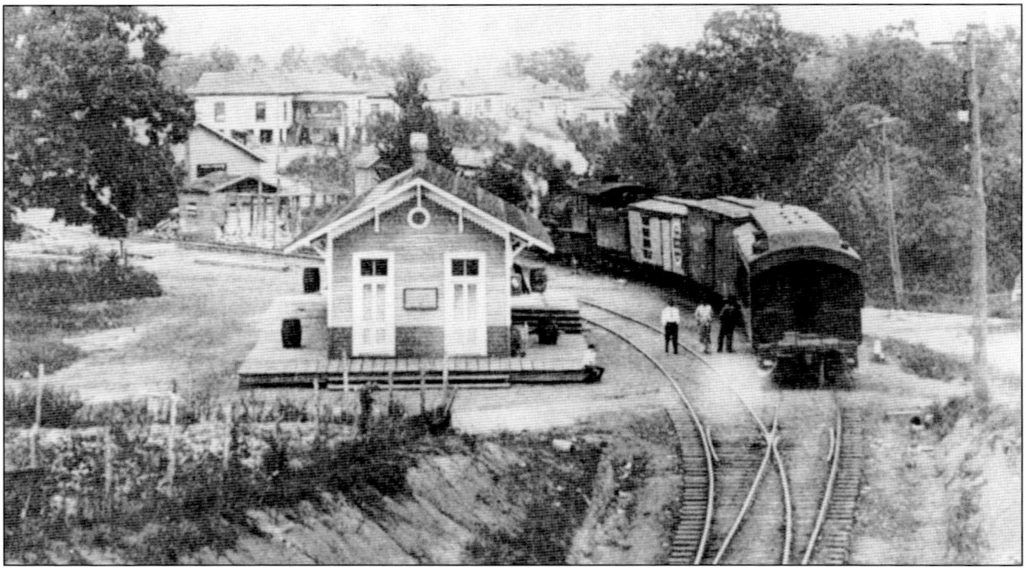

Ware Shoals Railroad. In 1904, the owners of Ware Shoals Manufacturing Company, later named Riegal Textile Mill in Ware Shoals, built a private short-line railroad to serve the mill and surrounding areas. For more than 80 years, the Ware Shoals Railroad served Greenwood County and its citizens through the transport of both freight and passengers. Pictured is the Ware Shoals Depot in 1914.

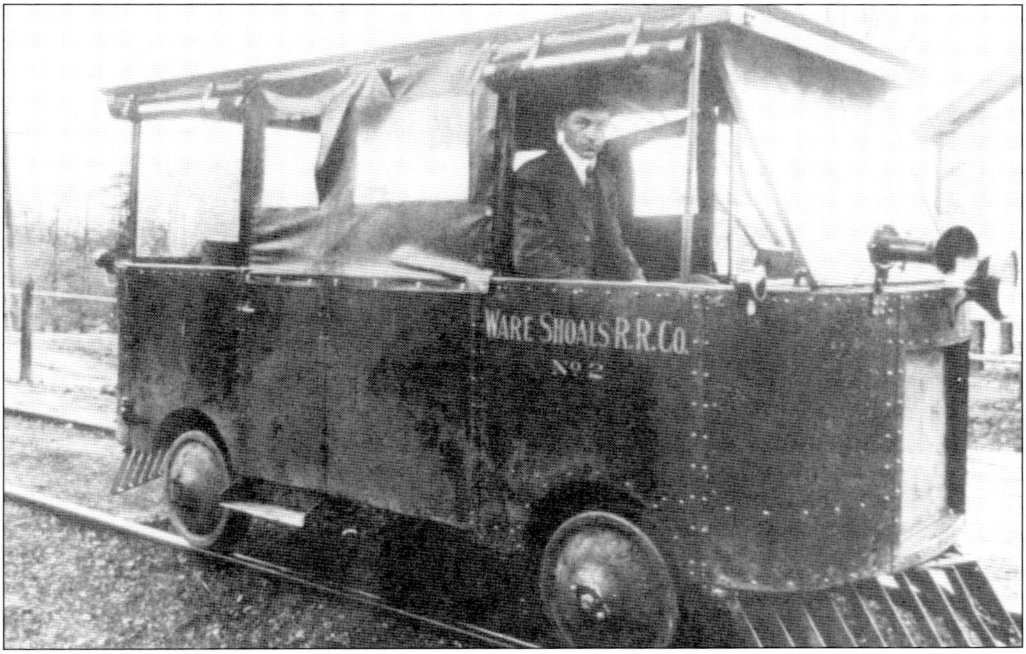

WARE SHOALS MOTOR CAR NO. 2. For one year, the six-passenger Ware Shoals Motor Cars transported passengers between Ware Shoals and Shoals Junction, South Carolina. The 20-minute trip must not have been popular, as motor cars were put into service during the year 1917 and taken out of service by January 1918.

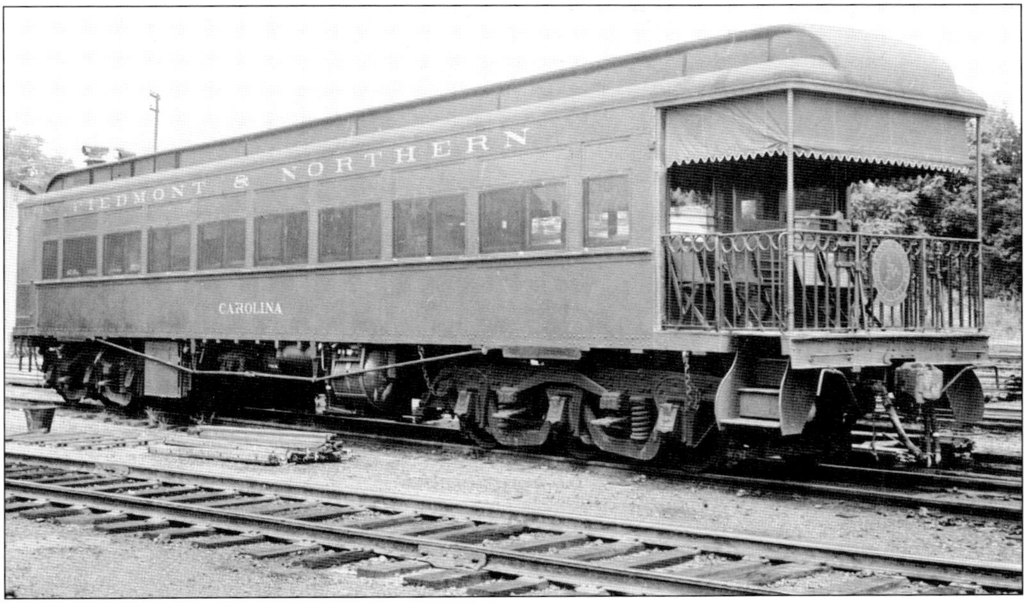

PIEDMONT & NORTHERN RAILROAD. In 1901, James B. Duke established the first and only electric railroad to run through Greenwood, the Piedmont & Northern Railroad (P&N). His original goal of connecting Upstate South Carolina with Charlotte, North Carolina, was never reached. However, the P&N ran from Greenwood to Spartanburg beginning in 1914. P&N became the first electric railroad to carry both heavy freight and passengers. Presidents of the railroad company, traveling between Spartanburg and Greenwood, used the office car, *Carolina*, pictured here.

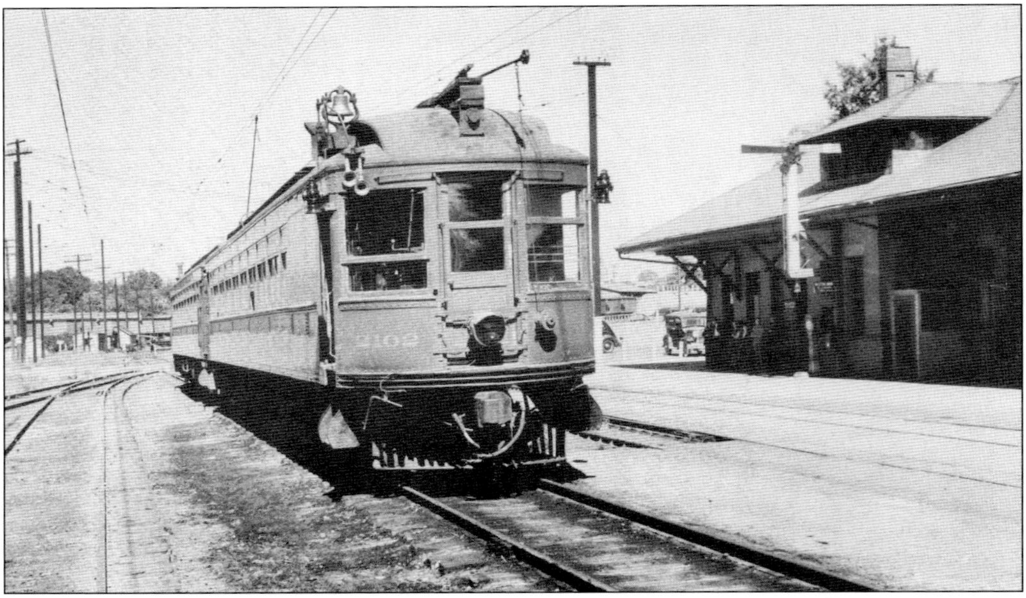

Trolley Service. P&N trolley service began on September 22, 1912, and ended on October 31, 1951. Engineer E.E. Sanders operated the first and last interurban Piedmont and Northern train. Electric lines were installed in Greenwood, through Shoals Junction, and up to Spartanburg. Pictured above is the Interurban Electric Car No. 2102 at the Greenwood passenger station on Maxwell Avenue before its daily trip to Spartanburg. The electric service proved most economical during wartime, and was often used by the all-female Lander College students traveling up to the all-male Wofford College athletic events. Railroad passengers would arrive in Greenwood at the Southern station, pictured below as it appeared in 1912, or Maxwell station (pictured above). (Above, courtesy of W.C. Janssen.)

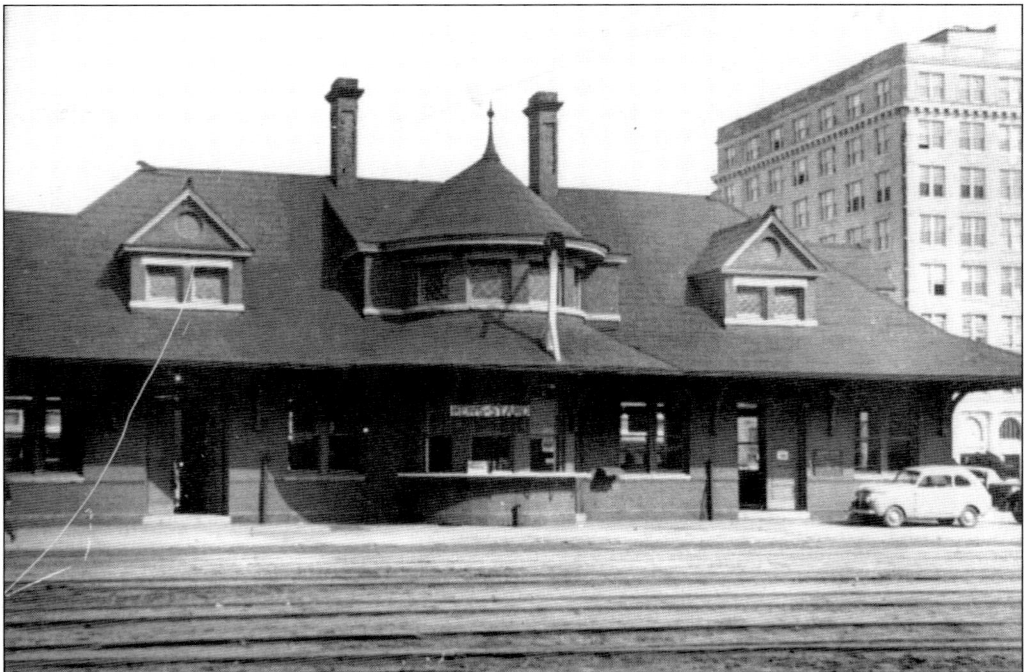

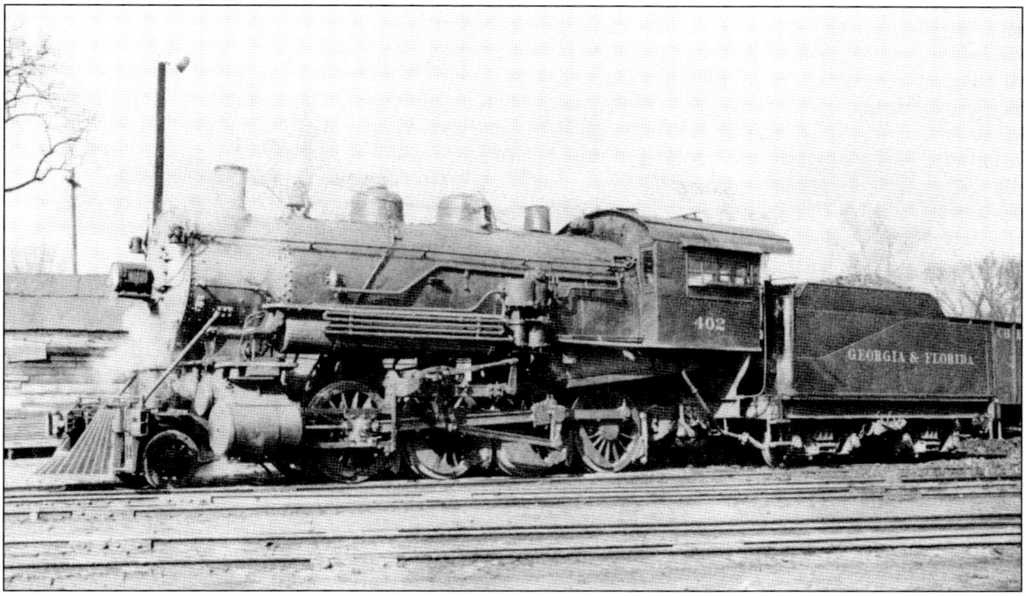

GEORGIA & FLORIDA RAILROAD. In 1929, the Georgia & Florida (G&F) Railroad arrived in Greenwood and was the last new railroad line built. The Greenwood Chamber of Commerce had worked tirelessly to ensure the creation of the new connection. (Courtesy of D. William Witbeck.)

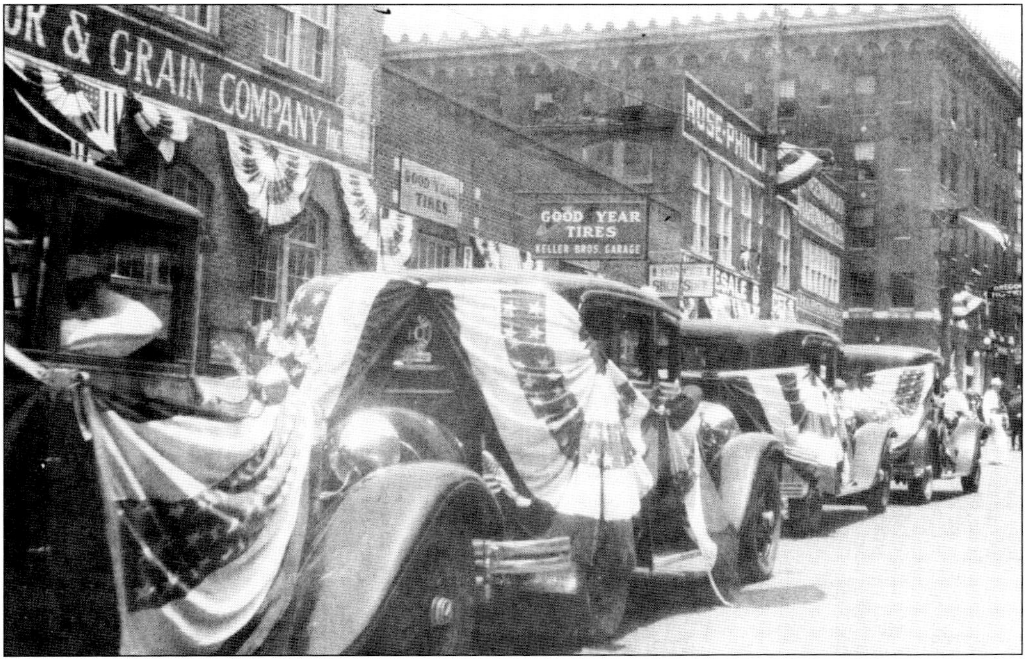

G&F DAY CELEBRATION. On June 19, 1929, cars decorated in red, white, and blue bunting lined up on Maxwell Avenue to receive visitors, who would be transported to Greenwood Fairgrounds for the celebration. Four special Georgia & Florida trains paved the way on the new rail line, bringing over 8,000 guests from Augusta.

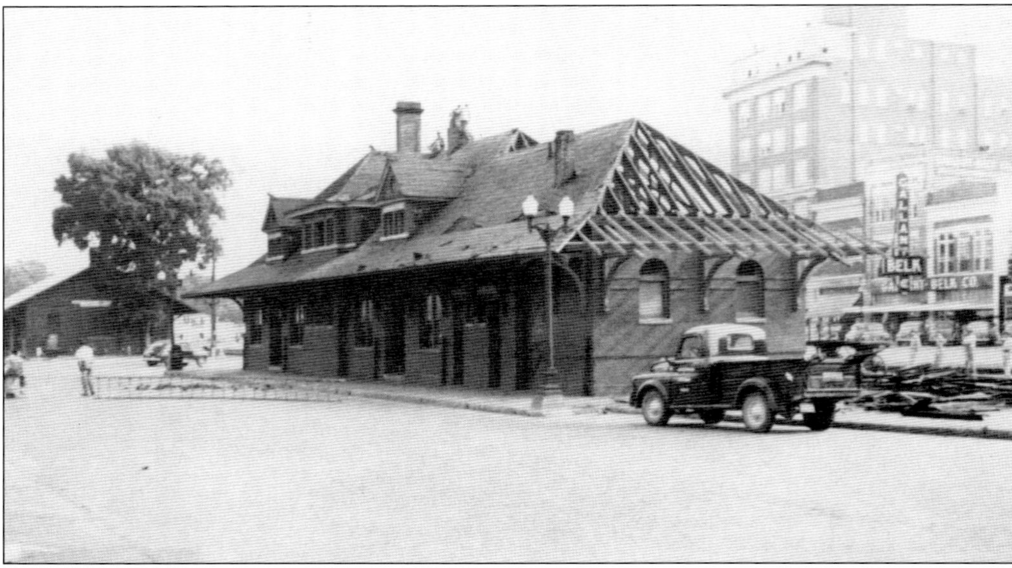

Southern Railroad Passenger Depot. The Southern Passenger Depot, otherwise known as Union Station, formed the very center of town and was the site of many parades, political rallies, and family reunions. The passenger depot was built in 1903 and is shown being deconstructed in 1952.

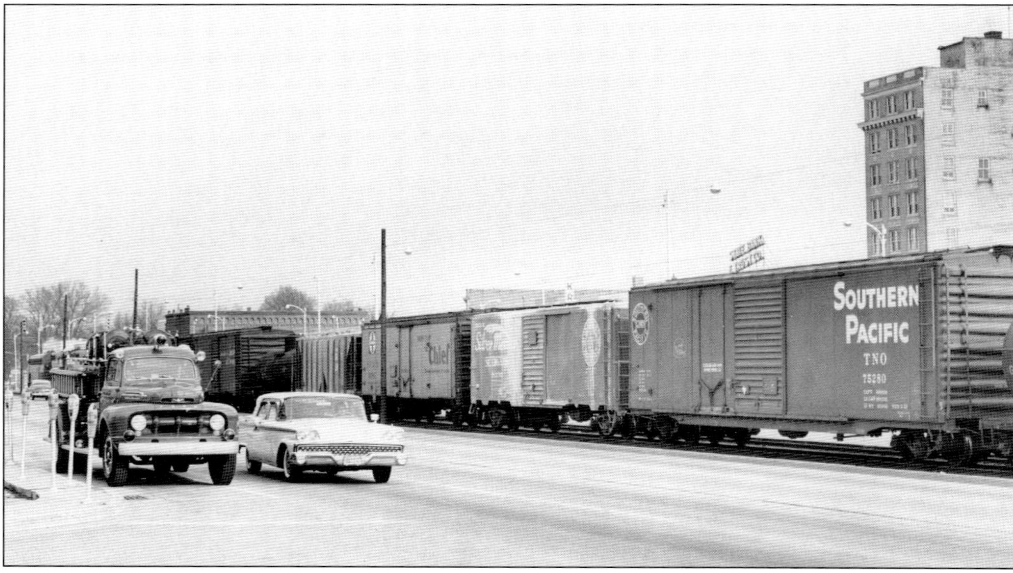

Railroad Popularity Faded. This photograph taken on December 1, 1952, shows a Seaboard Railroad freight train passing through the middle of downtown Greenwood. A fire engine and a car wait at a stoplight while the train passes alongside. In the 1950s, passenger train travel faded in popularity as long-distance commercial airline and car travel became more affordable for everyone.

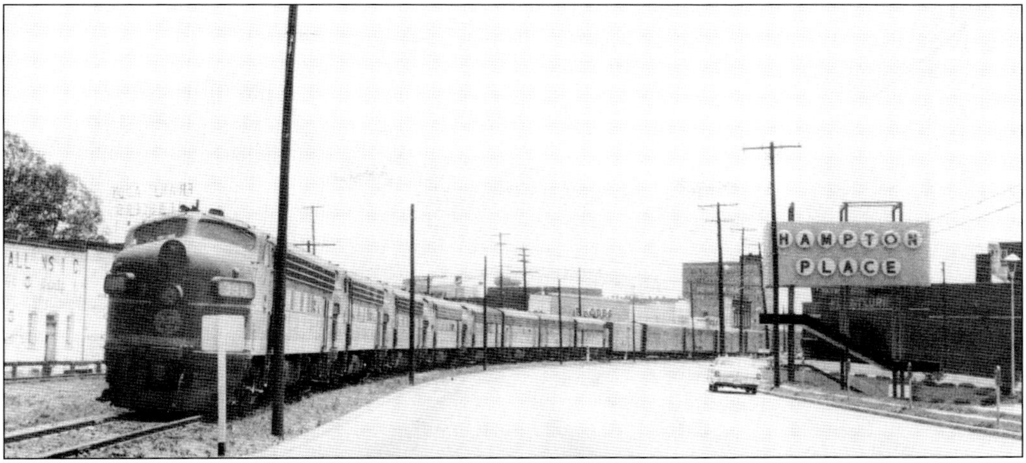

The Last Train. On November 4, 1982, the last train rumbled through Greenwood's square. The train was a special Southern Railroad passenger train, carrying government officials and politicians to the "Last Train" ceremony. This special day was long preceded by the last working train, a Seaboard Coast Line freight train, passing through the square on June 1, 1973.

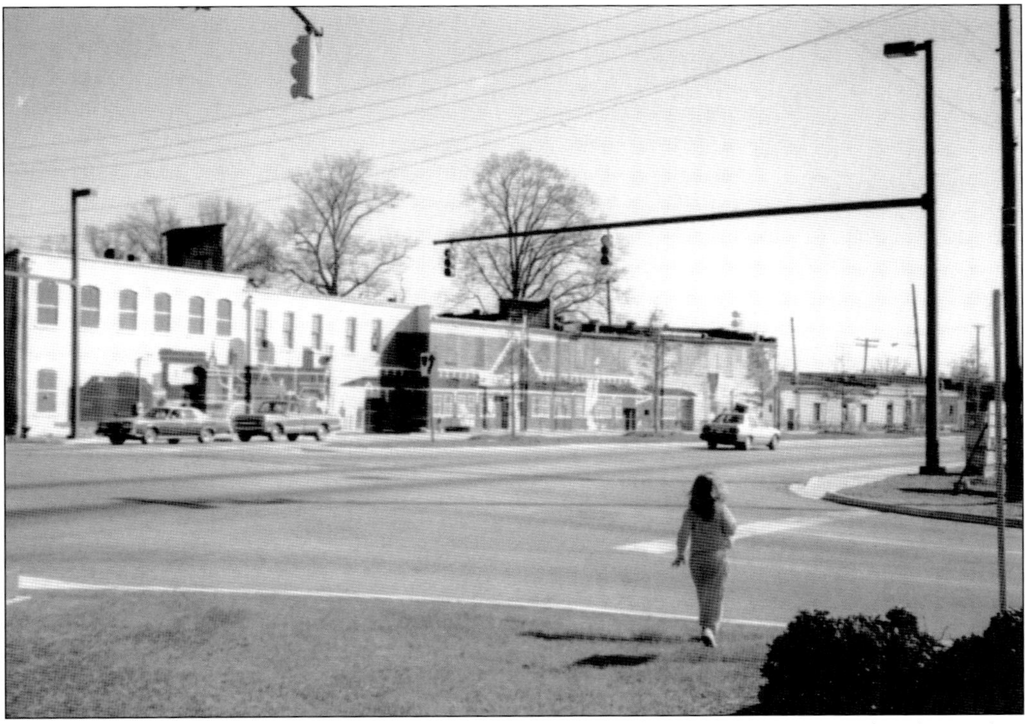

Train Art. Despite the removal of the last portions of track in 1982, Greenwood's relationship with the railroad could not be severed. Local artists painted this stunning mural of a train on the sides of Uptown buildings in honor of Greenwood's railroad legacy.

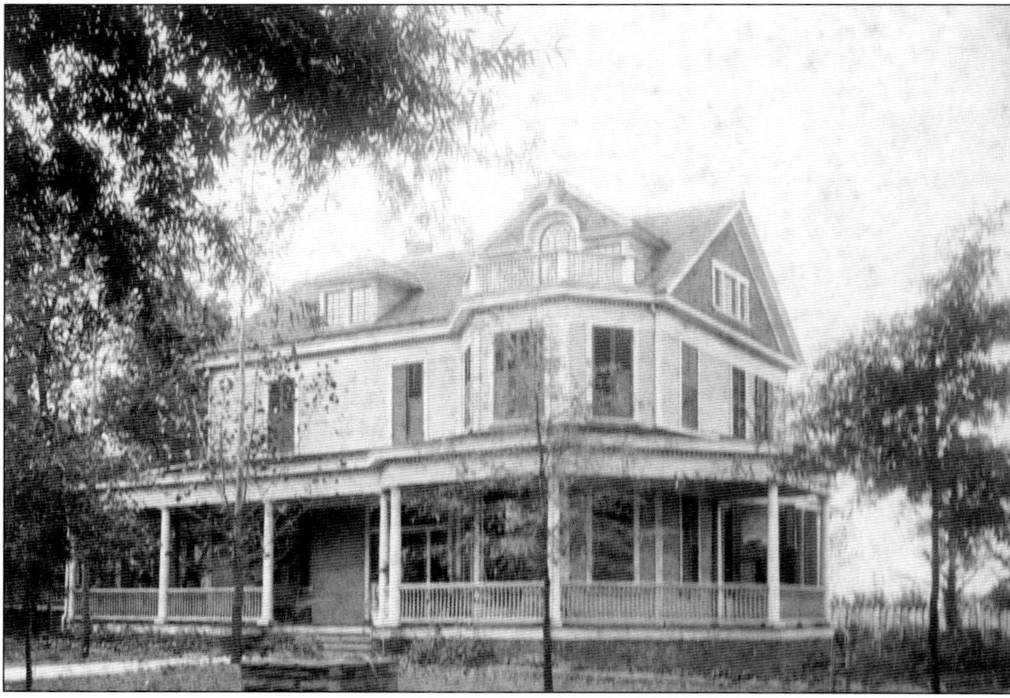

J.B. Park House. This historic house, built in the early 1900s, was hit by the tornado of 1944, and rebuilt with stone. Mr. and Mrs. L.B. Adams later purchased the house as they were preparing to create the Railroad Historical Center. The house became the railroad museum and housed memorabilia from the bygone era of railroads, including the 1904 Baldwin steam locomotive pictured below.

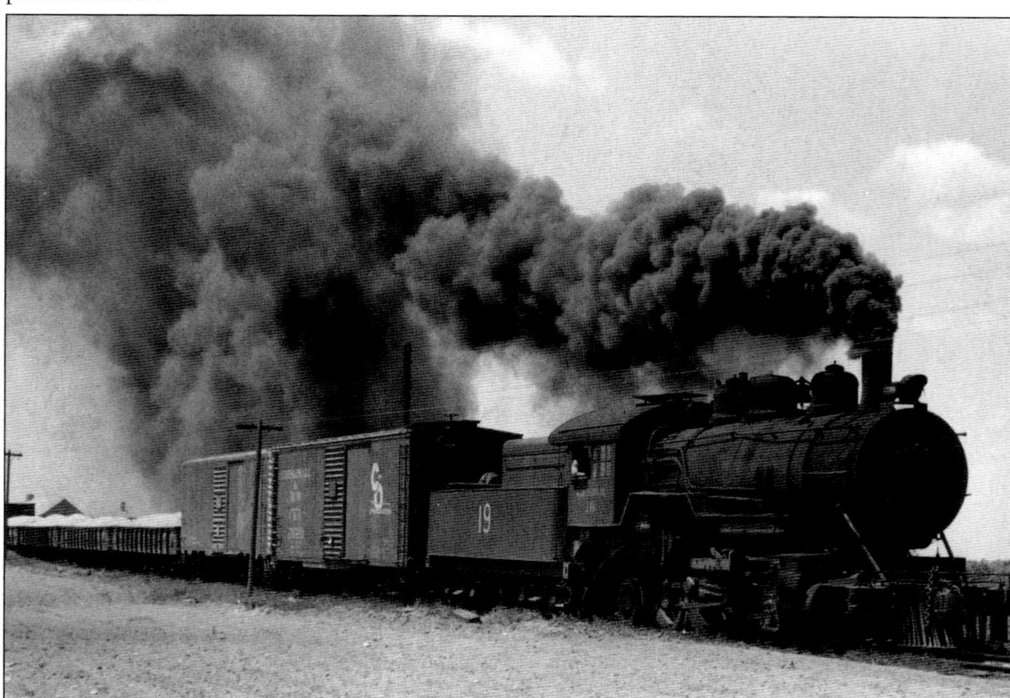

Three

TEXTILES

It is practically impossible to separate the story of Greenwood from the story of textiles. In fact, many of the early community leaders and entrepreneurs of Greenwood worked with the local mills, which began to spring up in earnest after the Industrial Revolution. The mills were owned and operated by men such as James Self, John Abney, A.F. McKissick, and others who were similar in character. They were unafraid of hard work and were willing to take risks.

Created in part as a means to provide economic opportunities for struggling white families, the mills and their surrounding communities soon became a way of life in Greenwood, Ware Shoals, and Ninety-Six. The mills themselves provided steady employment for many white members of the community. African Americans participated in the beginning stages of the textile process, such as picking, weighing, baling, and transporting cotton. At the mills, they often worked as yardmen, scrubbers, and sweepers. Despite this segregation, life in the mill community was close-knit. Mill corporations took special care to meet the needs of their employees, providing housing, education, and recreation.

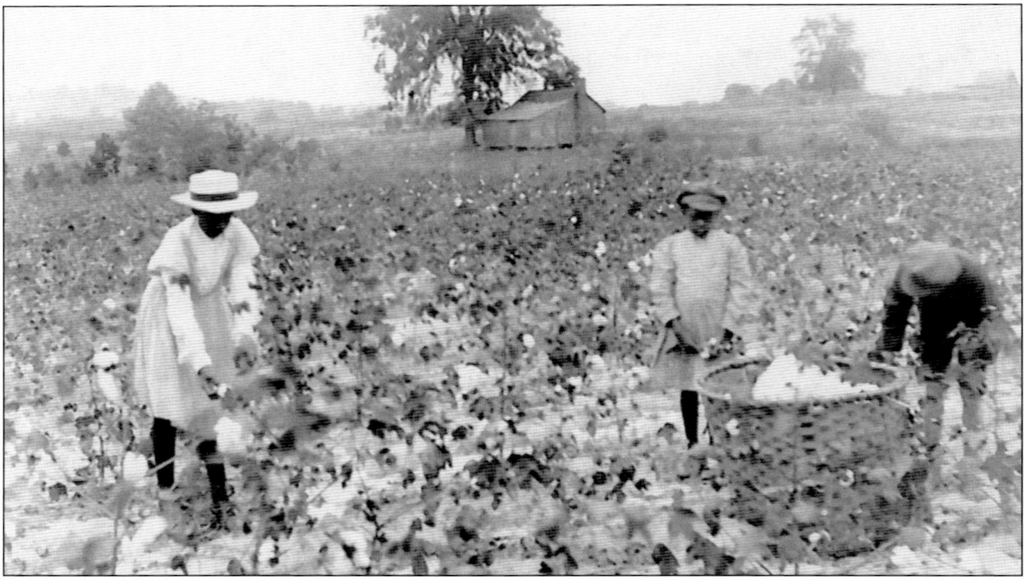

Preindustrial Textiles. Before the Industrial Revolution, textile manufacturing was a village industry. Spinning wheels and other instruments were located in people's homes or in a communal space, such as a loom shop, where the landowner would provide textile equipment for his tenants. From picking the cotton to producing the fabric, the community was involved in the entire process. Pictured are farmers picking cotton. This was very hard and demanding work, as a protective boll surrounds cotton fibers. Even after industry came to South Carolina, cotton was still harvested by hand, often by African Americans and for a very low wage.

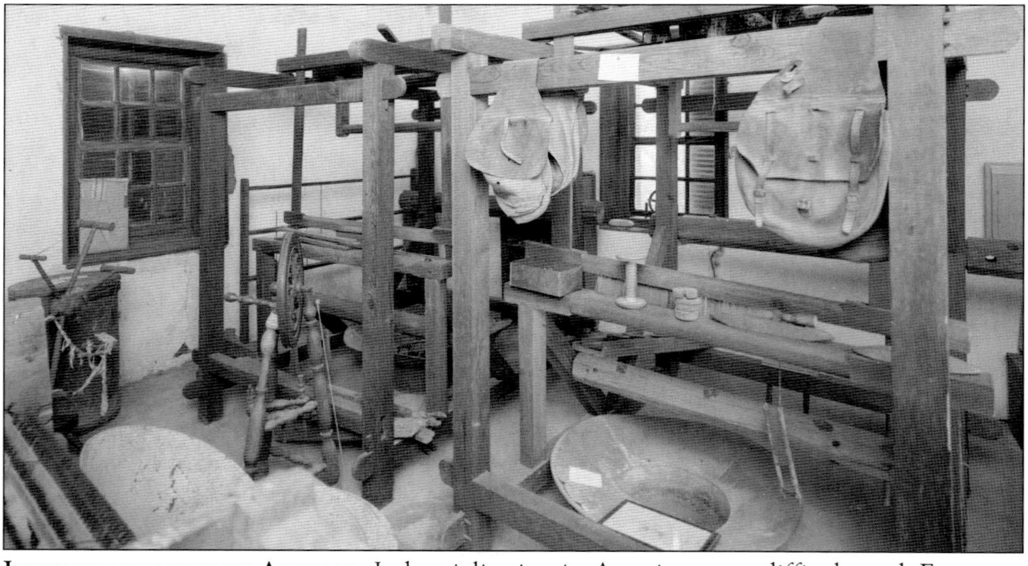

Industrialization in America. Industrialization in America was a difficult road. For many years, it was illegal for any drawings of looms or other equipment created in England to leave that country. There were even laws restricting textile workers from leaving. Despite this, information still found its way across the Atlantic, and inventors such as Samuel Slater made their way to the United States and helped industrialize the textile process. Looms like those pictured here would have been used in the late 1800s, at the dawn of the Greenwood textile industry . (Courtesy of the Library of Congress.)

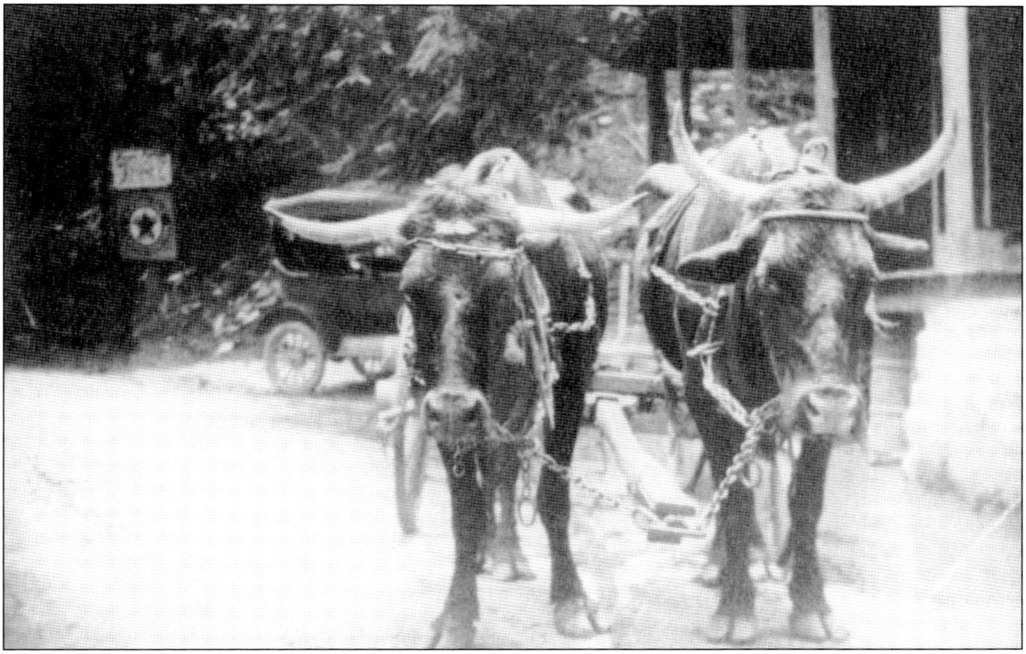

FARM ANIMALS. Cotton production would not have been possible without the aid of farm animals, such as oxen and horses. Traditionally, oxen, pictured here, were often strapped to a plough and used to break up soil. They were also used for transportation and powering preindustrial machinery. Furthermore, on a farm, draft horse breeds could be relied upon for heavy ploughing. Draft horses differ in size and strength to stock horses. They are known for their height, broad backs, and powerful hindquarters. (Courtesy of the Greenwood County Library System.)

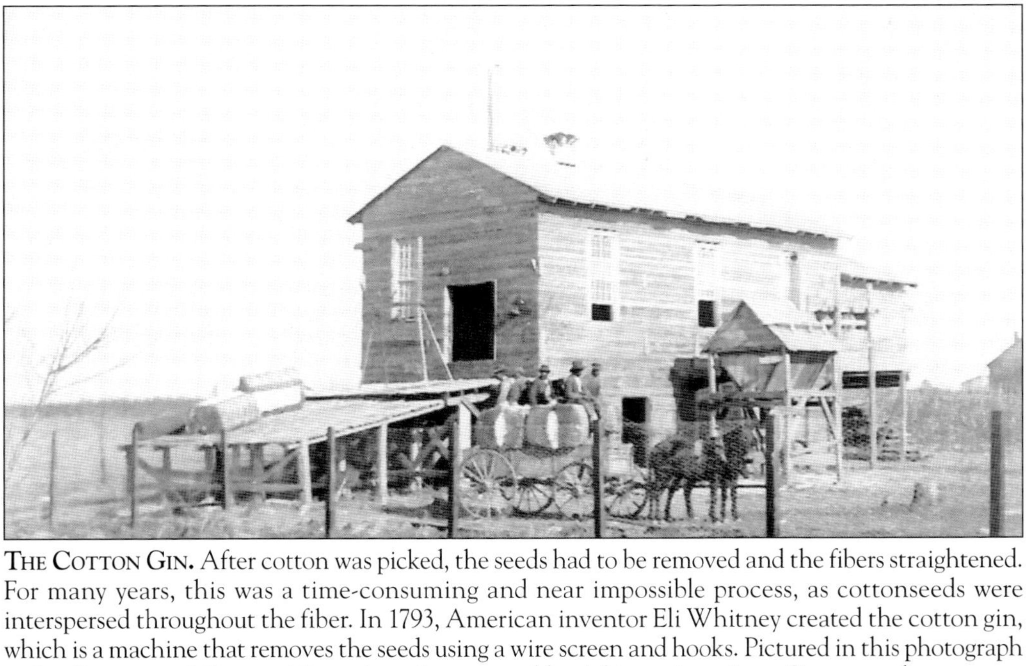

THE COTTON GIN. After cotton was picked, the seeds had to be removed and the fibers straightened. For many years, this was a time-consuming and near impossible process, as cottonseeds were interspersed throughout the fiber. In 1793, American inventor Eli Whitney created the cotton gin, which is a machine that removes the seeds using a wire screen and hooks. Pictured in this photograph is the Greenwood Cotton Gin, primarily operated by African American Greenwoodians.

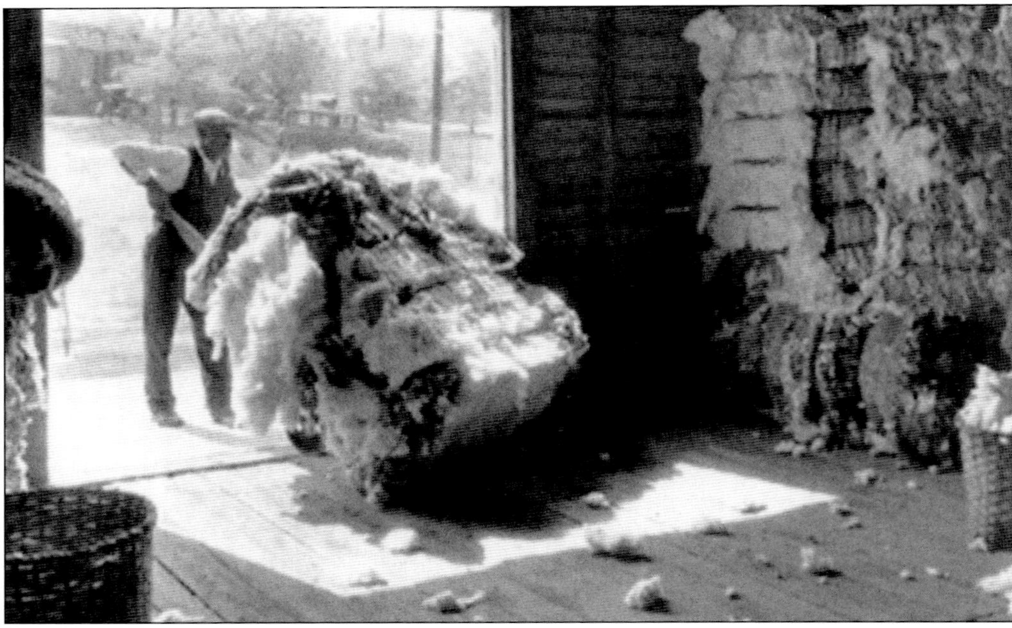

Preparing Cotton. After the cotton had been run through the gin, it had to be weighed and packed into bales for transport. In later years, cotton bales were secured with eight steel straps. An average bale weighed 500 pounds and included enough cotton to make over 300 pairs of jeans. In Greenwood, bales were carefully weighed before delivery. Pictured in the early 1900s is a man delivering a cotton bale in Greenwood.

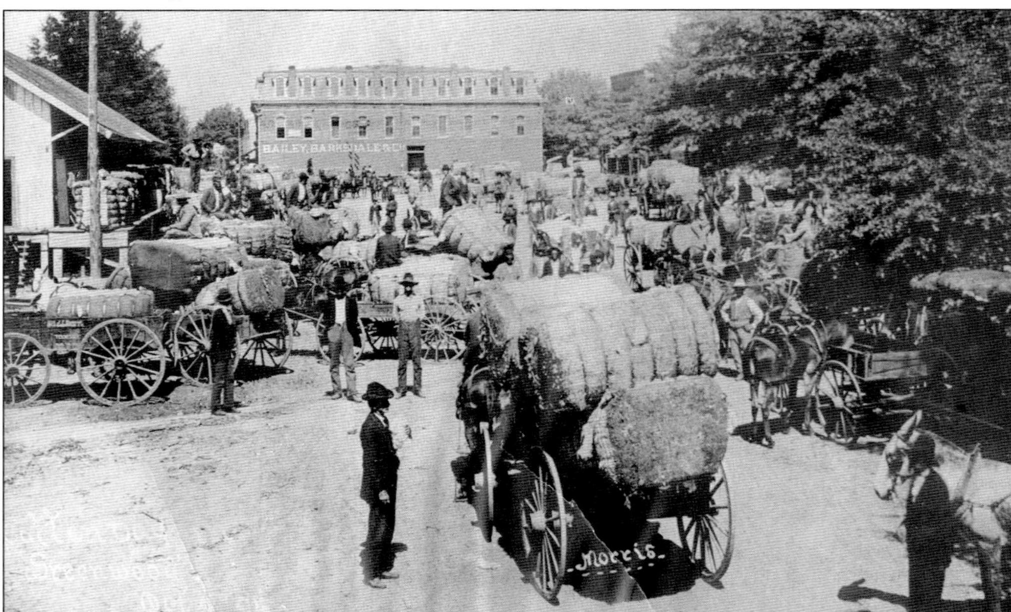

Greenwood Cotton Exchange. After the cotton was baled, it was taken to market by buggy. Farmers would negotiate with manufacturers and wholesalers for the best price. During harvest time, Greenwood's cotton exchange was a particularly busy location, as farmers from many different rural areas brought their goods to sell. This photograph of the cotton exchange was taken on a busy day in Greenwood's square on October 1, 1896. (Courtesy of the Library of Congress.)

Carding Cotton. Once purchased by the manufacturer, the cotton still needed to go through a process known as carding. This was where mill machines pulled the fiber into a web, allowing the threads to be disentangled. Before the advent of textile equipment, cotton was carded by hand using a pair of wooden paddles.

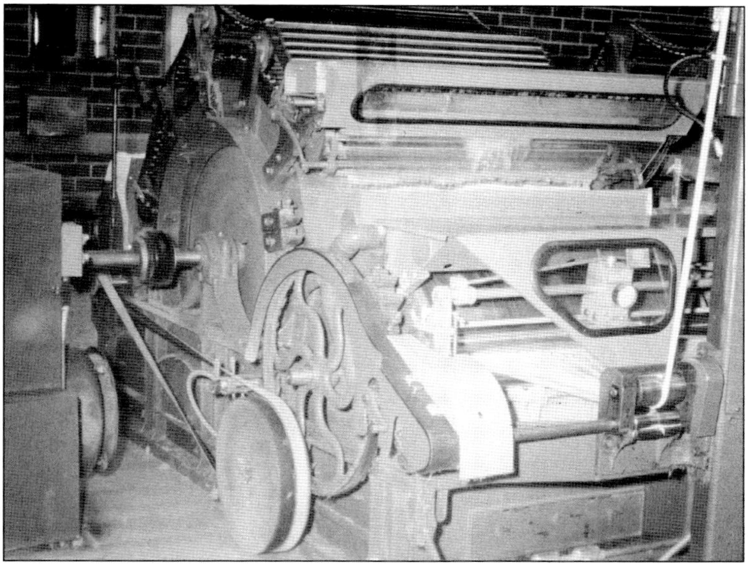

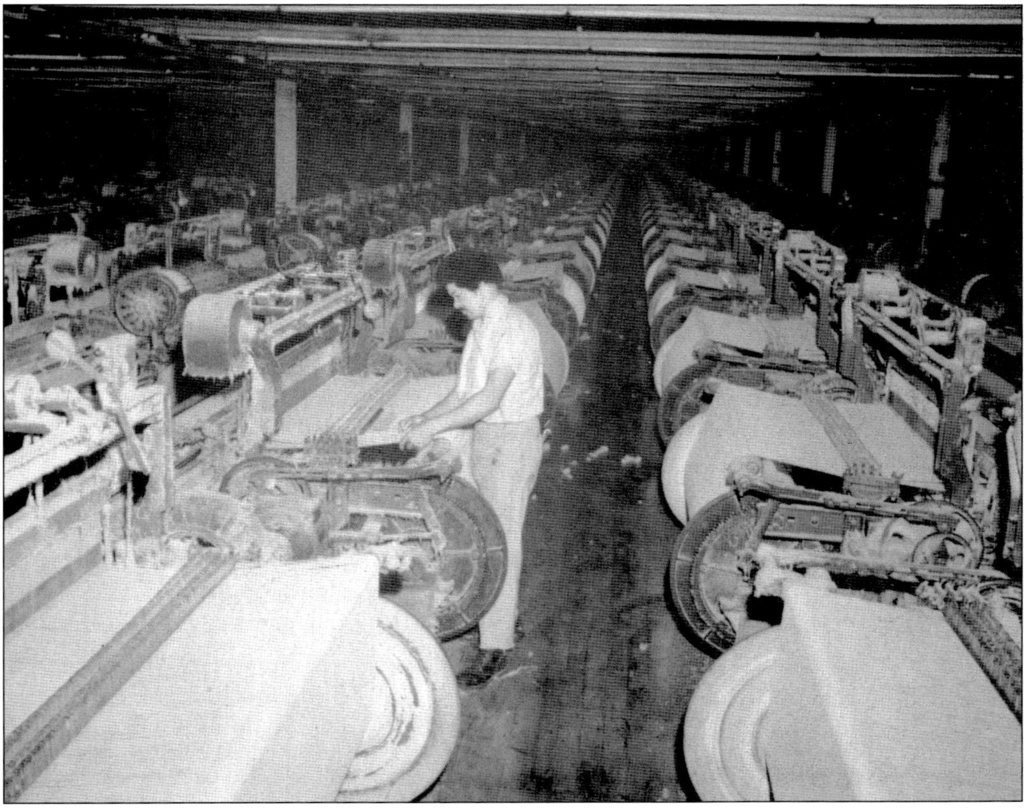

Weaving. Weaving is the process that turns thread into fabric. After 1785, in the textile industry, large power looms were used for this step. Longitudinal threads, called weft yarn, were passed over and under the warp yarn, or lateral threads. By tightly interlacing these two strands, fabric could be created.

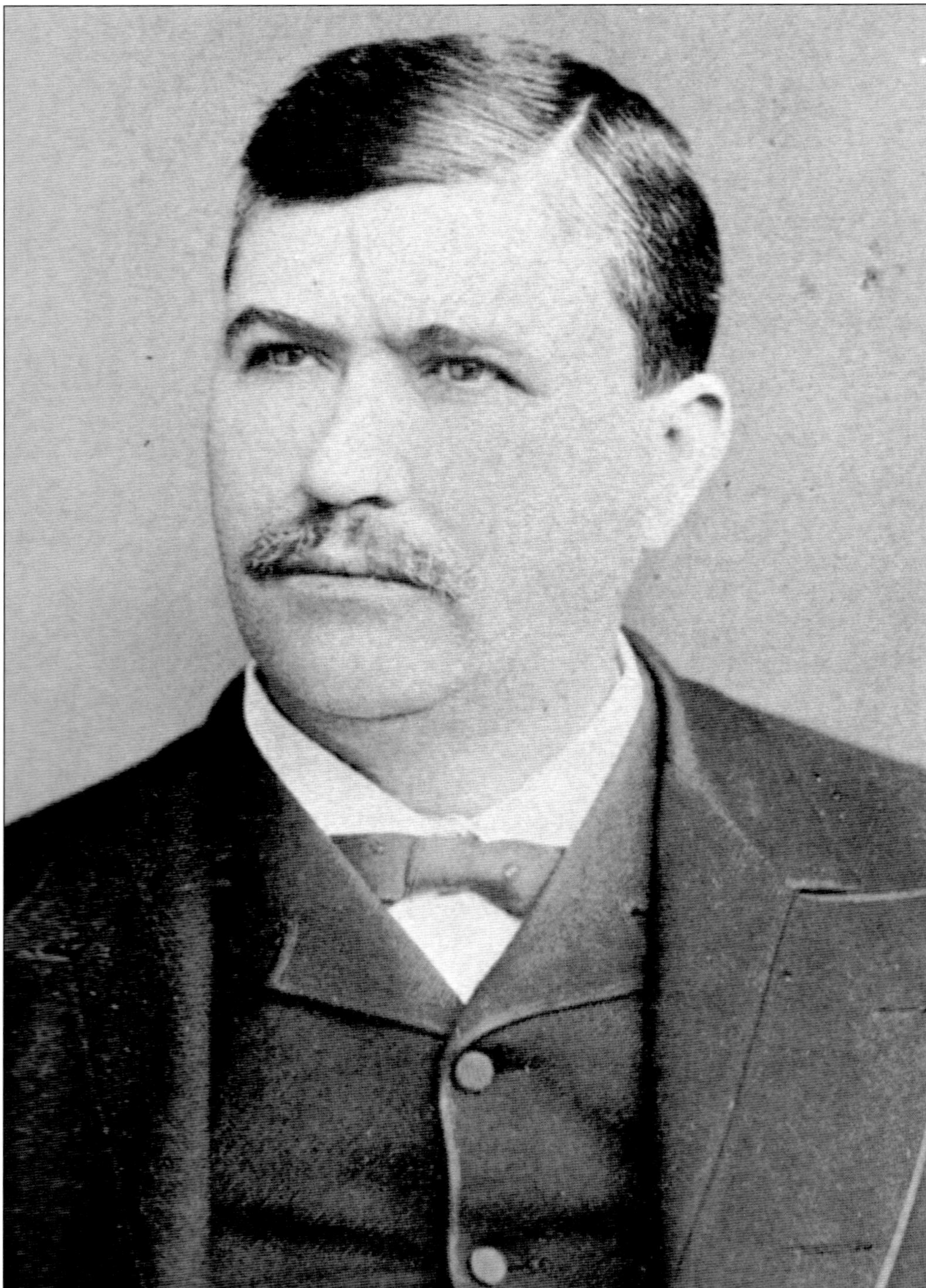

The Durst Brothers. William Lowndes Durst was the founder of the Greenwood Cotton Mill, the first textile mill in Greenwood. He and his brother John Kemp Durst were early entrepreneurs and ran both the Bank of Greenwood and the cotton mill. After William's death in 1902, John took over. William Lowndes Durst is pictured here.

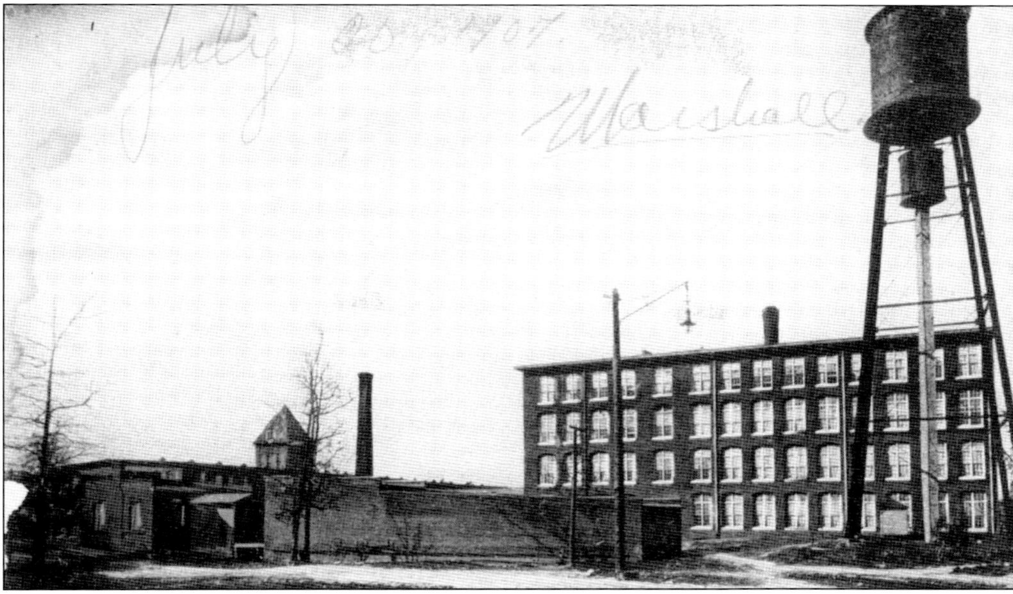

The Greenwood Cotton Mill. Opening in 1890, the Greenwood Cotton Mill was the first textile mill in Greenwood and operated with only 75 employees and four bales of cotton initially. As the business grew, the factory came to house 2,500 spindles and 84 looms. Kerosene was used to light the workspace, and water was sprinkled on the floor at scheduled intervals as a humidification system. Humidity plays a very important role in maintaining the properties of textile fiber.

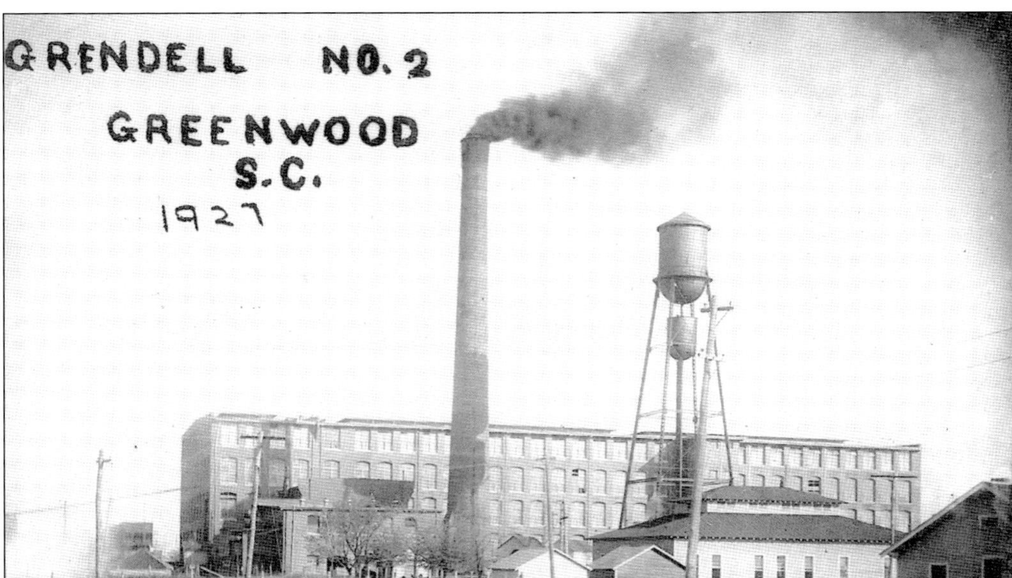

Grendel Mill. Greenwood's second mill, Grendel Mill, was chartered in 1896. Its first president was David Augustas Parker Jordan. In its first three years of operation, the capital stock of Grendel Mill tripled. After Jordan's death in 1901, A.F. McKissick took over Grendel Mill.

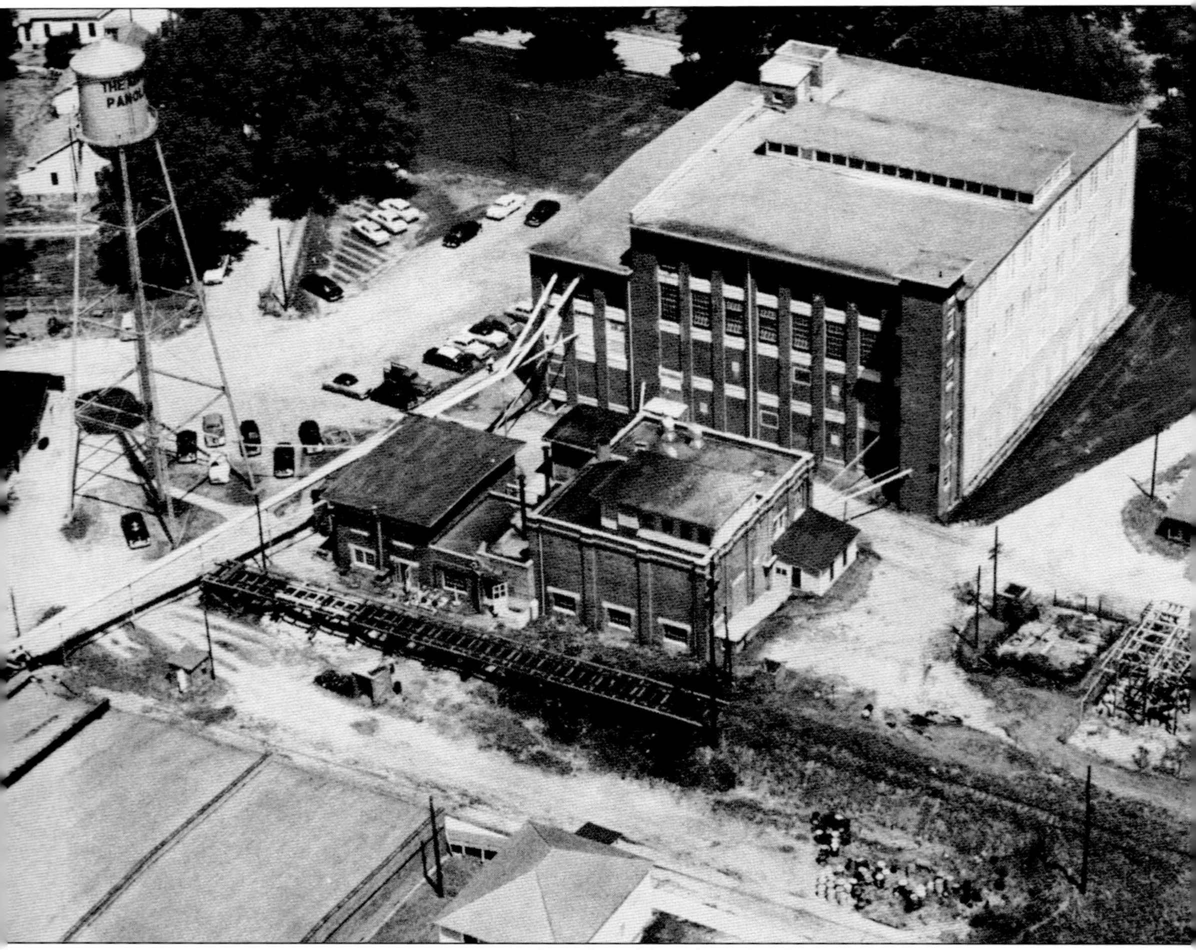

Samuel McGhee and Panola Mill. Thought to be named after a Native American word for cotton, Panola Mill was chartered in 1910 by Samuel McGhee, an attorney and banker. Besides owning this mill, McGhee also served two terms as a state senator, taught at a Marion County school, and owned a local newspaper. McGhee served as Panola Mill's president until 1921, when John Abney purchased it.

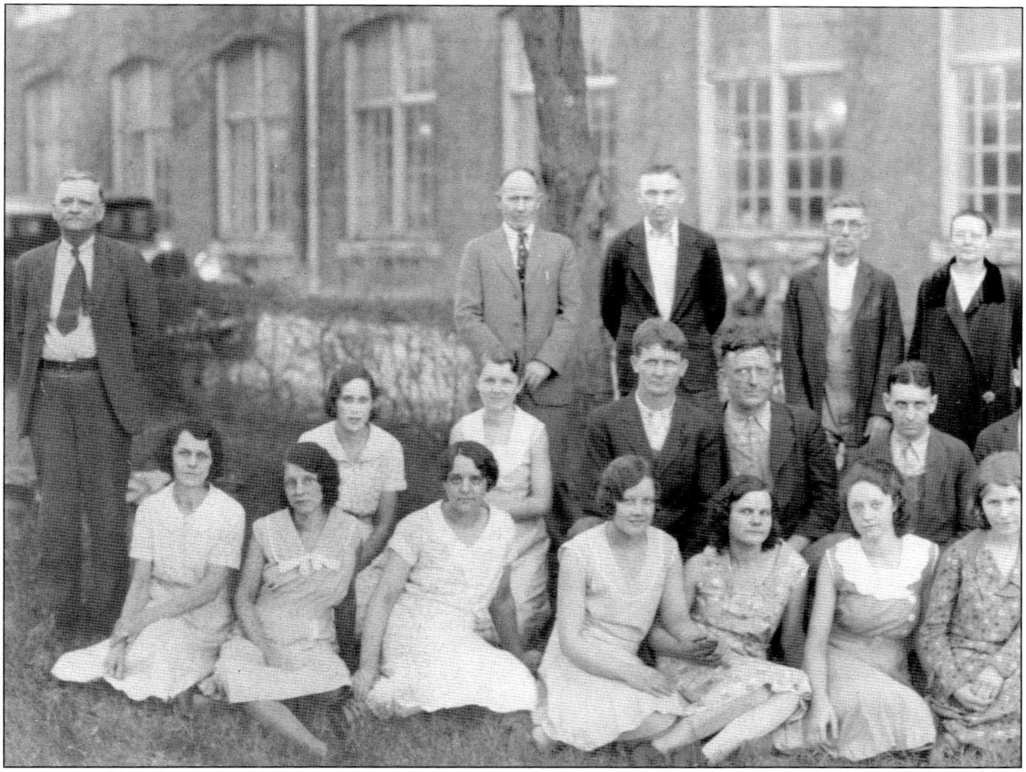

John Pope Abney and Abney Mills. Considered by some to be a "quiet man with the soul of a gambler," John Abney was unafraid to try new business ventures. Purchasing Grendel Mill from A.F. McKissick, Abney continued to purchase mills in Greenwood, Anderson, Belton, and Newry. Pictured is a group of day weavers at Grendel Mills posing for the camera in 1932.

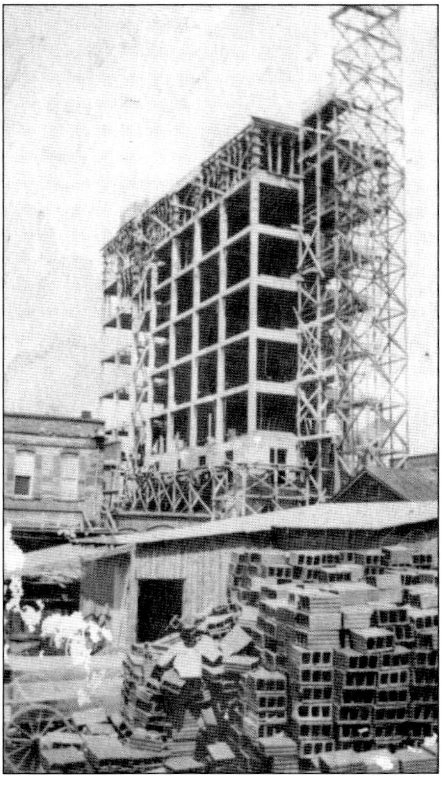

F.E. Grier and Abney Mills. After John Abney's death in 1942, Abney Mills was taken over by F.E. Grier at the request of John's family. Grier ran the mills in such a way that the business continued to expand. By 1946, Panola Mill, Grendel Mill, and Anderson Cotton Mill were renamed Abney Mills. Eventually, Grier ran 27 mills in South Carolina, North Carolina, and Mississippi, employing over 15,000 people. Pictured during construction around 1920 is what became known as the Grier Building, named in honor of F.E. Grier's accomplishments.

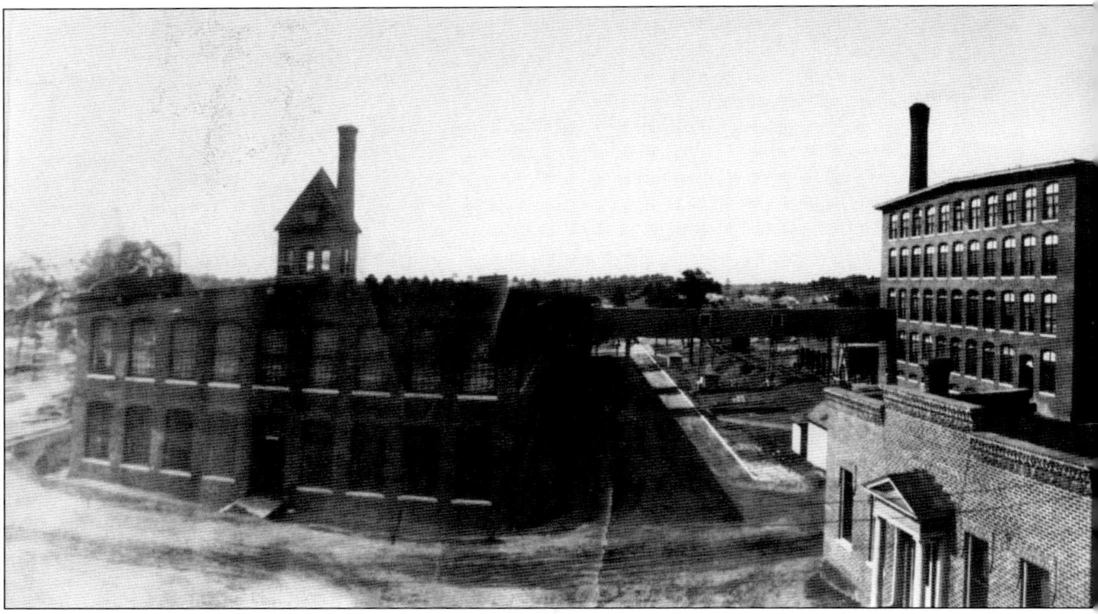

Greenwood Mills. James Self took over the mill during a time of financial hardship. One of the plants had closed, and the other surely would unless new machinery could be purchased. He immediately went to New England to visit the Draper Loom Corporation in order to acquire it. In a show of extraordinary gumption after George Draper backed out of the deal his brother

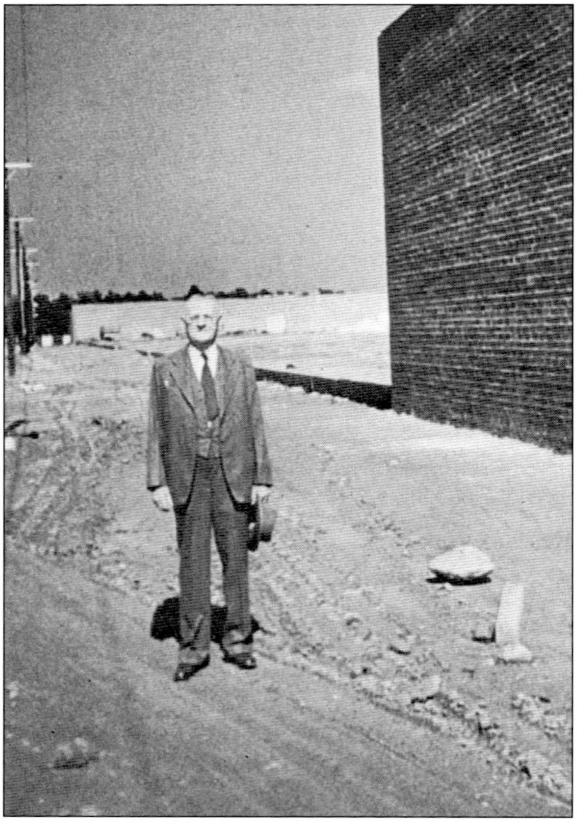

James Cuthbert Self. Born on July 1, 1876, James C. Self's name eventually became synonymous with the textile industry in Greenwood. His introduction into business began in 1899, when he started at the Bank of Greenwood. There, he came into contact with John Kemp Durst, president of the Greenwood Cotton Mill. By 1908, James Self took over this mill, and by 1931, he owned four of the seven mills in Greenwood County. In this photograph, Self is at the construction site of Durst Plant, the last he ever built. (Courtesy of the Self Family Foundation.)

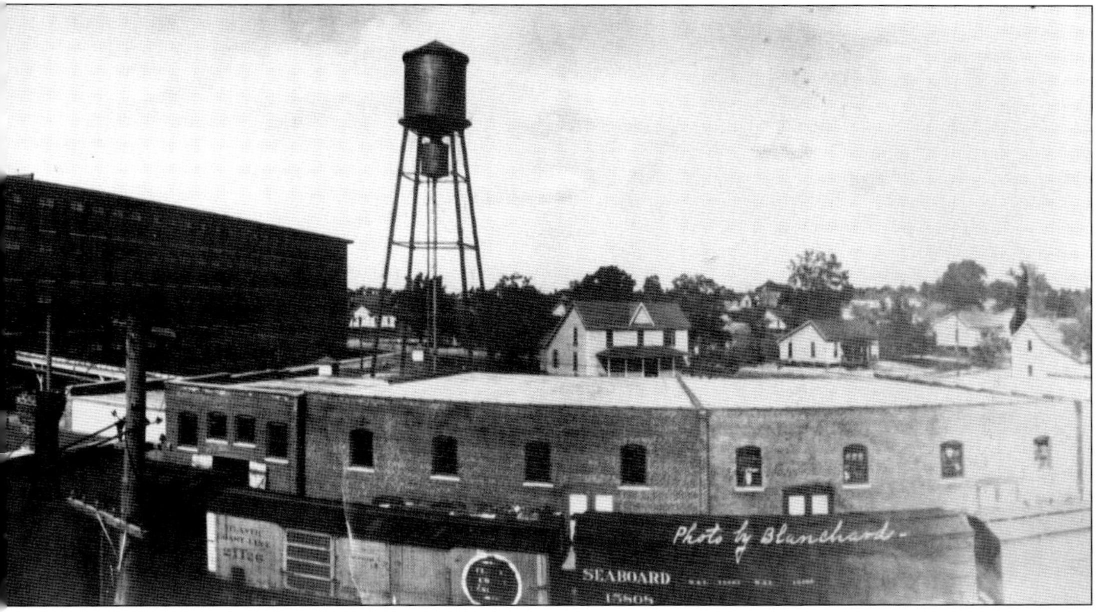

promised, Self came back into his office and stated, "In the South, sir, we do what we promise." His character was apparently enough to secure the looms, and the mill did not close down. In this photograph, the Greenwood Cotton Mill is captured in a panoramic view. (Courtesy of Lander University.)

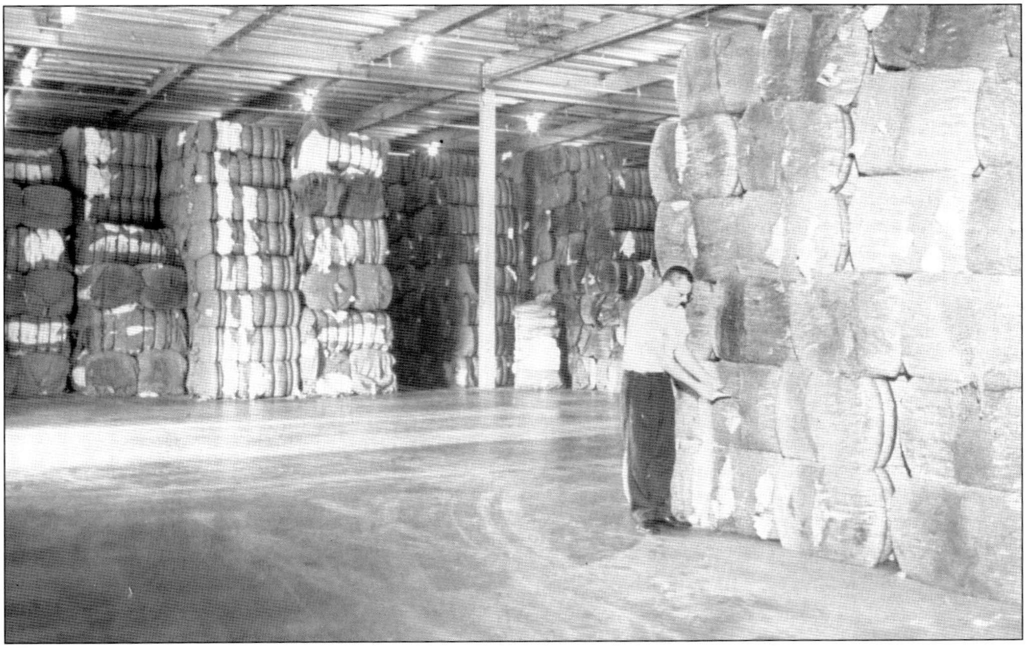

GREENWOOD MILLS AND THE GREAT DEPRESSION. The textile industry, like many others, suffered during the Great Depression. However, Self continued to look for opportunities to grow and make a profit. He purchased extra cotton for the storehouse in case of a shortage, and in 1921, he purchased the Ninety-Six Mill. Despite financial difficulties, James Self was still able to meet payroll, and when some of the banks closed, he paid his employees with cash. Greenwood Mills continued to stockpile cotton after Self's tenure. Pictured is a Greenwood Mills cotton warehouse in later years.

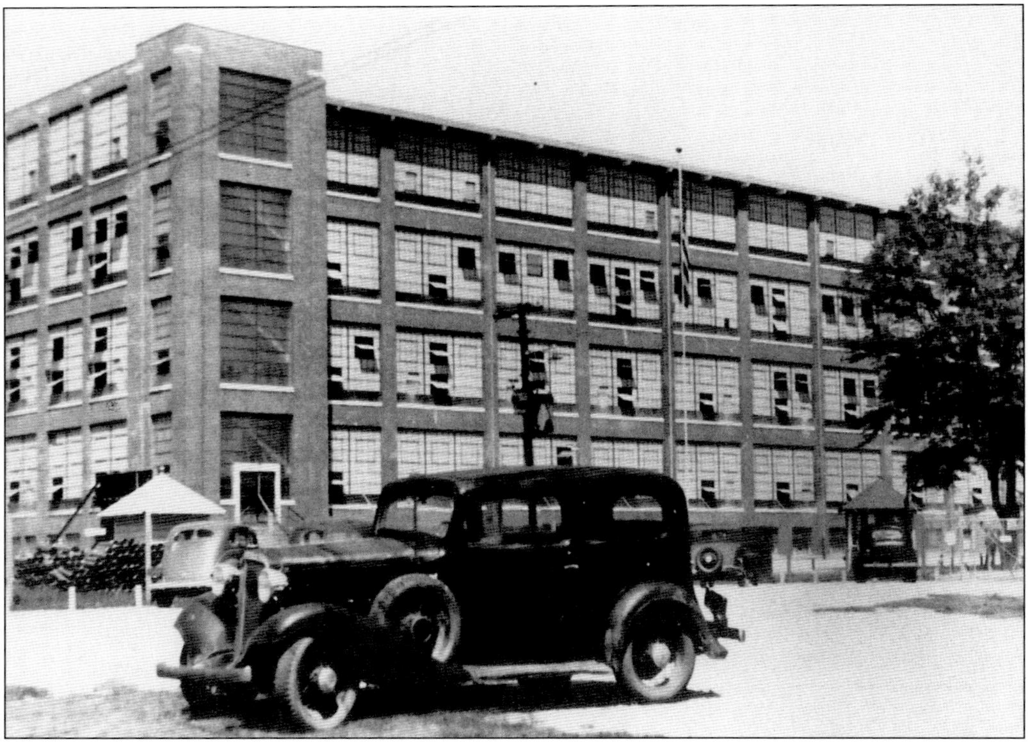

TEXTILE UNIONS. In the 1930s, attempts were made to unionize textile workers. In many states, these attempts were met with violence, and mills were forced to shut down. Although there was picketing and some factories did close for a short period of time, there were no recorded acts of violence in Greenwood's mills. Mathews Mill, a Greenwood Mill, is shown in this 1930s photograph.

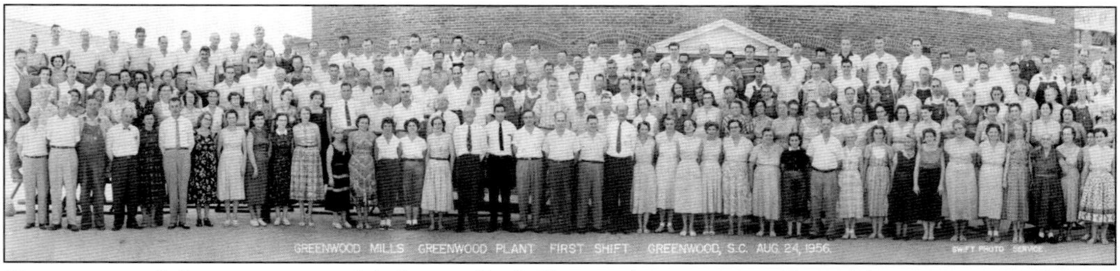

GREENWOOD MILLS AFTER 1955. James C. Self passed away in 1955, and his son Jim took over the operation of Greenwood Mills. The company continued to expand, working with other organizations, such as Clemson University, to meet new demands in the textile industry. Greenwood Mills continues to be a family-owned business, operated by members of the Self family. In the background of this photograph, the Greenwood Plant, once called the Greenwood Cotton Mill, is shown. The first-shift employees gathered for this picture on August 24, 1956, 66 years after the opening of Greenwood Cotton Mill.

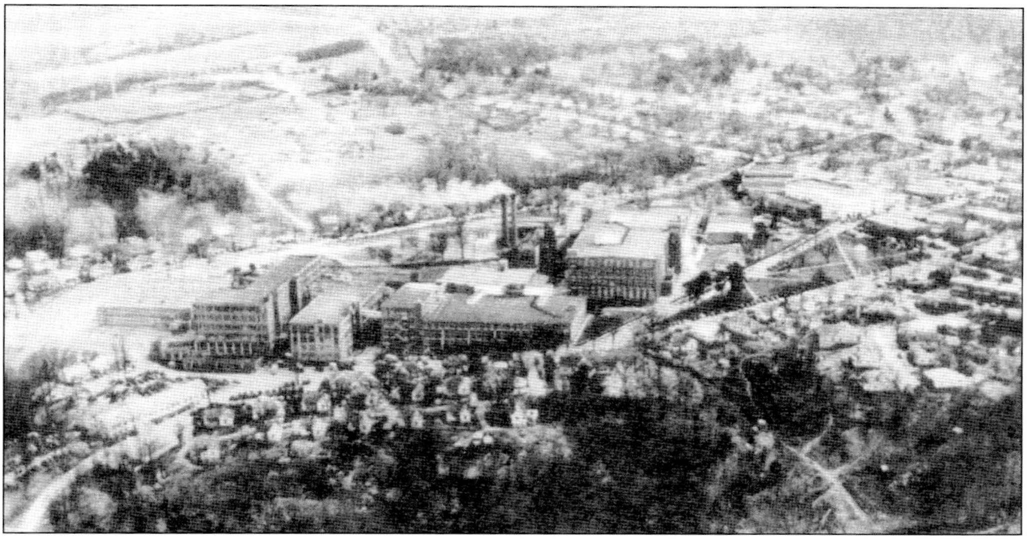

Riegel Mill. Benjamin Riegel of New York believed that profit could be found in a project taking form off the banks of the Saluda River. In 1902, he established Ware Shoals Manufacturing Company as well as the town of Ware Shoals. By 1916, this mill housed over 70,000 spindles and 1,000 looms. Riegel Mill was responsible for building Ware Shoals's first school and providing other services, such as electricity and banking.

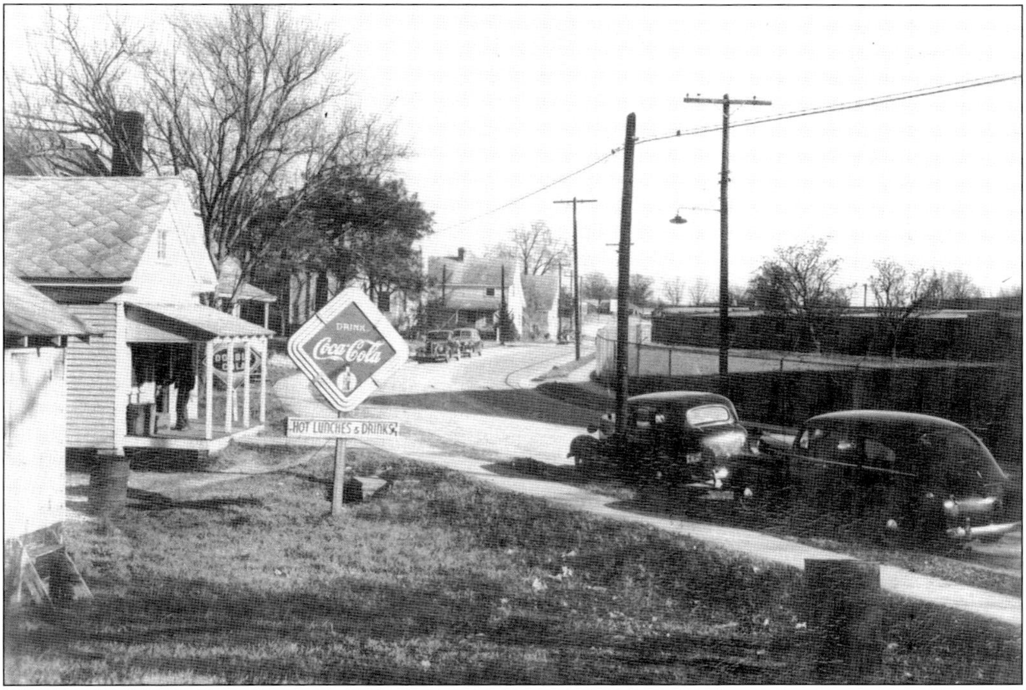

Mill Villages. The state of mill villages varied all over the country based on the attitudes of mill executives. Self set the standard for mill villages in this area, showing that he was deeply concerned with his workers' quality of life. He began working on these mill villages in the 1920s, creating a community with wide streets, sturdy homes built of brick and tile, schools, churches, and other recreational facilities. Millions of dollars were spent on these villages, while only $1 per room per week was charged to tenants.

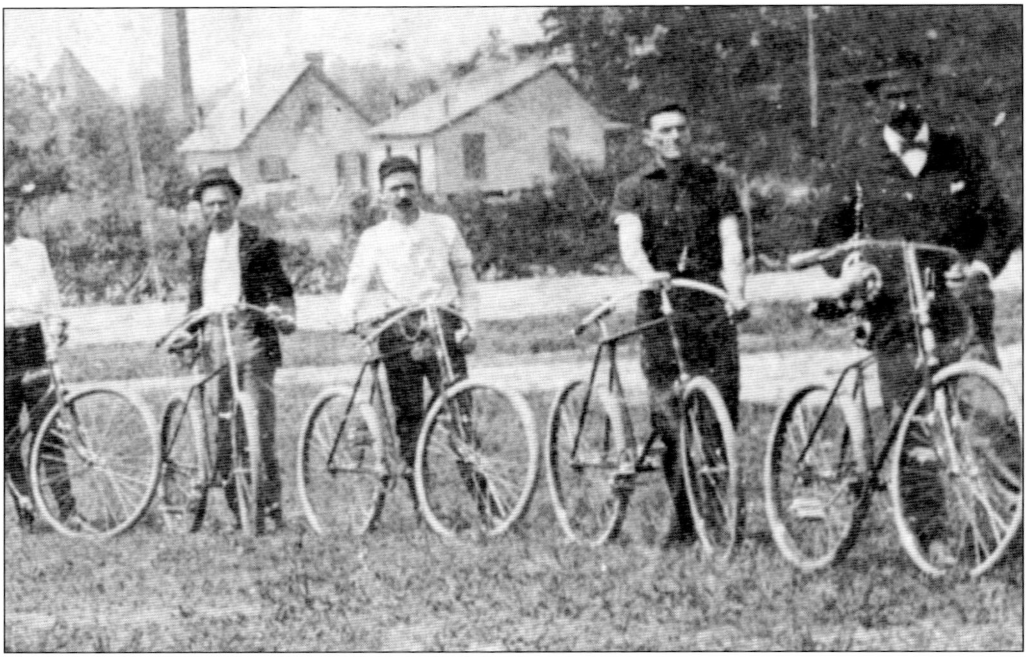

Mill Life. The mill was a way of life for surrounding community members. Mill corporations provided many different services to their employees, including schooling for their children, recreational activities and athletics, fairs and festivals, and even general stores. All of these led to a close-knit community centered around each mill in Greenwood. Pictured above are employees of the Greenwood Cotton Mill with their bicycles. This picture was taken on July 4, 1893, and some of the earliest mill houses are visible in the background. Pictured below is a woman spinning bobbins in a Greenwood Mill in the 1960s.

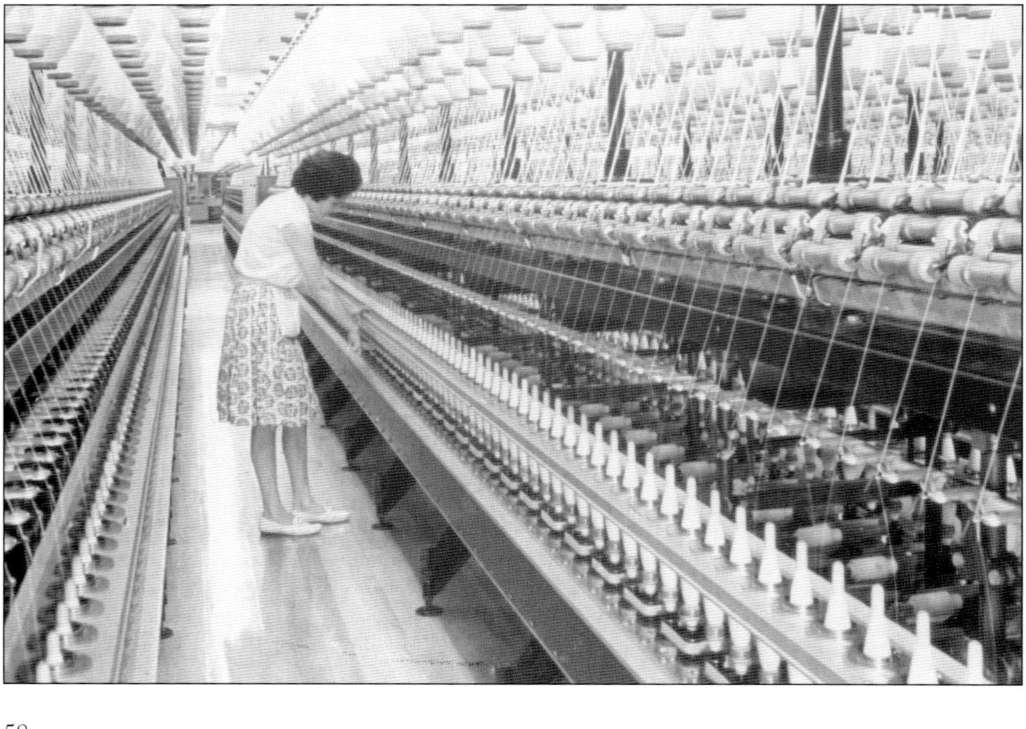

Four

Community Services

Community services can be seen as the "signs of life" in a town or region. Undoubtedly, they serve as proof that a town's population has grown to such an extent that certain services are now necessary. To modern minds, it is hard to imagine living in a place without law enforcement, a fire department, clean water, steady electricity, a hospital, or even a local library. However, Greenwood, as a fledgling establishment, would not have had these things automatically. They would have had to be put into effect by forward-thinking and community-minded individuals. Certainly, there are many people to thank for establishing the services that contribute to today's safety and security, such as the Greenwood Sheriff's Department (established in 1897), the Greenwood Library (1901), the Greenwood Fire Department (1909), the Greenwood Hospital (1911), the Greenwood County Health Department (1915), and many more.

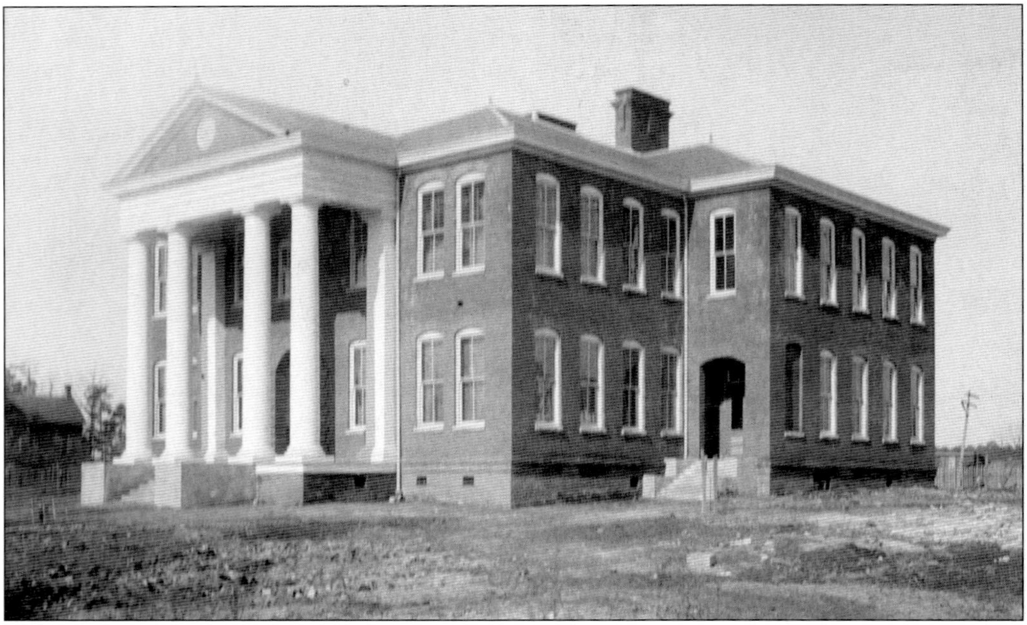

Connie Maxwell Children's Home. A native of Newberry, John Chappell Maxwell moved to Greenwood after the end of the Civil War. In 1890, he donated 470 acres of land for a Baptist orphanage. Named after his daughter Connie who died of scarlet fever when she was only eight years old, Connie Maxwell Children's Home opened its doors in 1892. This institution also ran a school for its children until 1931.

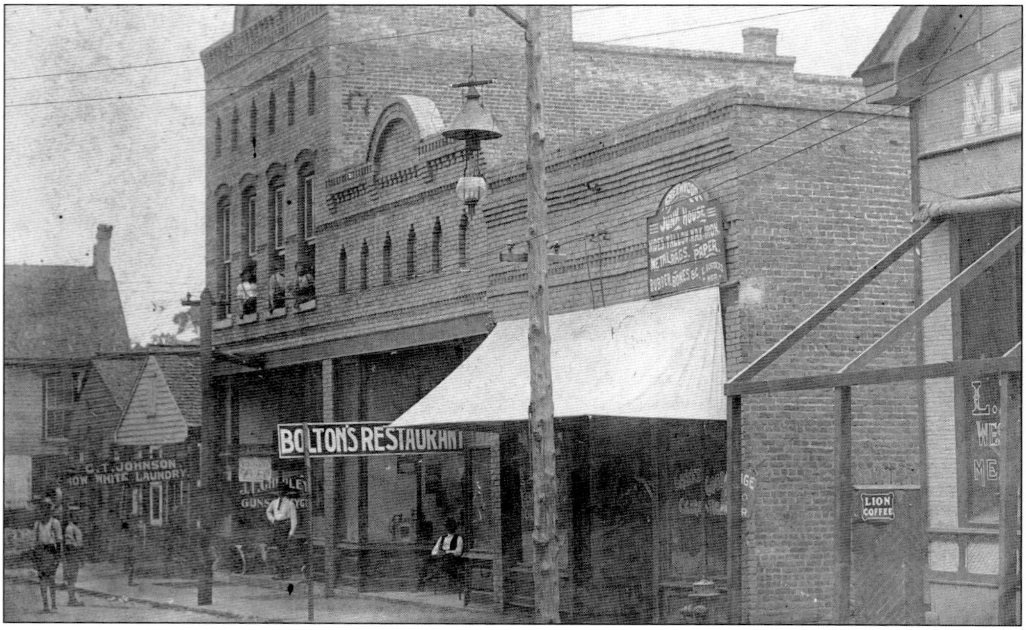

Commission of Public Works. The Commission of Public Works was originally created on October 26, 1896, although it was not officially given this name. It was created to provide the people of Greenwood County with streetlights and porch lights; however, the original 25-year charter with the city council was ultimately extended, and it was given its current name. Early electric streetlights can be seen in this photograph looking down Waller Avenue.

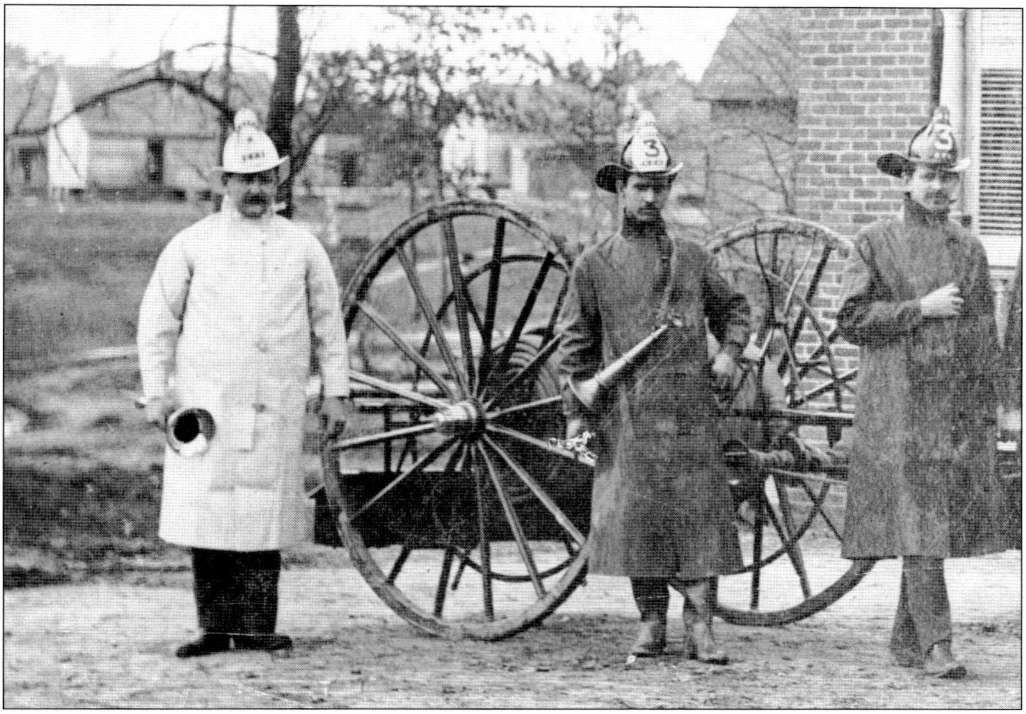

GREENWOOD COUNTY FIRE DEPARTMENT. The creation of a fire fighting organization in Greenwood was spurred on by J.T. Simmons's warehouse fire in March 1895. After this, city council ordered a hook and ladder truck for the community. In its first years, the Greenwood County Fire Department was entirely staffed by volunteers. However, by 1910, the organization had five officers, four paid staff members, and 36 "call men." Also, they had two substations with hand-reel hoses at both Greenwood and Grendel Mills. Another landmark for the Greenwood County Fire Department was the purchase of its first factory-built fire truck in 1937.

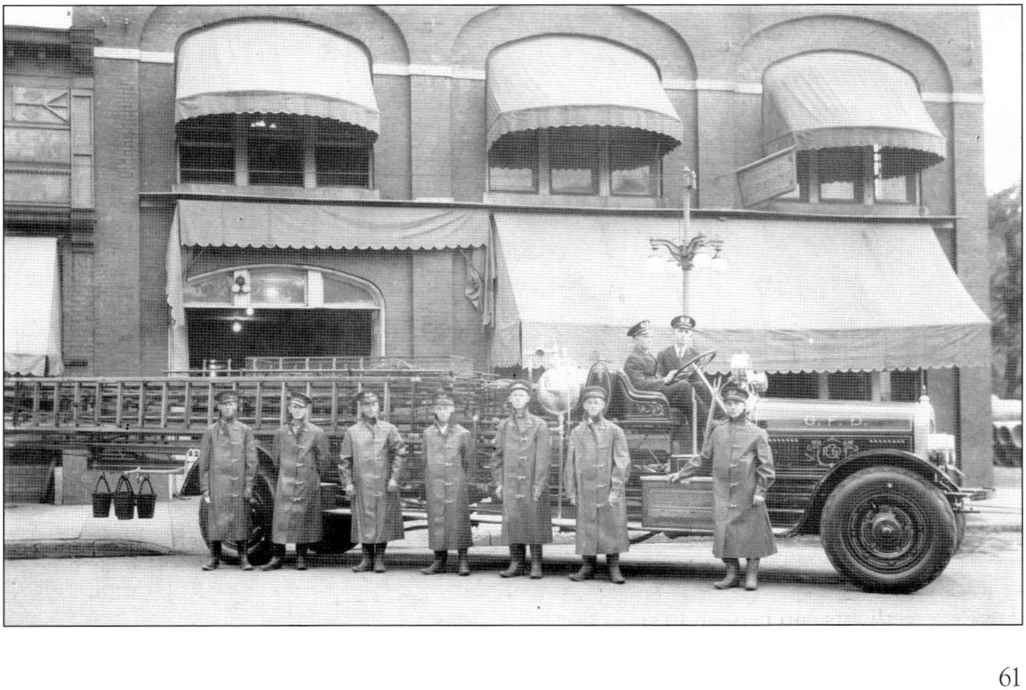

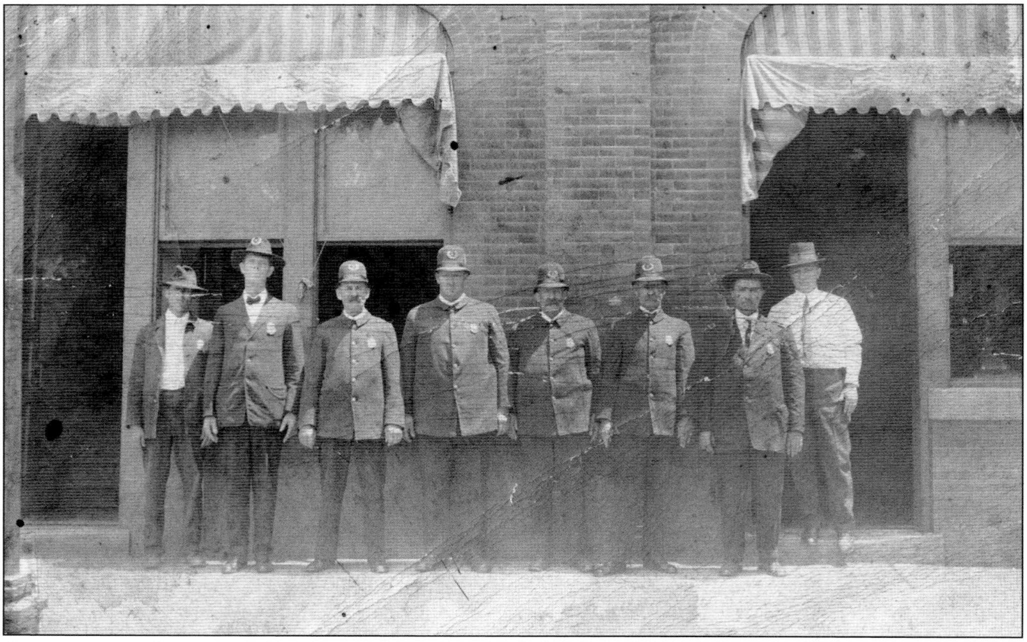

GREENWOOD COUNTY SHERIFF'S DEPARTMENT. The first sheriff of Greenwood, Robert Foster McCaslan, was selected in 1897. This photograph was taken not long after the department was formed.

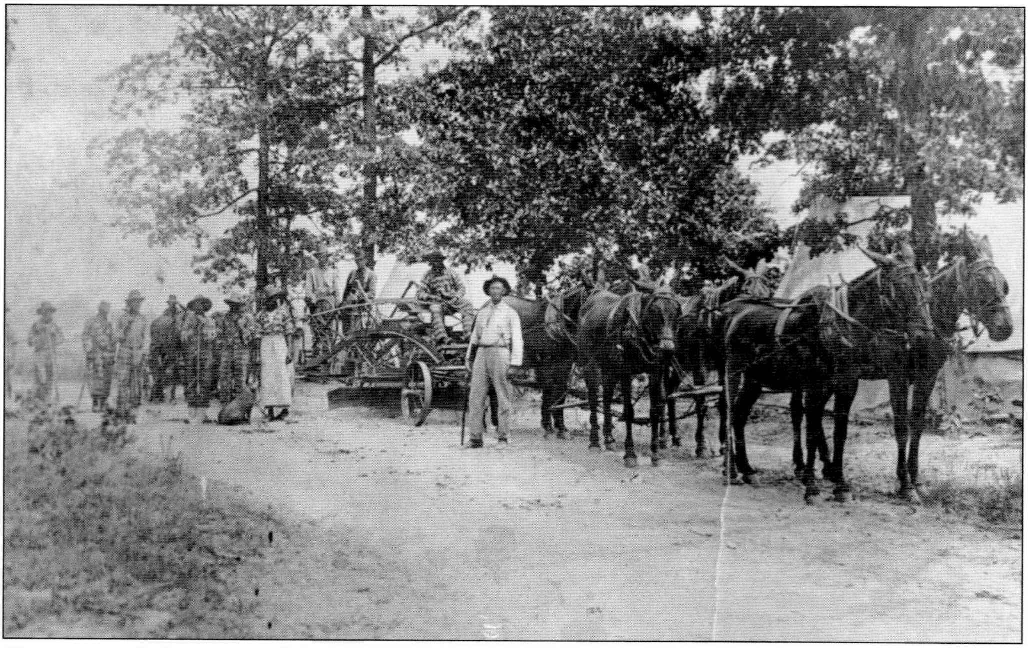

GREENWOOD'S STREETS. There were three major roads in the village of Greenwood in its earliest years, forming a triangle for businesses and residences to develop. The first of these was approved in 1778, but was not actually laid out until 1785. From these humble beginnings, roads began to spring up, connecting schools, homes, churches, and businesses in a web of community life. When laying out streets, citizens were invited to help, and in later years, work crews from the local jail provided labor. Pictured is S.E. Hodges overseeing one of the work crews.

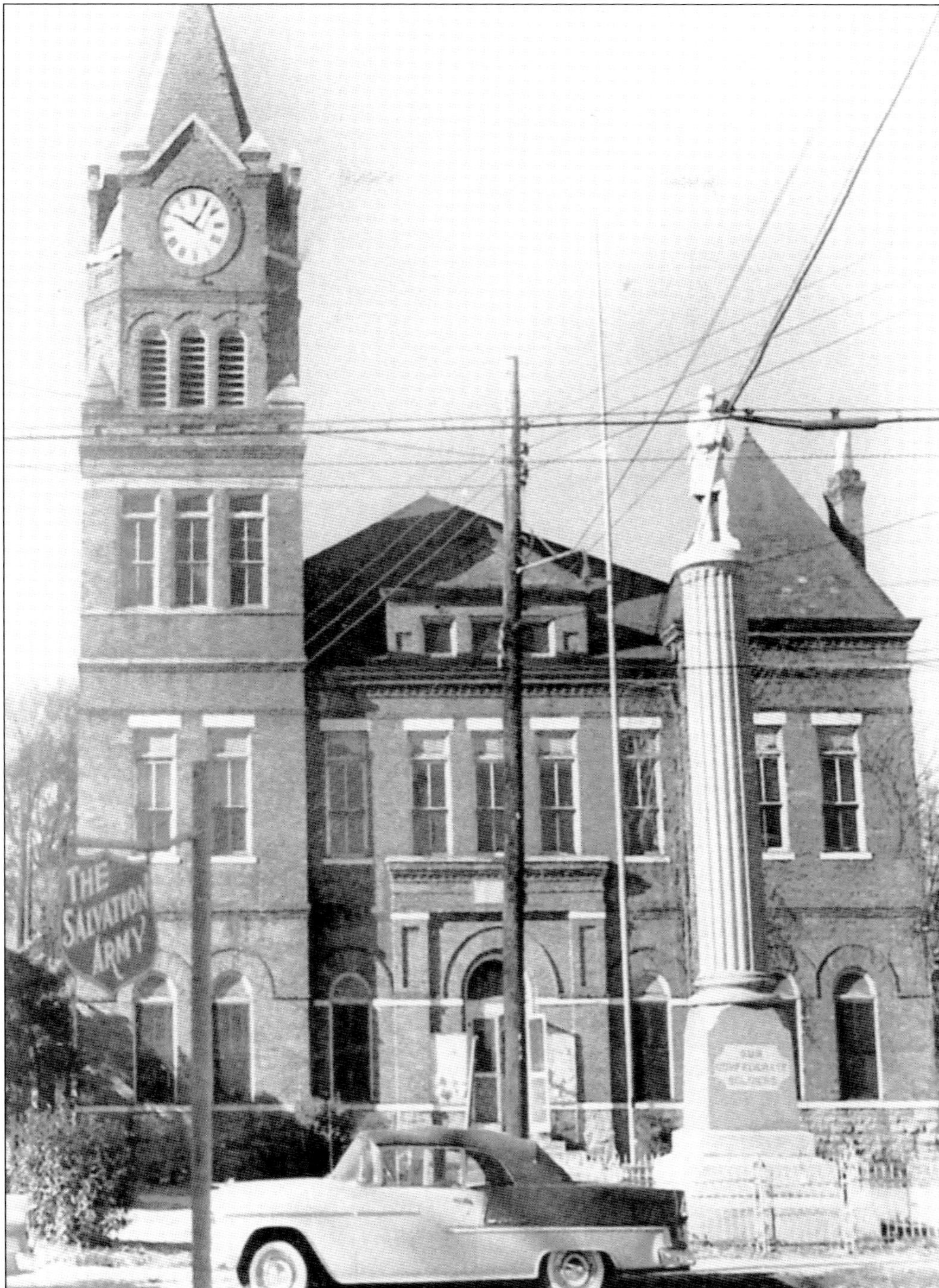

GREENWOOD COUNTY COURTHOUSE. Completed in 1898, the Greenwood County Courthouse contained office space on its first level and a courtroom on its second. It opened amidst a flurry of newspaper articles and legal problems, ultimately leading the original contractor to pull out in March 1898. The courthouse was replaced in the 1960s by a building that cost about $1 million to build, and was created by C.Y. Thomason and Company.

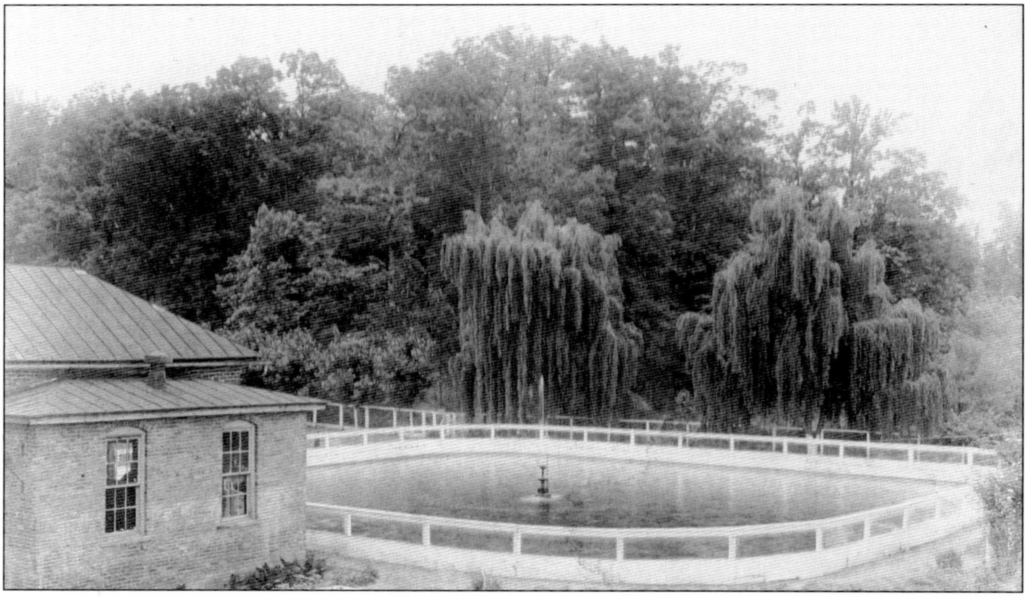

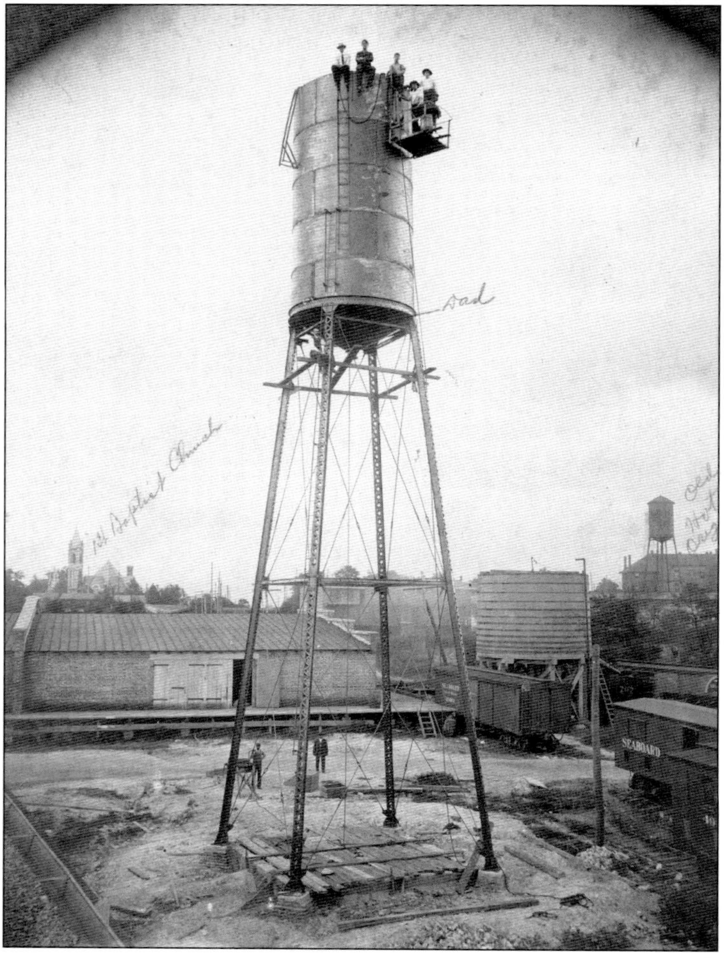

Greenwood Reservoir. In 1898, Greenwood opened the first municipally owned water and light plant in the state. A site at Yoe Springs was chosen because of the adequate supply of water; this spring produced 60 gallons of water per minute. Besides producing light and water for the town of Greenwood, this site also held the "powerhouse," which was a park and picnic area frequented by the locals. A water tower, pictured at left, was constructed on Oregon Avenue to maintain a supply of water should there be an emergency shortage.

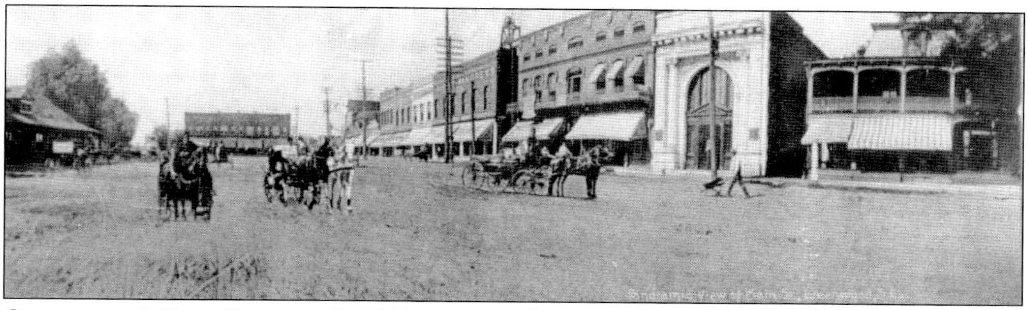

Greenwood's First Library. In 1901, a group of 28 women in Greenwood formed the Library Association. They collected books from members of the community, and when the first library opened, they boasted a collection of 178 titles and were only open six hours a week. Originally housed in a room overlooking a local business, by 1916, members of the community began to plan for a separate local library in earnest. Horse-drawn buggies would have been the mode of transportation for those visiting the library in 1901. This photograph shows how the square looked when the library was located above a storefront on Maxwell Avenue. Notice that the horse and carriage in the foreground were added after the photograph was taken. (Courtesy of William John Park.)

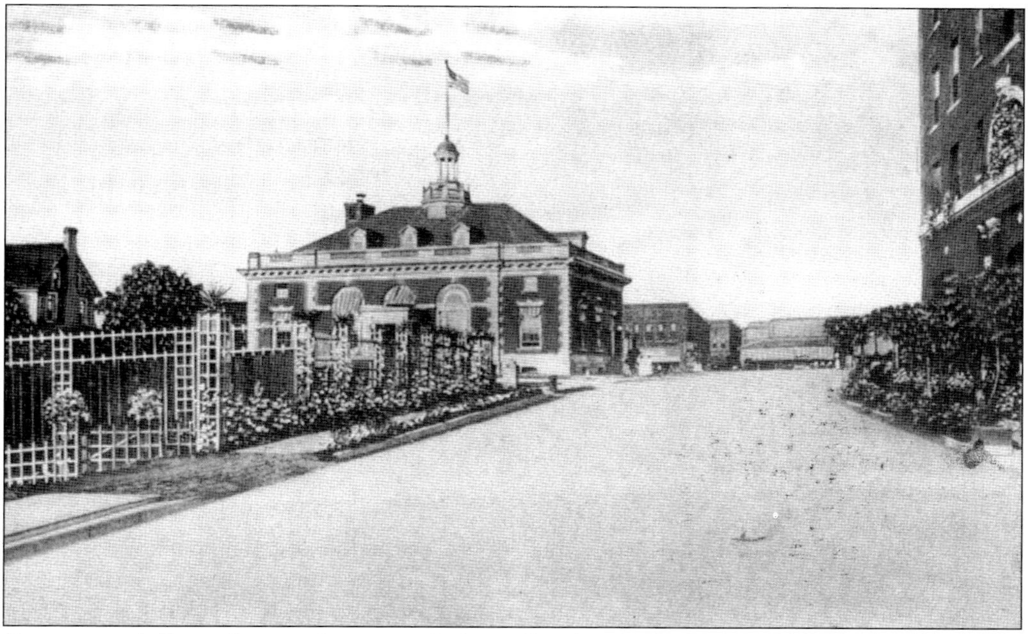

Greenwood's Post Office. Greenwood's first official post office was established in 1912 in the Federal Building. Before this time, makeshift post offices in Greenwood were located in stores and even people's homes! Due to the size of the city, Greenwood did not have a free mail service until 1906.

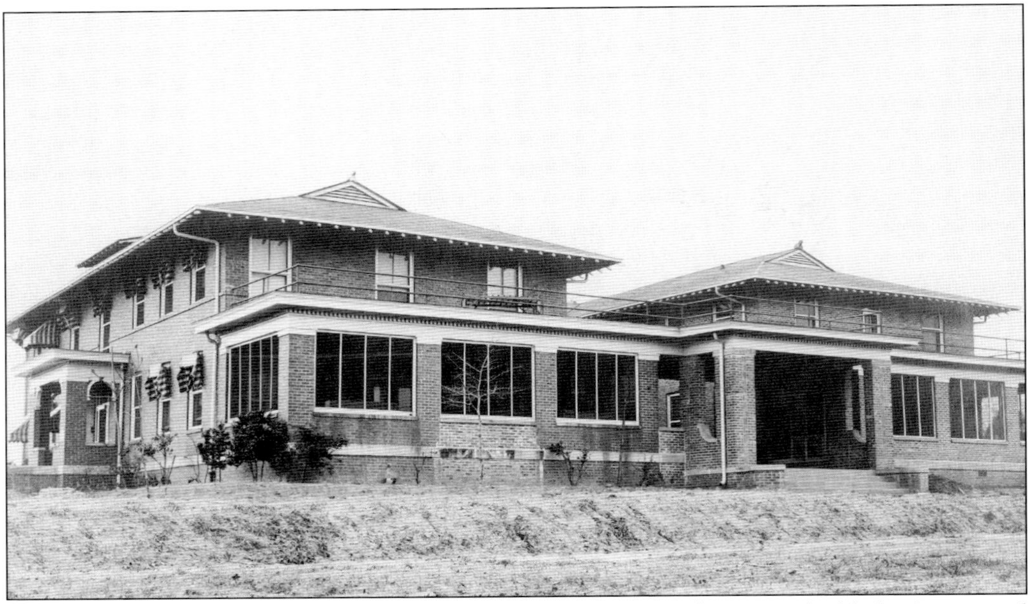

GREENWOOD HOSPITAL. Opened in 1912 and costing approximately $12,000 to build, the Greenwood Hospital only contained 35 patient rooms until a second wing was added in 1924, which brought the capacity to 52. The Greenwood Hospital also operated a Nursing School from 1914 through 1937 and again after the end of World War II. This hospital was devastated by the tornado that hit Greenwood in 1944. (Courtesy of the Greenwood County Library System.)

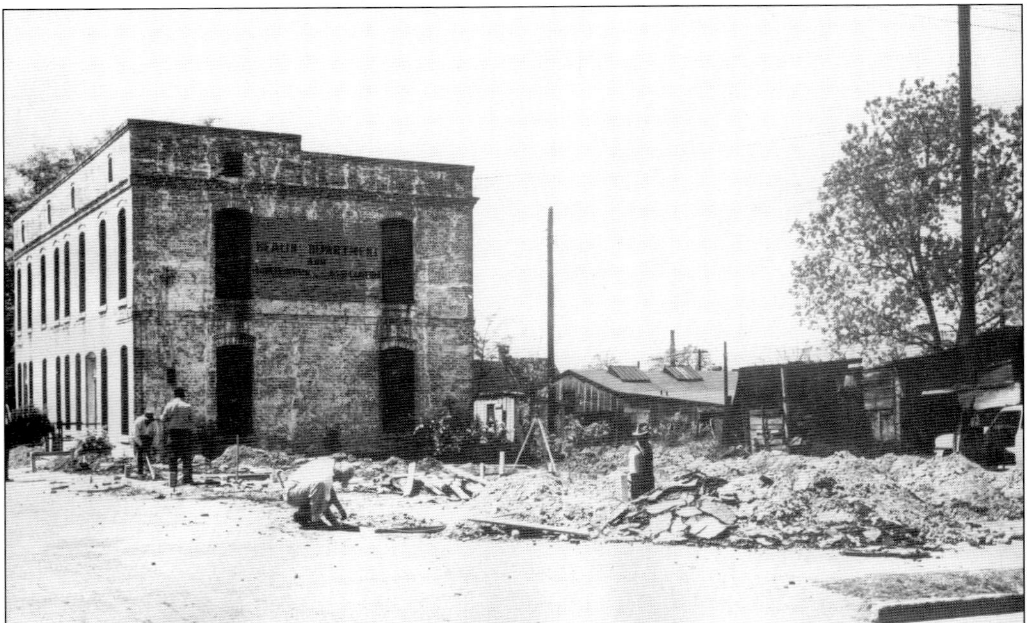

THE HEALTH DEPARTMENT. Greenwood County had one of the first two health departments in the state of South Carolina. Located on Monument Street and funded in part by the Rockefeller Foundation, this organization, which opened in 1915, was originally dedicated to monitoring the water quality and milk pasteurization requirements in Greenwood County. The health department is pictured after a fire devastated adjacent buildings.

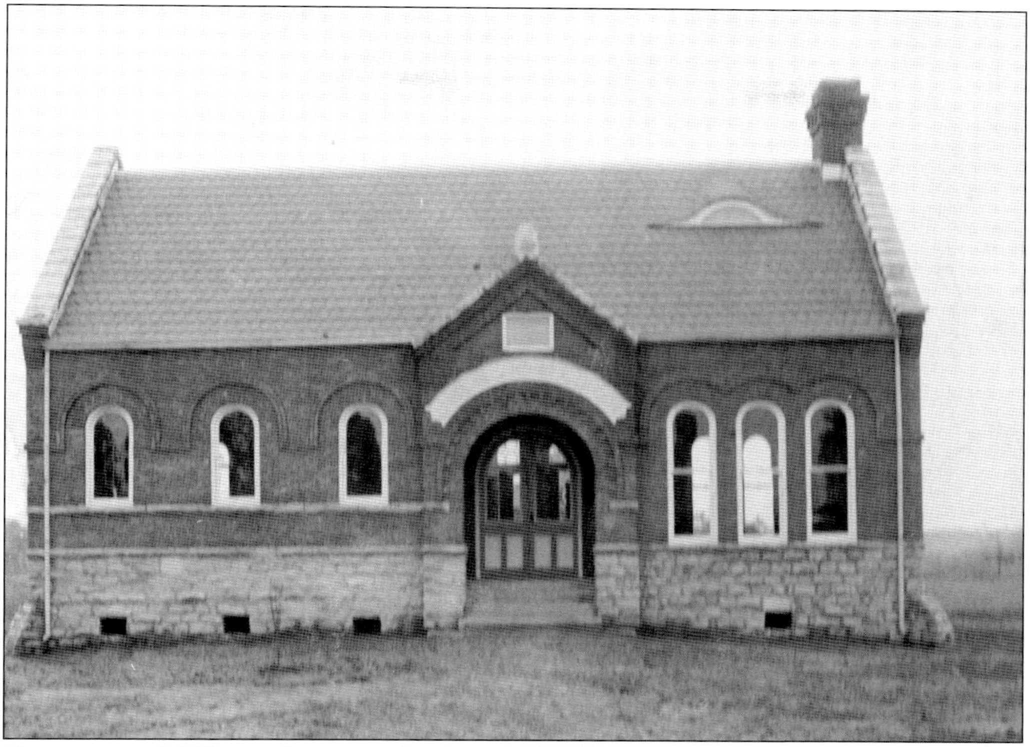

Carnegie and McKissick Libraries. By 1916, another library graced the landscape of Greenwood. Over $12,000 was obtained from Andrew Carnegie for this new project. Besides this facility, which featured 4,000 books, McKissick Library, pictured here, served as the library for the children of Connie Maxwell Children's Home.

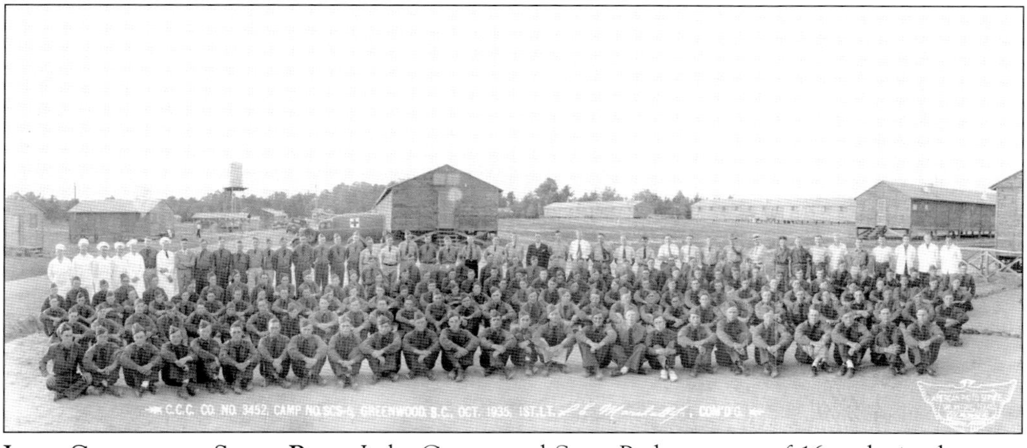

Lake Greenwood State Park. Lake Greenwood State Park was one of 16 parks in the state developed by the Civilian Conservation Corps, an organization formed by the federal government during the Great Depression. Lake Greenwood State Park is composed of five different peninsulas, 915 acres of forest, and facilities for boating, skiing, camping, and more.

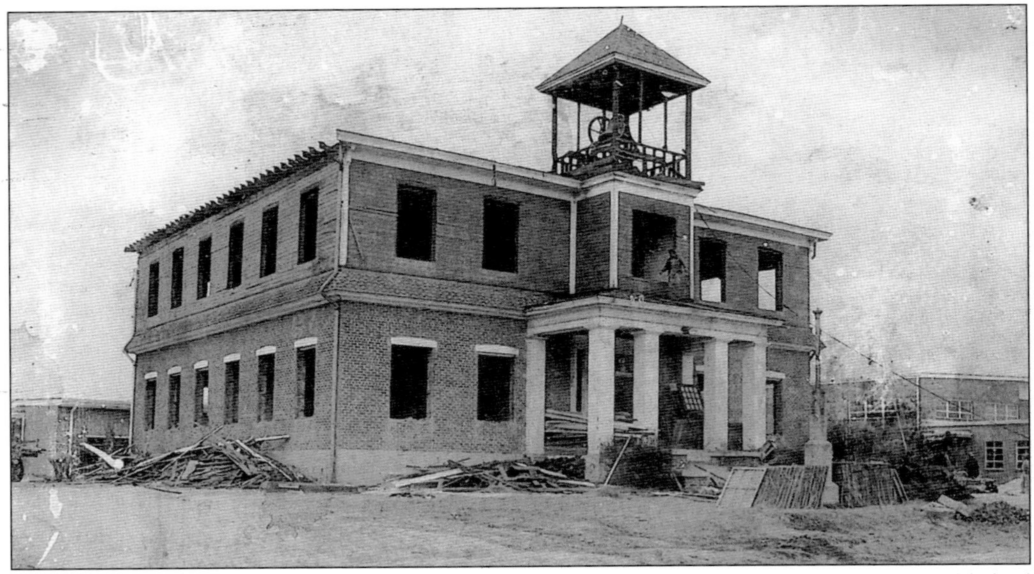

Brewer Hospital. This African American hospital opened its doors in May 1924. Established on the same property as the Brewer Normal School, this hospital contained 30 patient rooms. Some improvements were made to the facility over the years of its operation, such as the addition of a sprinkler system in 1955. The hospital is pictured here during construction. (Courtesy of the Greenwood County Library System.)

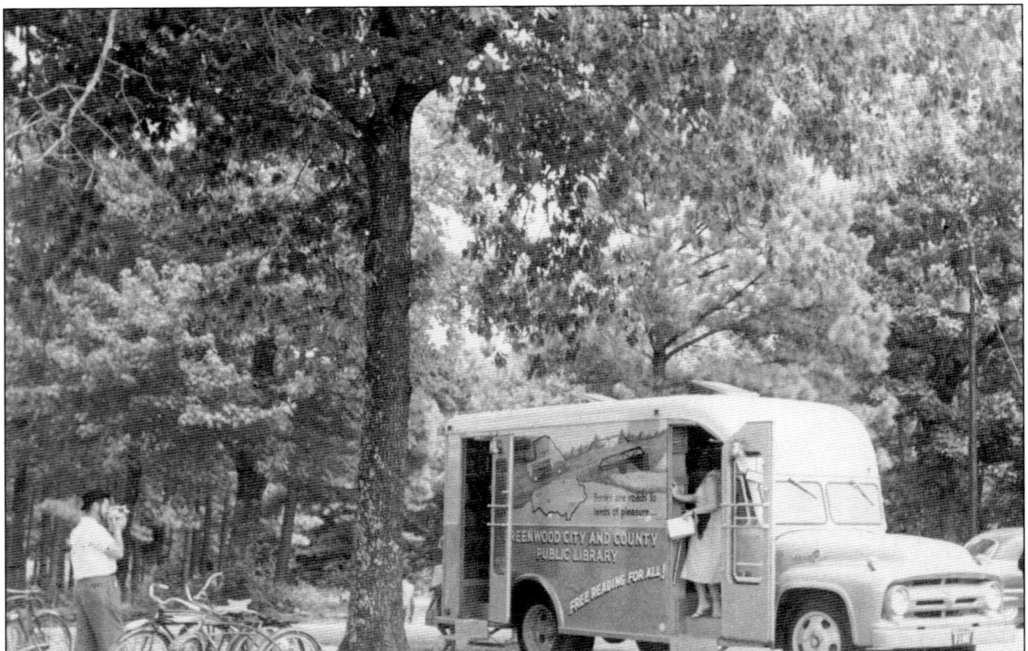

The Book Mobile. Started by the Greenwood County Council of Farm Women in 1937 as a way to bring literacy to rural communities in the county, this book mobile consisted of shelves added to the back of an ordinary pickup truck. Kathleen McCabe served as the first "truck librarian" and visited over 20 different locations twice a month. (Courtesy of the Greenwood County Library System.)

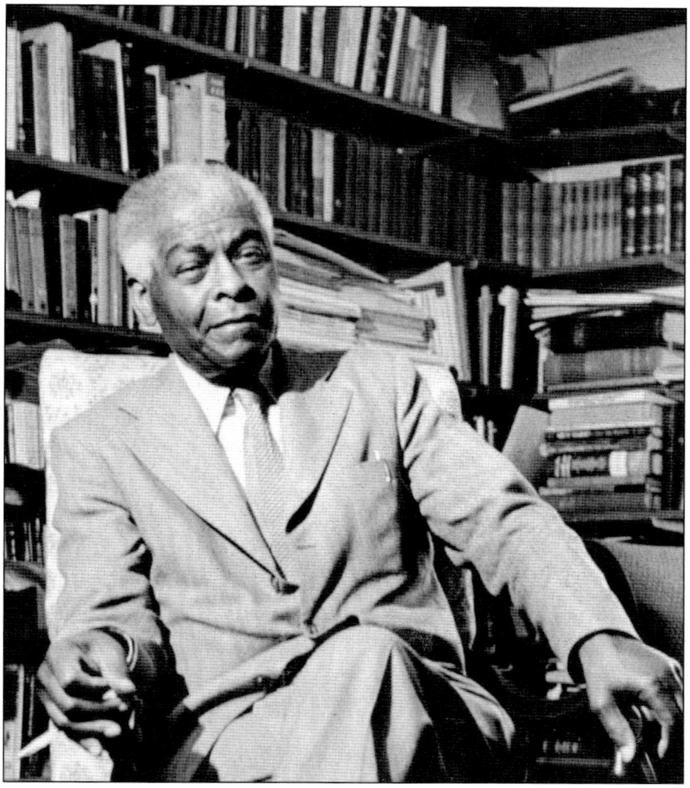

Mays Library. This library, which served the African American community through 1971, was housed at Brewer Normal School starting in 1940. It contained a selection of about 50 books and was named in honor of Dr. Benjamin Mays. Beginning in 1951, the Greenwood County Book Mobile served African American children. The main branch of the library was finally integrated by the late 1960s. Pictured is Dr. Benjamin Mays, president of Moorehead College. He was born in Greenwood County to parents who had been enslaved, and was an inspiration to all.

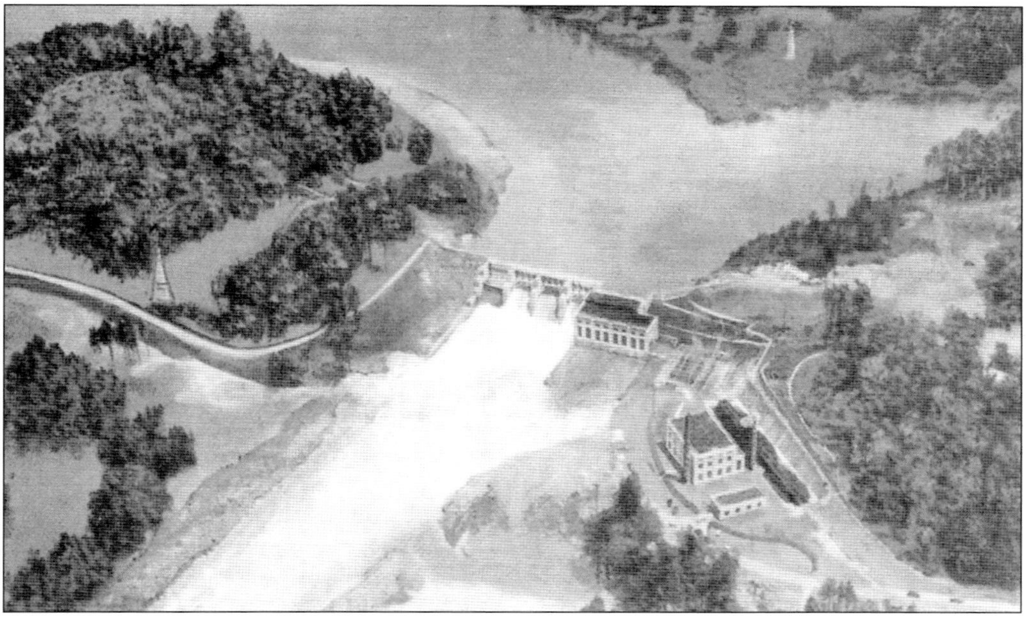

Buzzard's Roost Power Plant. After the Public Works Administration was created in 1933 to help combat the unemployment of the Great Depression, Greenwood put in an application to create a dam and power plant on the Saluda River. This plant would not only create jobs, but would also provide power to rural Greenwoodians. After a lengthy legal battle, which ultimately ended at the Supreme Court, Buzzard's Roost Power Plant opened on August 20, 1940.

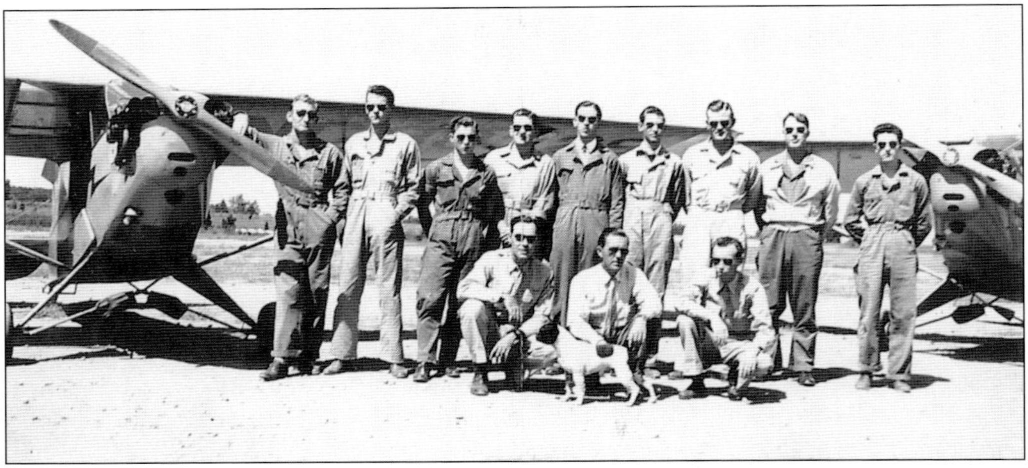

Coronaca Army Air Field. After 1940, as part of the federal Development of Landing Areas for National Defense program, many air bases were created across the United States, including Coronaca. This air field served as an auxiliary field for the Army Air Base in Greenville. The Coronaca Army Air Field closed soon after the end of World War II. This photograph shows a group of young pilots, including World War II flying instructor Jack Whatley. (Courtesy of Ginger Whatley Bell.)

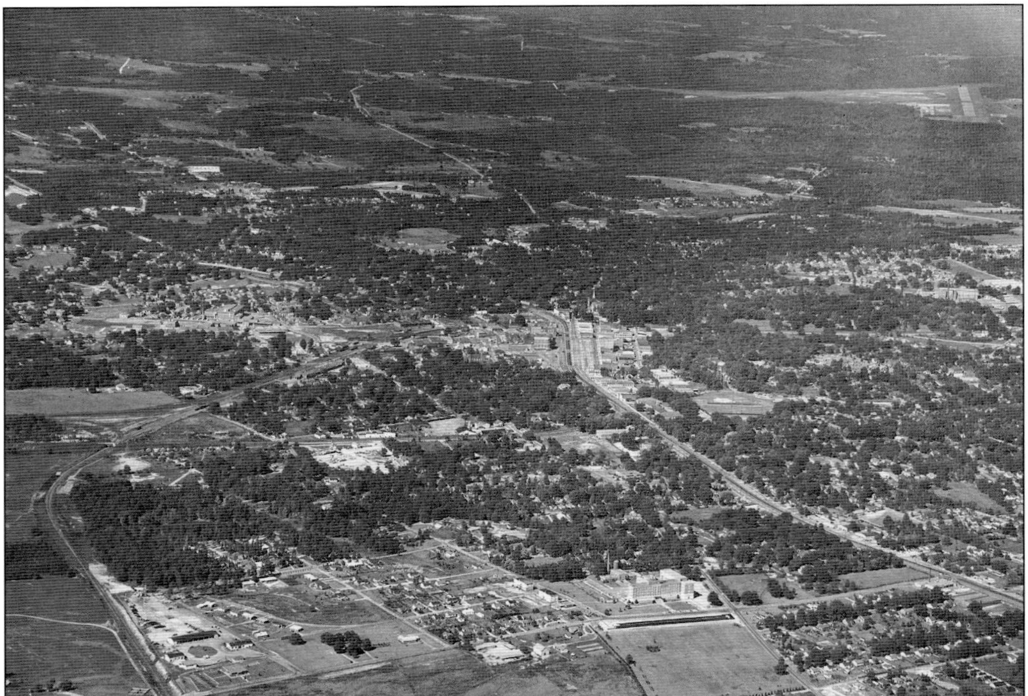

Greenwood County Airport. Through the efforts of the newly formed Greenwood Airport Commission, 1,500 acres, including the location of Coronaca Army Air Field, were obtained from the federal War Assets Administration after World War II. The airport was in use by 1949, and 10 years later, the Federal Aviation Administration installed a VOR navigation beacon. This aerial view includes the landing strip at top right, captured in 1956 by Pettigrew photography. (Courtesy of Ginger Whatley Bell.)

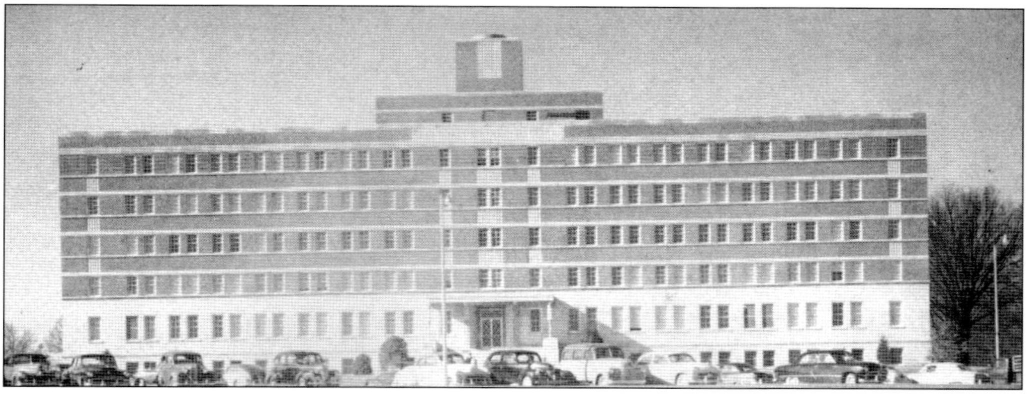

SELF MEMORIAL HOSPITAL. After the 1944 tornado, James C. Self announced that the Self Family Foundation would build a new hospital for the Greenwood community. Opened in November 1951 and capable of serving 179 patients at a time, the Self Memorial Hospital was a state-of-the-art facility that underwent several building projects before 1980.

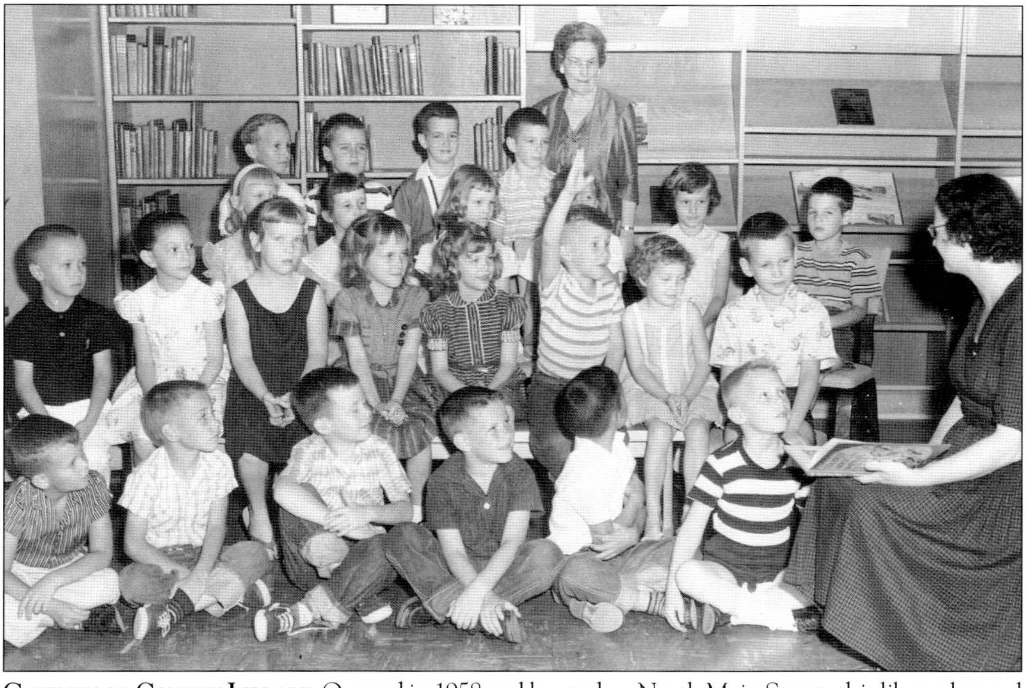

GREENWOOD COUNTY LIBRARY. Opened in 1958 and located on North Main Street, this library housed over 30,000 volumes in its first year. The Greenwood County Library employed seven librarians, and over the next several years, it continued to grow, adding a smaller branch in Ninety-Six and one in Ware Shoals. In this photograph, Miss Mansfield conducts story hour for a group of children visiting the library in the 1950s. (Courtesy of the Greenwood County Library System.)

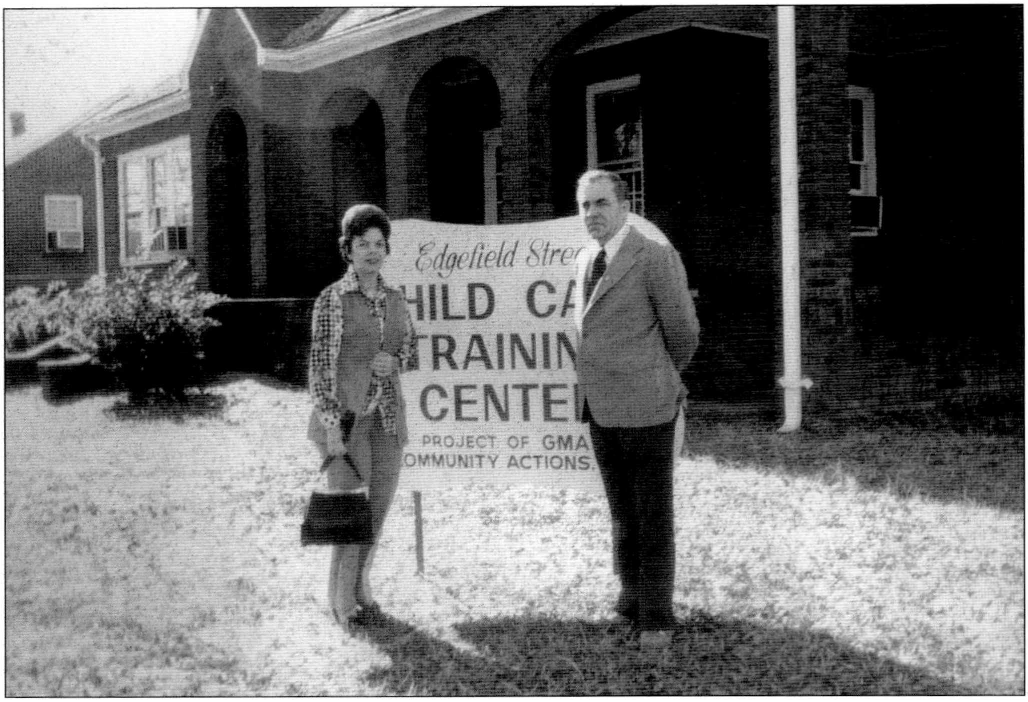

THE BURTON CENTER. This organization, which supports mentally handicapped individuals, was birthed out of the 1958 Greenwood County Association for Retarded Citizens. Felton and Doris Burton spearheaded this organization after the birth of a daughter with Down's syndrome. In 1971, this Hope Center, which exposed handicapped individuals to educational programs and vocational opportunities, was established. A residential program was established in 1974.

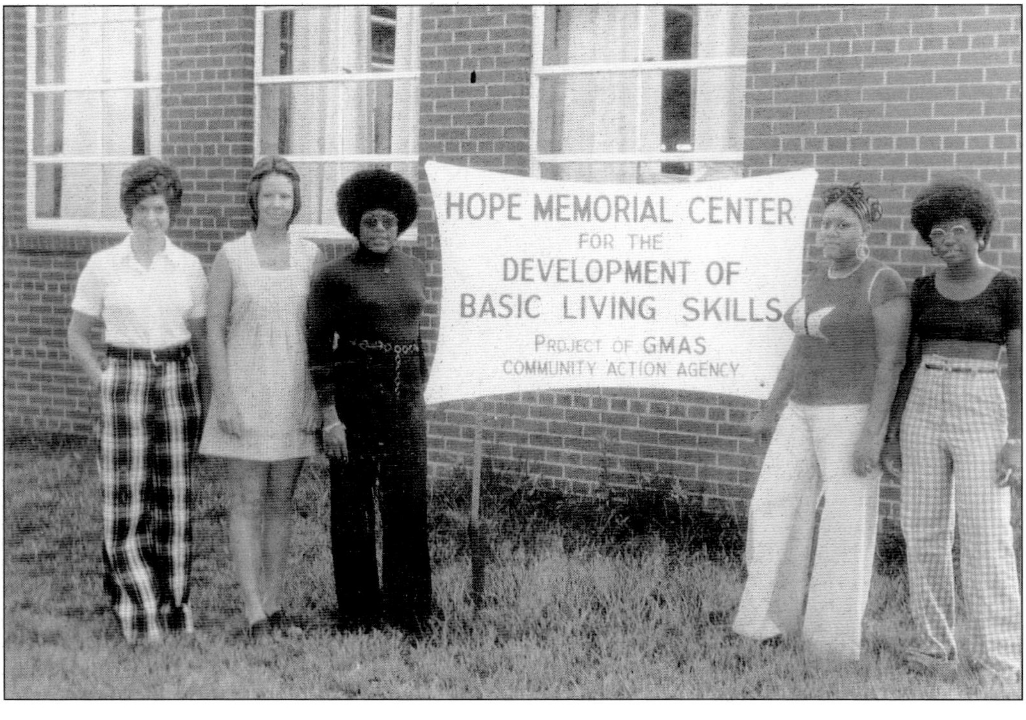

Five

Athletics, Arts, and Culture

A town or county is certainly more than the sum of its industries, schools, and services. Another defining characteristic is its cultural or recreational activities. When moving to a new town or city, people want to know what kinds of things they will be able to experience. From the very beginning, Greenwood was concerned with offering its residents the best in athletics, arts, and culture. From fairs and parades to theaters and museums, Greenwood has always been a town that strives for creativity and quality. An advertisement from a 1914 edition of the *Index Journal* further reflects this, as it states, "Every healthful man, woman or child demands and should have different classes of recreation and entertainment." Greenwood has always supported the idea that culture matters, and many officials and organizations continue to advocate this belief today.

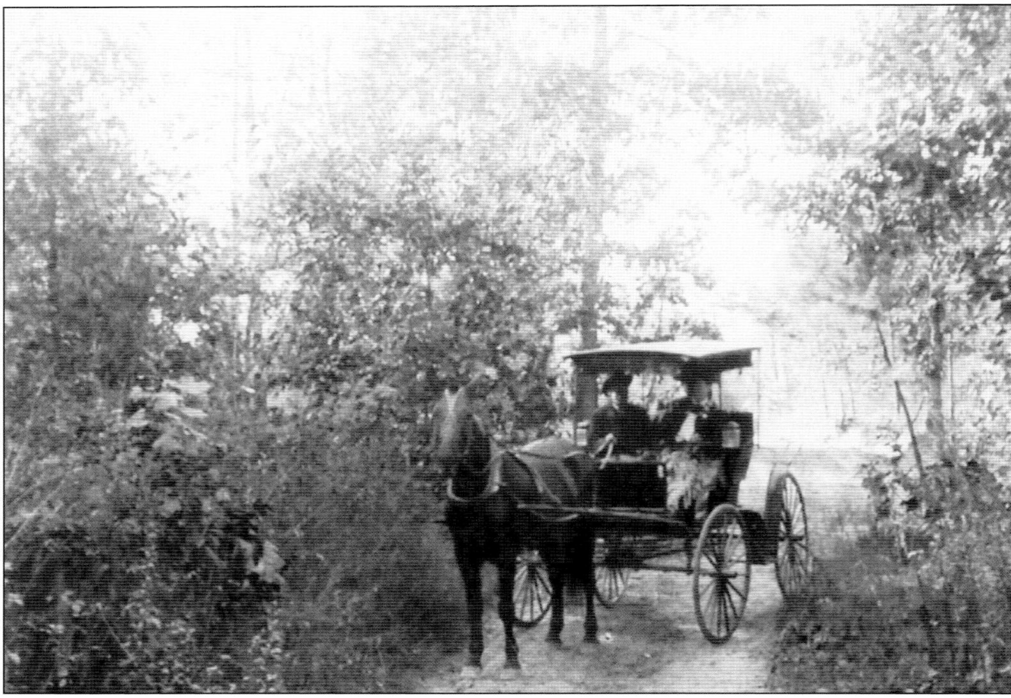

Surrey. Rob Roy Robinson drives this surrey down a country road in Greenwood County early on October 28, 1905. Miss Bates and Miss Hickock enjoy the scenery while sitting in the back seat. (Courtesy of Alvin Fennell.)

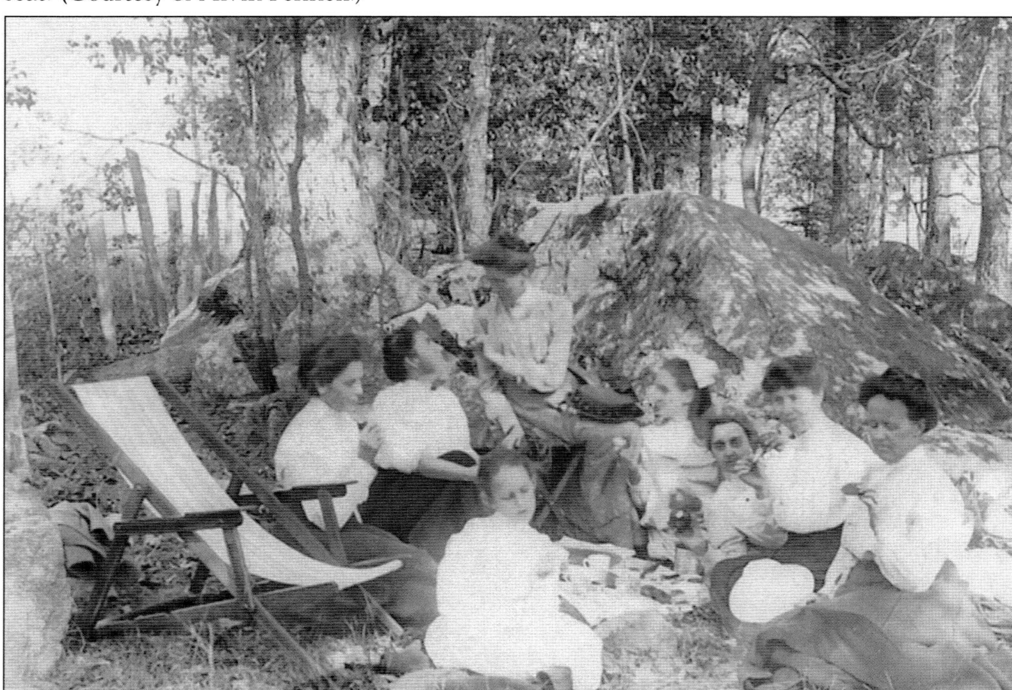

Richter Farm. Eight ladies enjoy a summer picnic on Mr. Richter's Farm in 1907. (Courtesy of Alvin Rucker.)

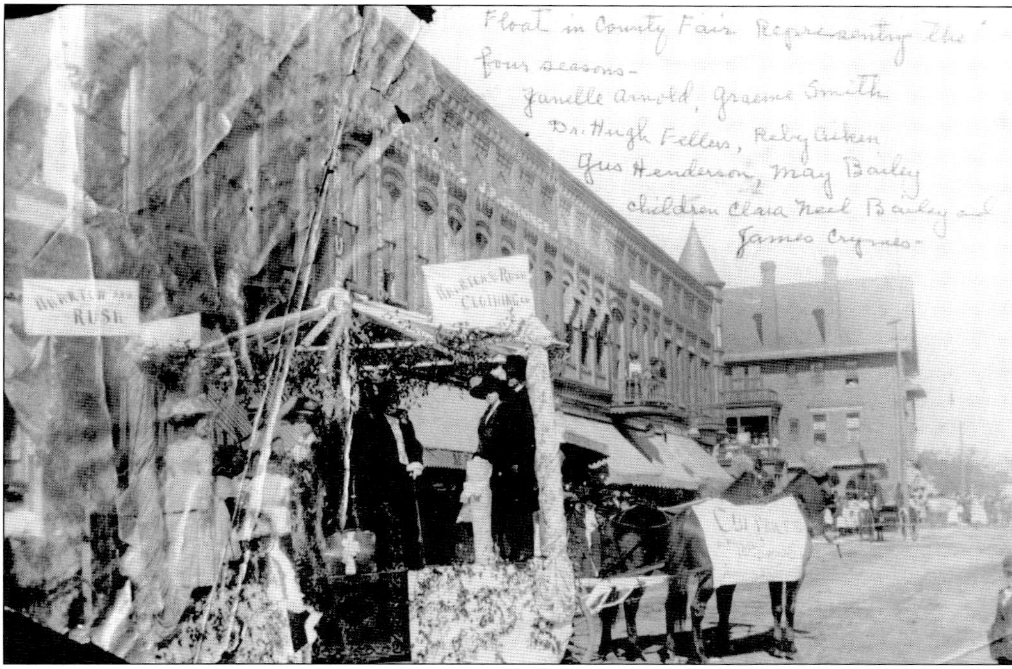

GREENWOOD COUNTY FAIR PARADE. In 1910, the local fair was considered "one of the leading county fairs" in South Carolina. Known for its great selection of hogs, horses, and other livestock, the start of the Greenwood County Fair was cause for much celebration.

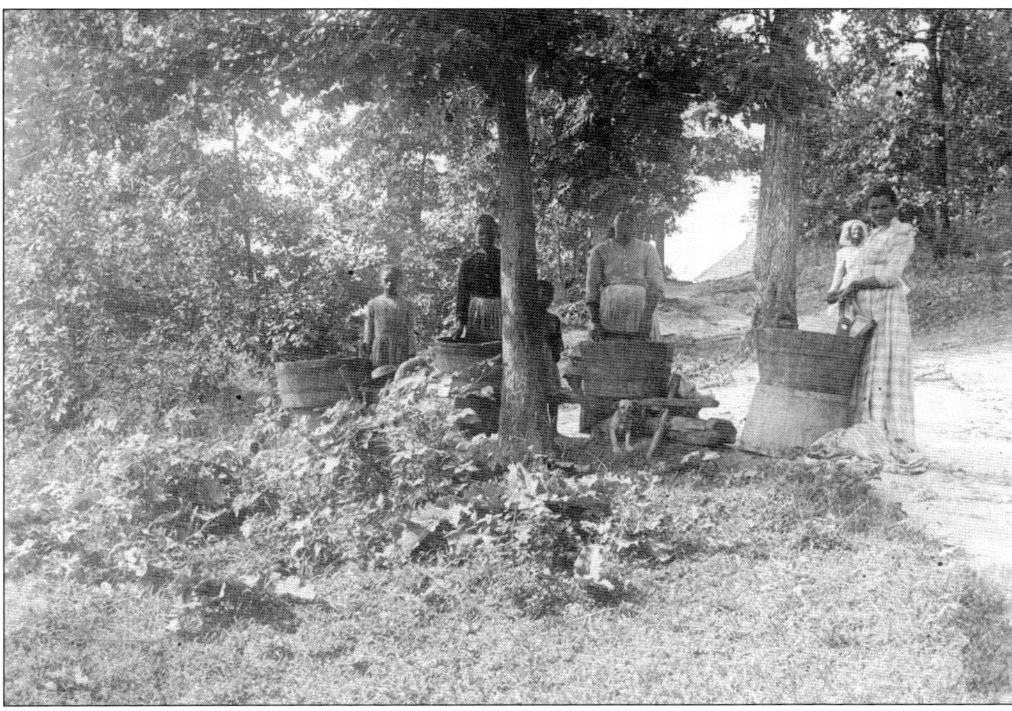

WASH DAY. Before the advent of electrically powered water supplies, citizens of Greenwood used creeks or springs to fulfill household tasks such as washing clothes. This is a group from the Brewer School washing clothing.

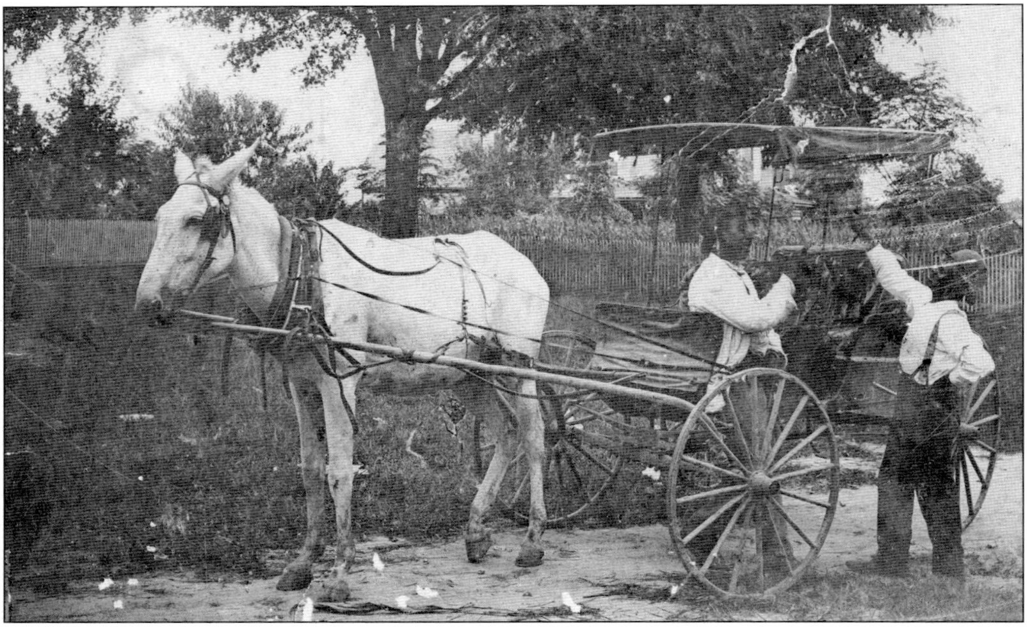

EARLY TRANSPORTATION. Bob Hackett, a representative in the state legislature, is pictured here with his friend Ab McIntosh, a porter for the Express Company. Hackett drove his horse-drawn buggy to Greenwood's Union Station to meet passenger trains six to eight times a day. Travelers needing local transportation could pay a quarter per ride. (Courtesy of the Greenwood County Library System.).

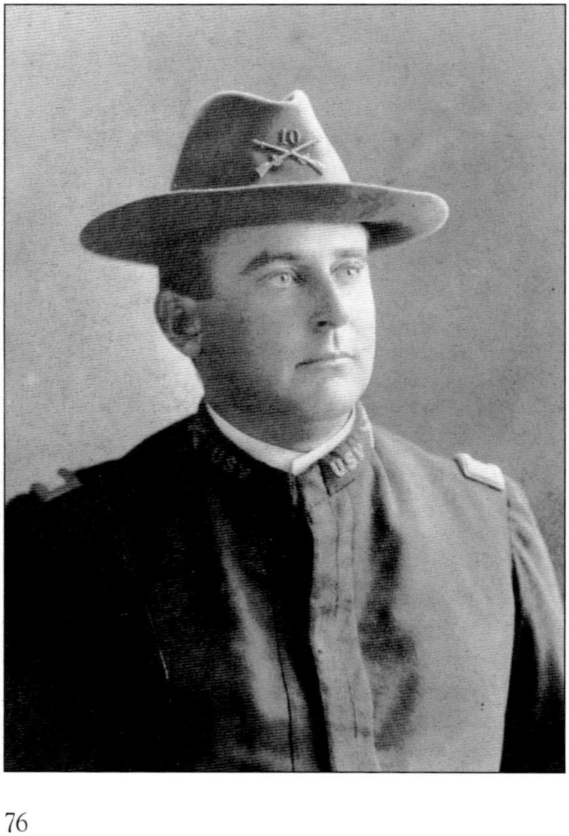

THE *GREENWOOD INDEX* AND THE *GREENWOOD JOURNAL*. William Gregg Chafee, pictured here, established the *Greenwood Index*. The *Index* began producing papers in 1897 from its location on Waller Avenue. The *Greenwood Journal*, which opened three years earlier, had Rufus B. Wilson as its editor. (Courtesy of the Greenwood County Library System.)

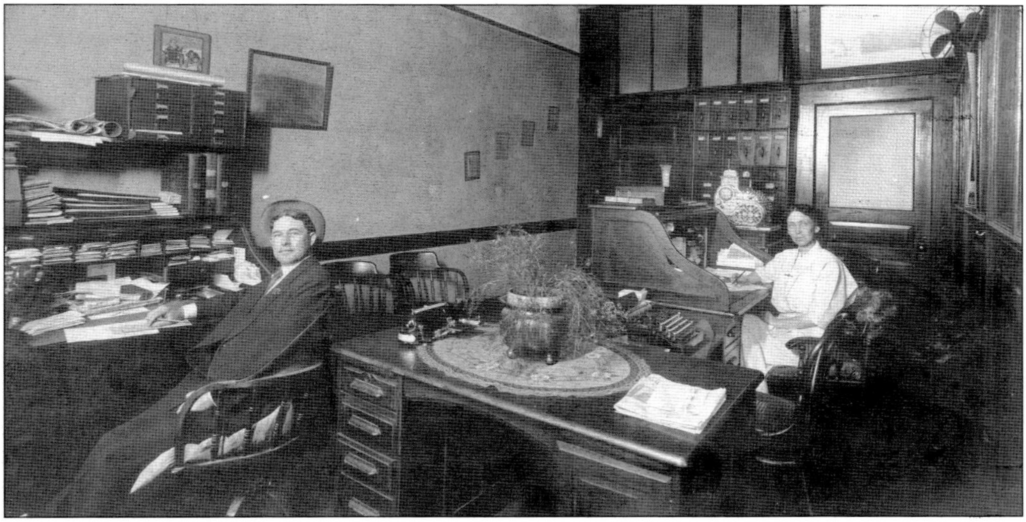

The Index Journal. Before 1890, there were over five weekly papers in Greenwood. The *Index Journal* was formed in 1919 after the merger of the *Greenwood Journal*, established in 1894, and the *Greenwood Index*, established in 1897. Harry L. Watson was the first owner of this newly established paper. He served as a Greenwood newspaperman for over 50 years. Shown here is the office of Joel S. Bailey and Agnes Puckett at the *Greenwood Index* prior to the merger. (Courtesy of the Greenwood County Library System.)

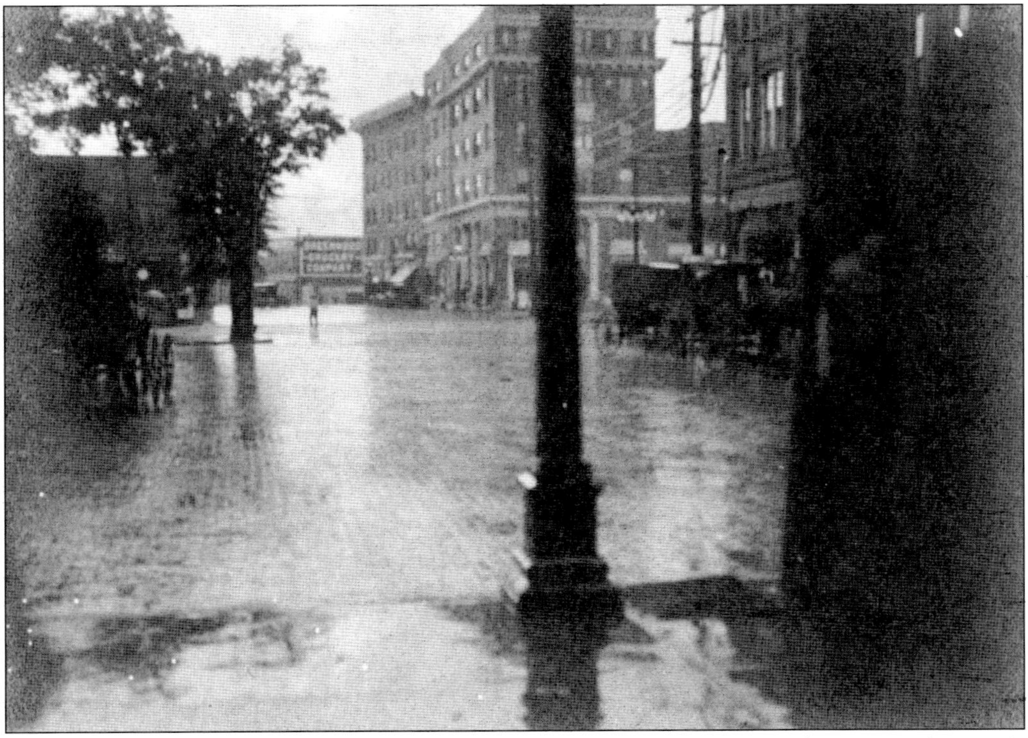

Maxwell Avenue View. This is a view down Maxwell Avenue in 1915. The National Loan & Exchange Bank Building stands in the center, and the Barksdale Building is to the north, on the right side of the photograph. A member of the Hodges family took the photograph one rainy evening, with the family's storefront immediately behind the photographer.

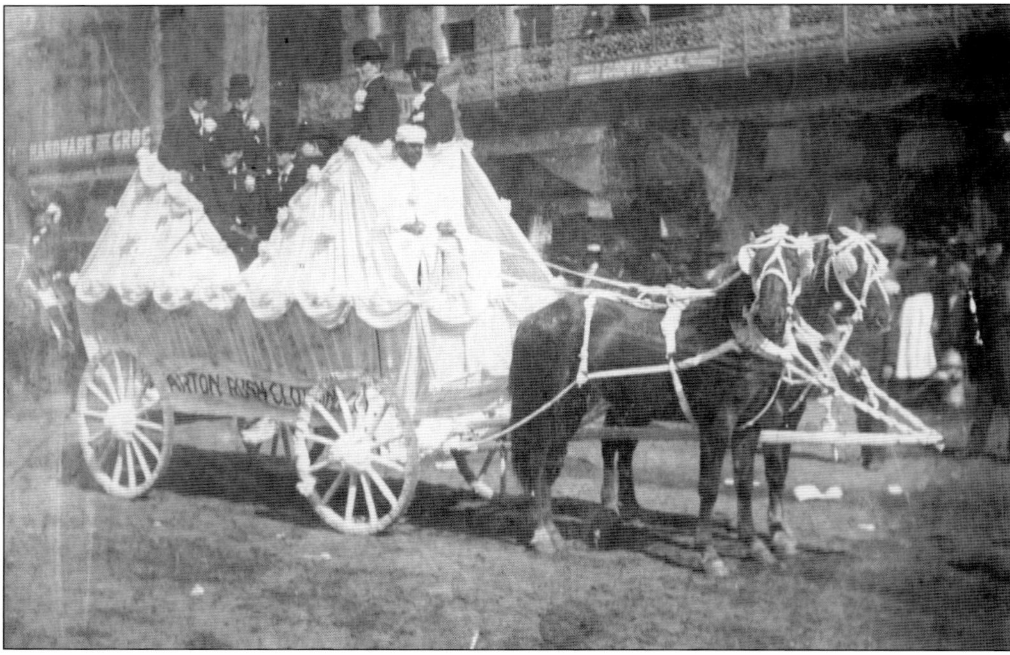

WHARTON AND RUSH. Greenwood was a place of great entrepreneurial spirit, as evidenced in this 1915 photograph of one of Greenwood's first parades. Pictured is a float sponsored by Wharton and Rush Clothing, a store located inside the Oregon Hotel. The pair also owned another business, Wharton and Rush Dry Goods.

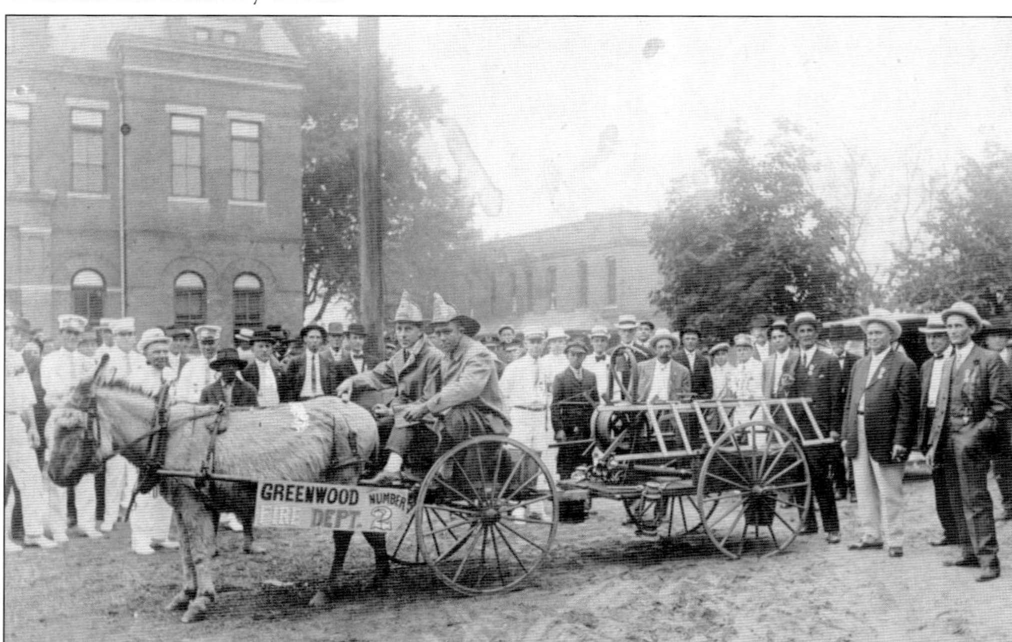

FIRE DEPARTMENT PARODY. At the state firemen convention held in Greenwood, John K. Durst and Fred Andrews played the part of comedians, when they dressed as firemen and rode a mock engine down the street. Both men were respected members of the community, and Durst was the proud owner of the Durst-Andrews Company.

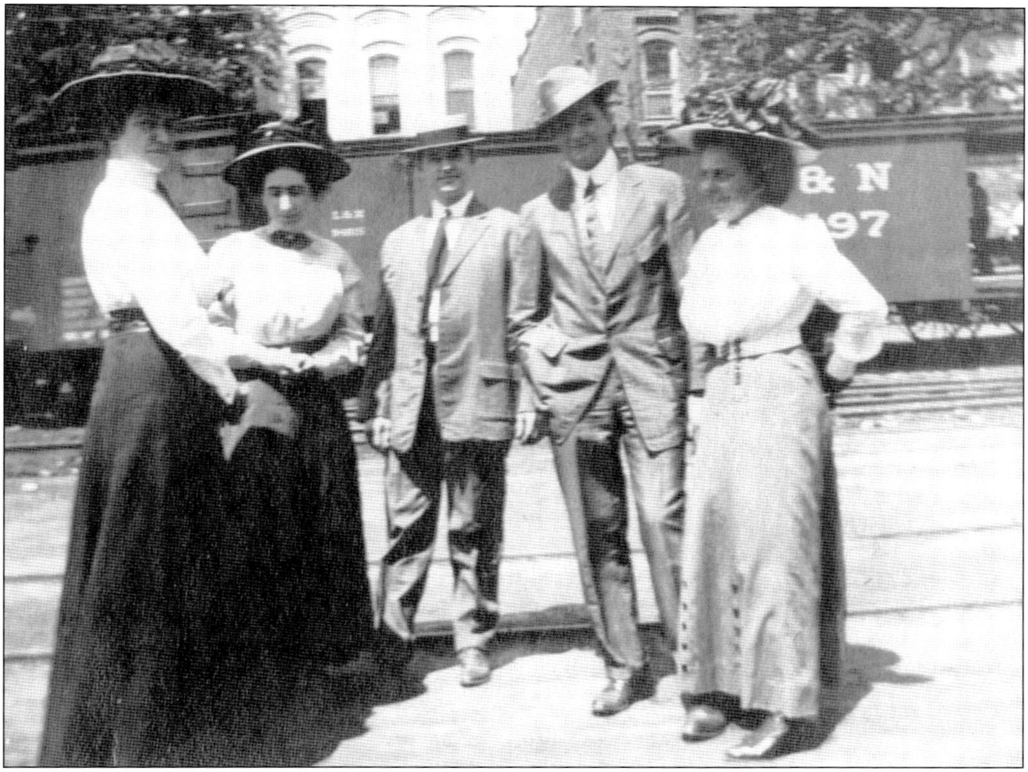

GREENWOOD CITIZENS. In this early 1900s photograph, a group of Greenwoodians converses in front of the Wharton and Rush store, as a freight train goes by.

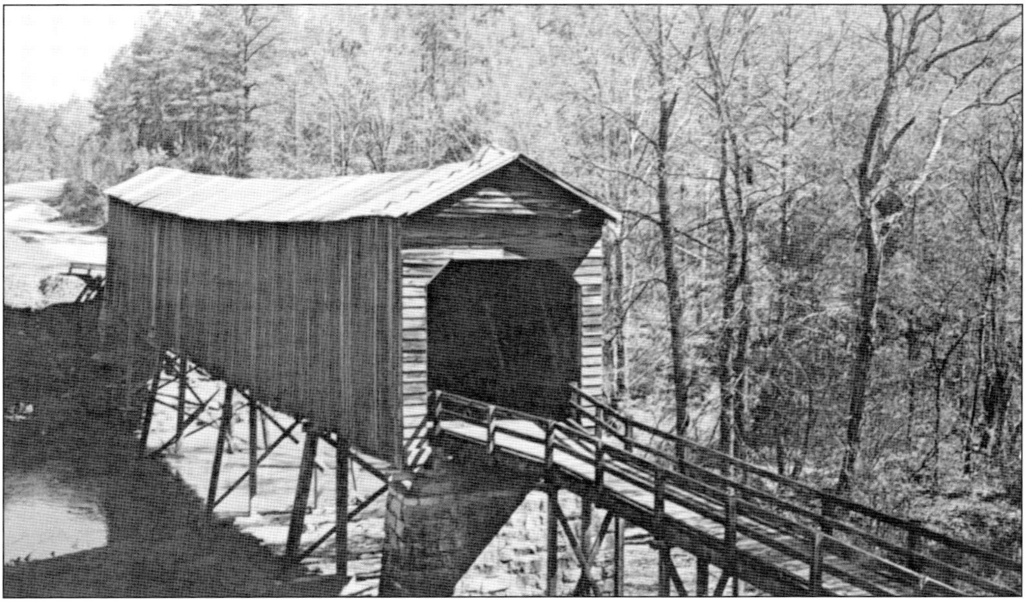

LONG CANE COVERED BRIDGE. At one time, the Long Cane Covered Bridge was one of 400-plus covered bridges in South Carolina; at the time of its destruction, it was one of only three remaining in the state. It burned down on July 7, 1979. Two years before it burned, the bridge was listed in the National Register of Historic Places. (Courtesy of Jean Whatley.)

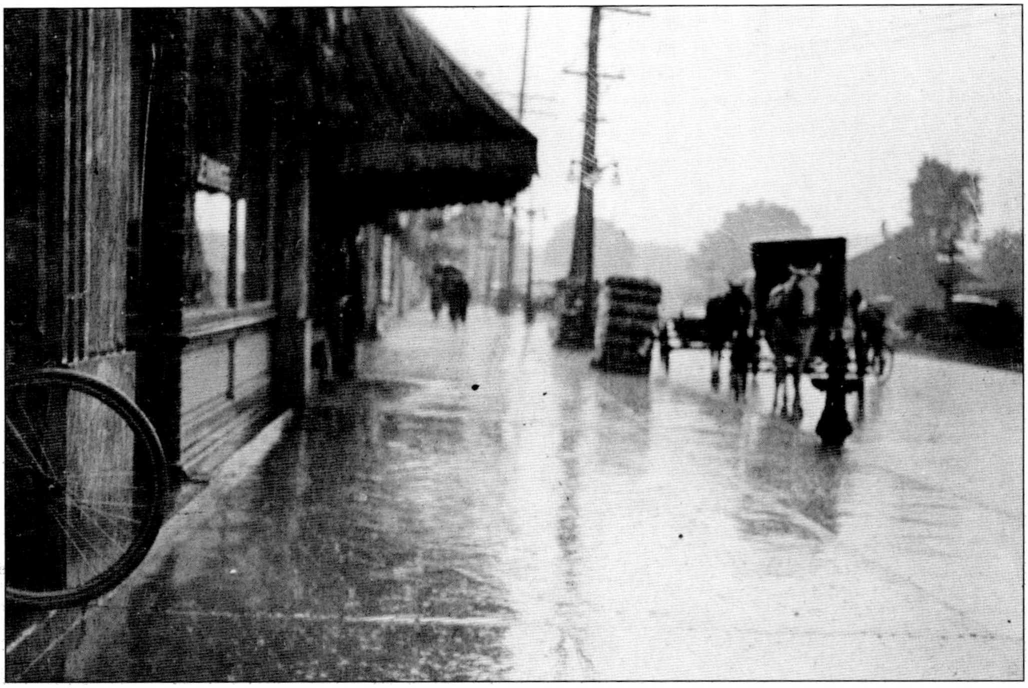

Rainy Day in Greenwood. In 1915, cotton bales line Greenwood's streets, and a horse-drawn buggy waits for its owner outside of Rosenburg's Department Store. In the foreground, a cyclist is on his way out of a shop's doorway.

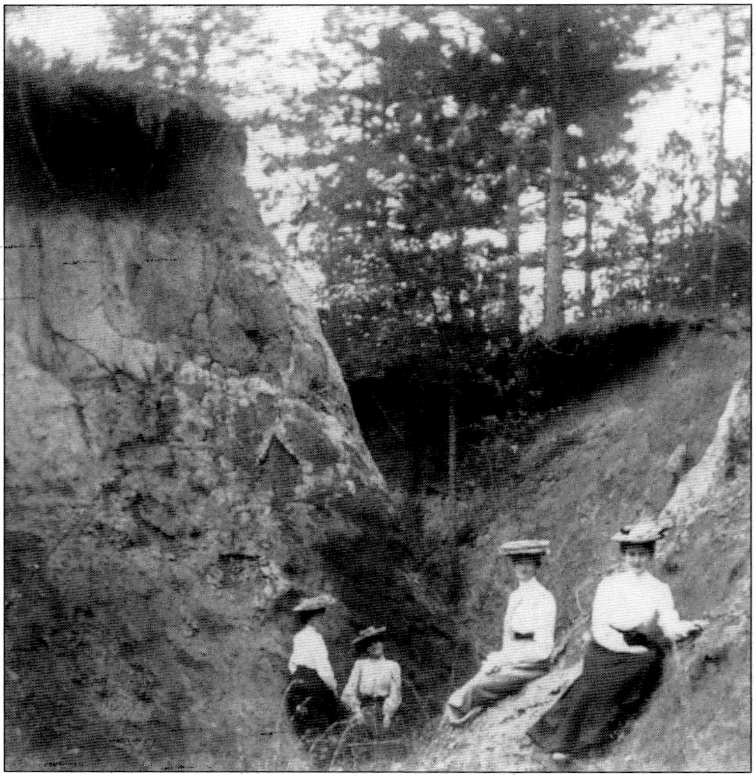

Teachers' Day Out. Teachers at the Brewer Institute in Greenwood enjoyed time together and posed for this photograph as they sat in a washout on April 16, 1904. (Courtesy of Alvin Fennell.)

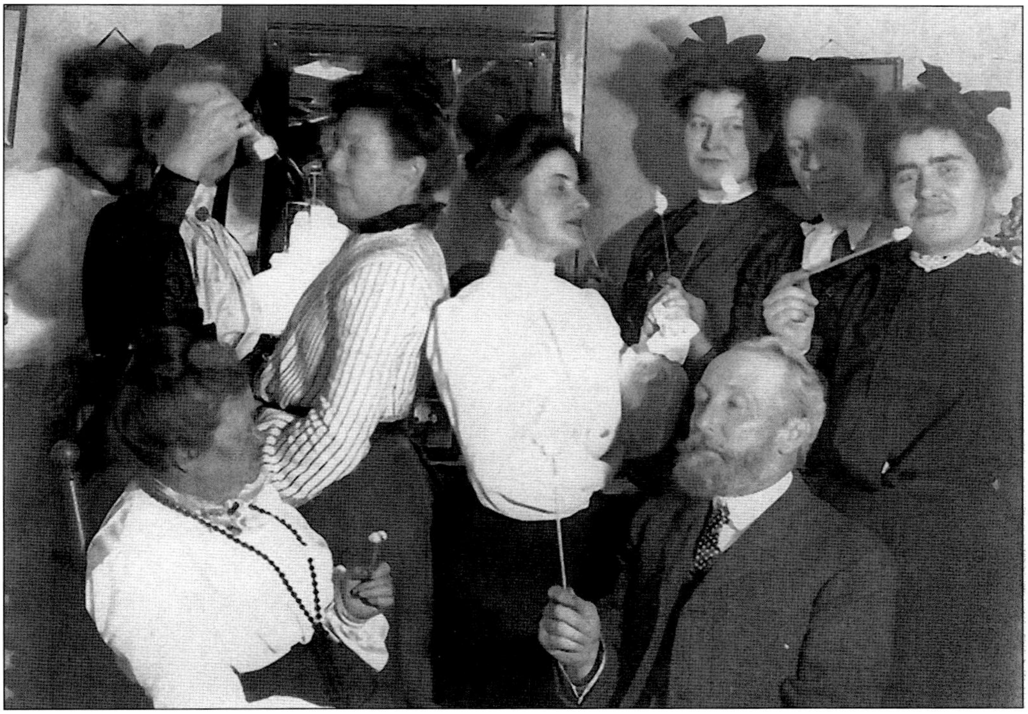

Marshmallow Roast. Faculty members of the Brewer School are enjoying a fun marshmallow roast in this photograph, taken in 1903.

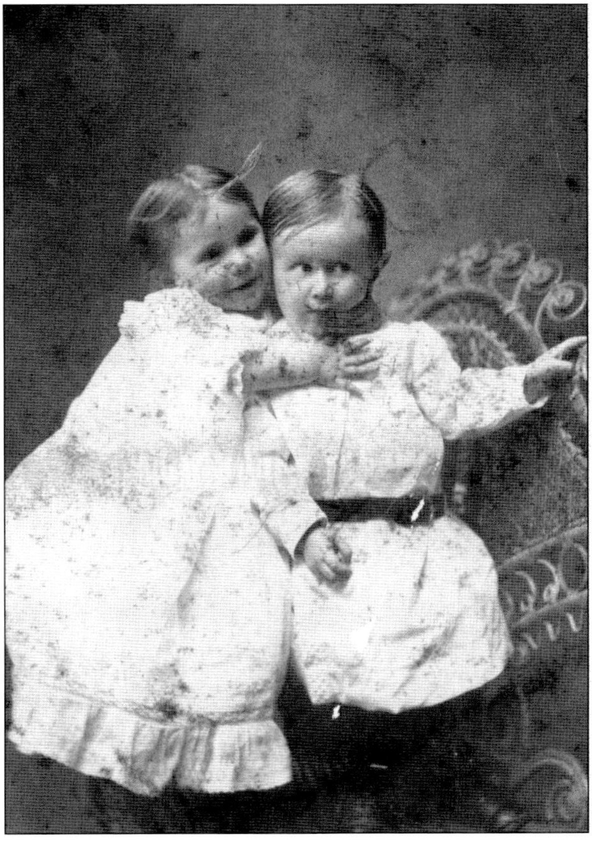

The Unwanted Embrace. Winona Barksdale steals a hug from James Durst just as this photograph was snapped in the summer of 1902.

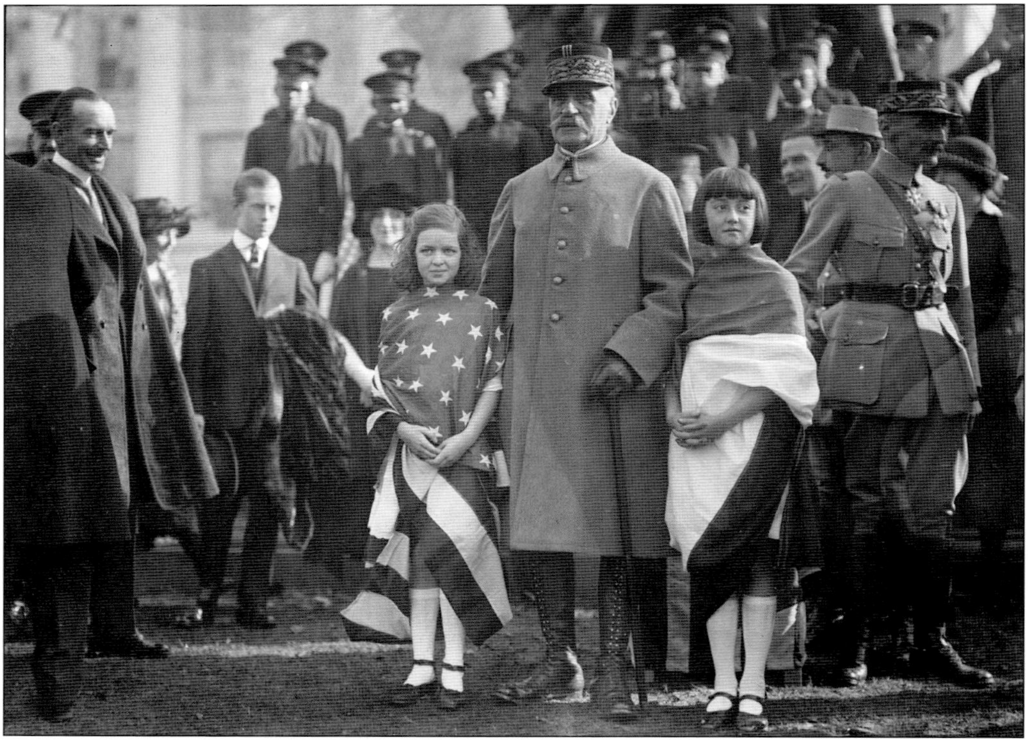

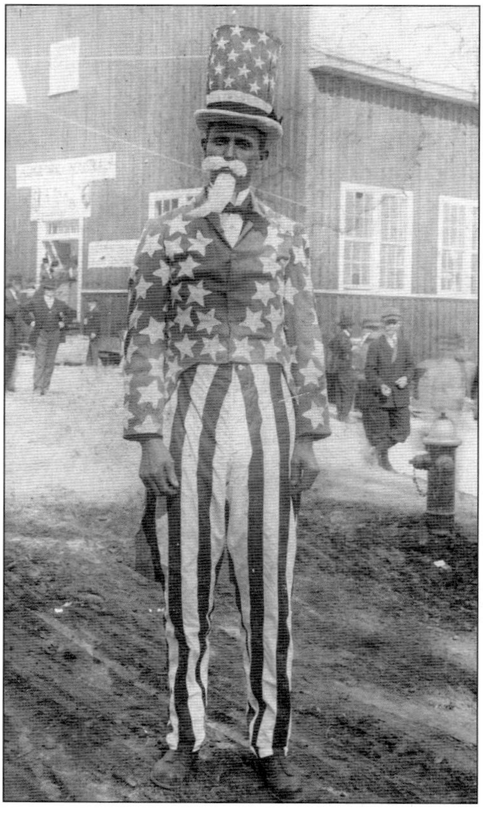

Foch Day. On December 9, 1921, all of Greenwood was in an uproar preparing for the arrival of Marshal Ferdinand Foch. Foch served as one of the great field marshals for the Allied forces during World War I. During his official goodwill tour, Foch visited Greenwood, and the entire city was decked out for the occasion, with bunting and flags and even a wooden replica of the Arc de Triomphe. Pictured is Foch in Washington, DC, during his tour of America in 1921. (Courtesy of the Library of Congress.)

Uncle Sam. Calvin Poore is dressed as Uncle Sam for a patriotic event in downtown Greenwood.

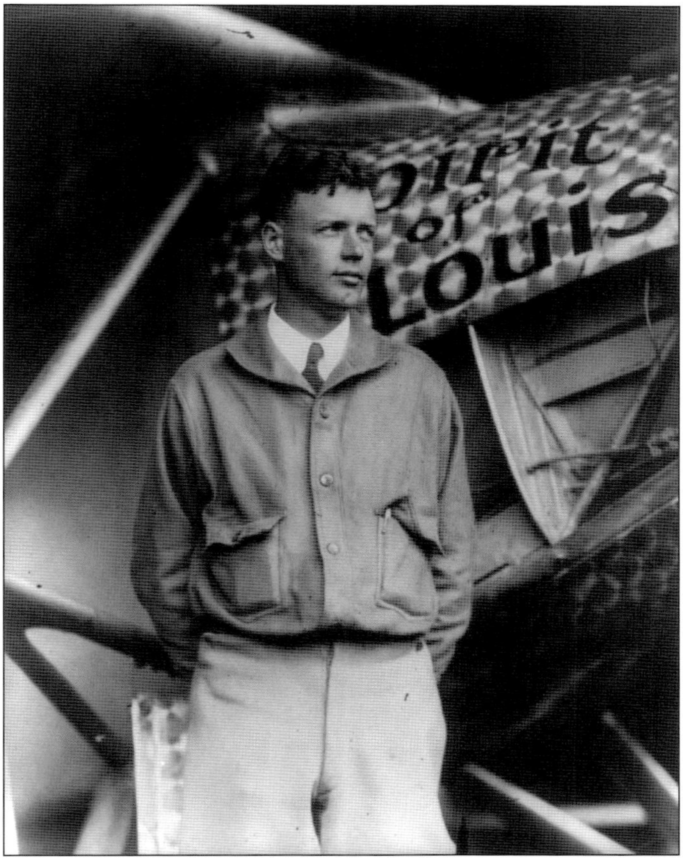

CHARLES LINDBERGH AND THE *SPIRIT OF ST. LOUIS*. On October 12, 1927, Charles Lindbergh circled twice over Greenwood at the request of city officials. He also dropped a letter, contained in a cloth bag, from his plane. This letter of greeting was retrieved in front of Efrid's Department Store and was displayed there. Charles Lindbergh's flight over Greenwood marked the opening of the Piedmont Fair for that year. (Courtesy of the Library of Congress.)

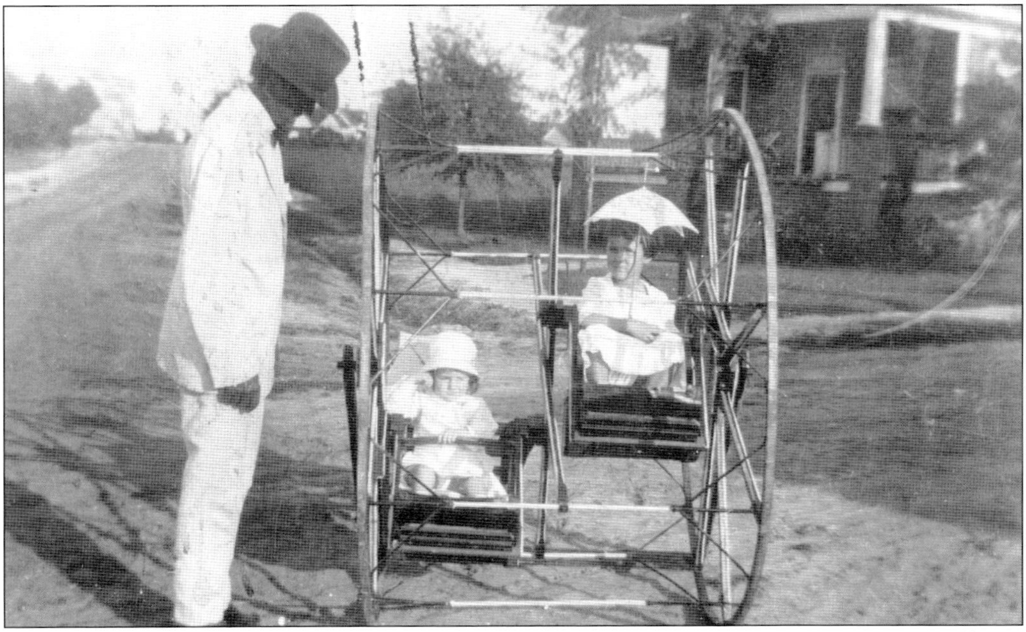

HANDMADE PRAM. C.M. Calhoun created this special pram for his daughter Mary Etta Calhoun (Moore) seated to the left. It operated very similarly to a tiny Ferris wheel.

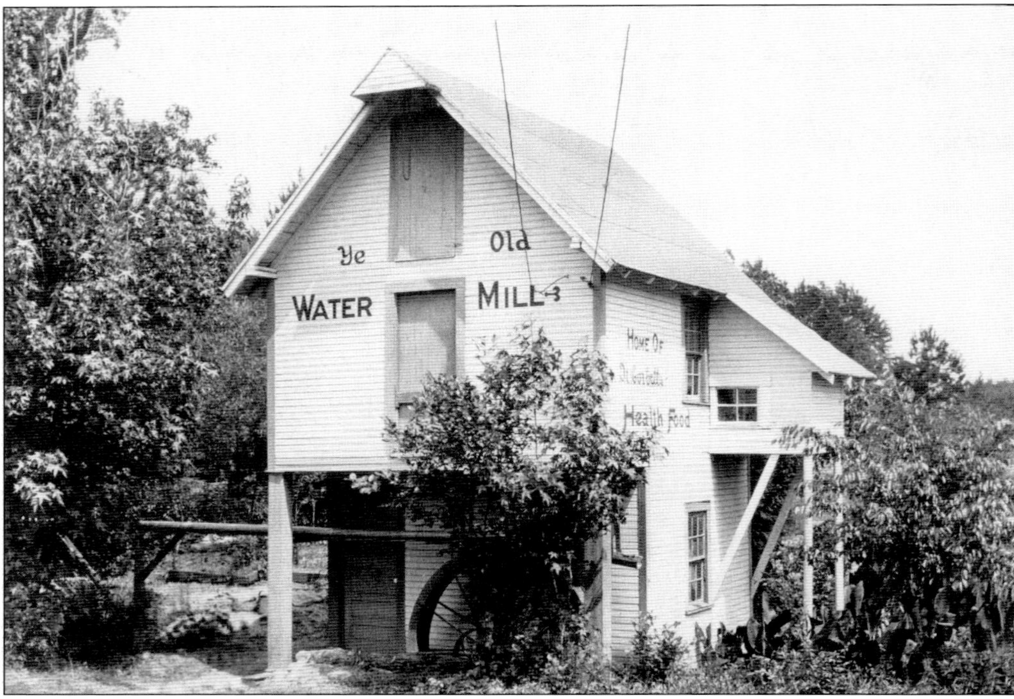

YE OLD WATER MILL. Park Seed Company was established on 17 acres of beautiful land, which originally housed recreational facilities for the people of Greenwood. This site already featured a bathing pool, boating area, and picnicking facilities. The Park Seed Company added a mill with a waterwheel to grind ingredients for a substance known as Dr. Corbett's Health Food. The inventor of the food gave his recipe to Park Seed Company. (Courtesy of William John Park.)

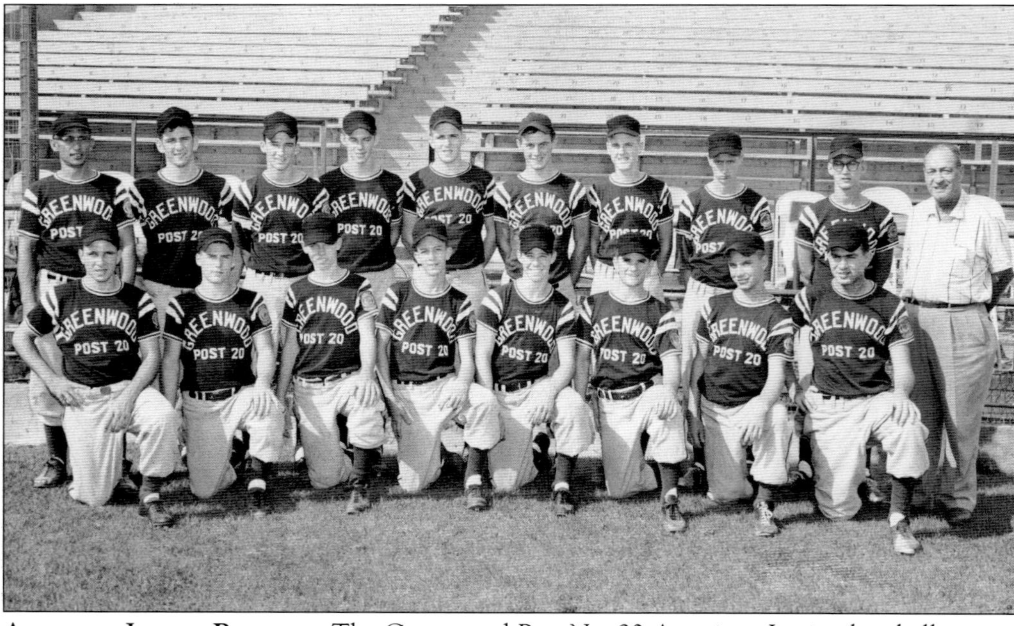

AMERICAN LEGION BASEBALL. The Greenwood Post No. 20 American Legion baseball team is pictured in 1958 in front of the Greenwood High School stadium. J.C. Boozer coached the team, and Joseph Seal served as athletic officer.

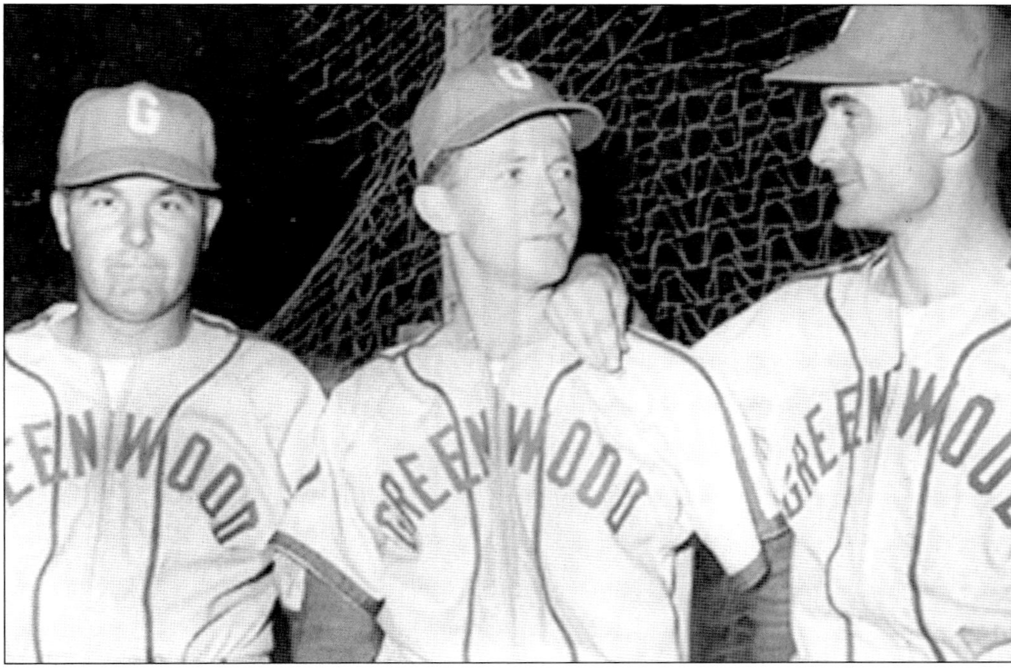

TEXTILE LEAGUE BASEBALL. With the growth of mill communities in Greenwood, mill-sponsored activities also became a huge part of life, and none more so than baseball. Baseball teams began to form, and the 1930s saw the height of the mill leagues, with players such as Bill Voiselle going on to play Major League ball. In this photograph, team members on the Greenwood Mills team discuss the game.

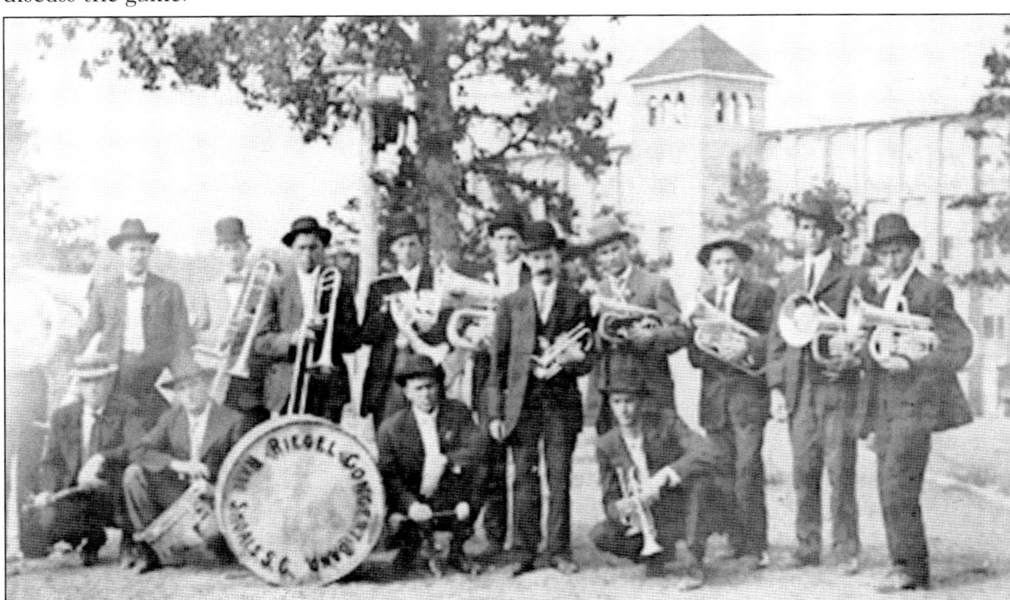

RIEGEL BAND. Riegel Stadium was built in Ware Shoals in 1931, and its baseball field was rumored to be so large that virtually no one could hit the ball over the center field fence. The Riegel Stadium hosted African American baseball teams as well as teams in the women's textile league. The Riegel Band, pictured here, regaled sports enthusiasts at many of these events.

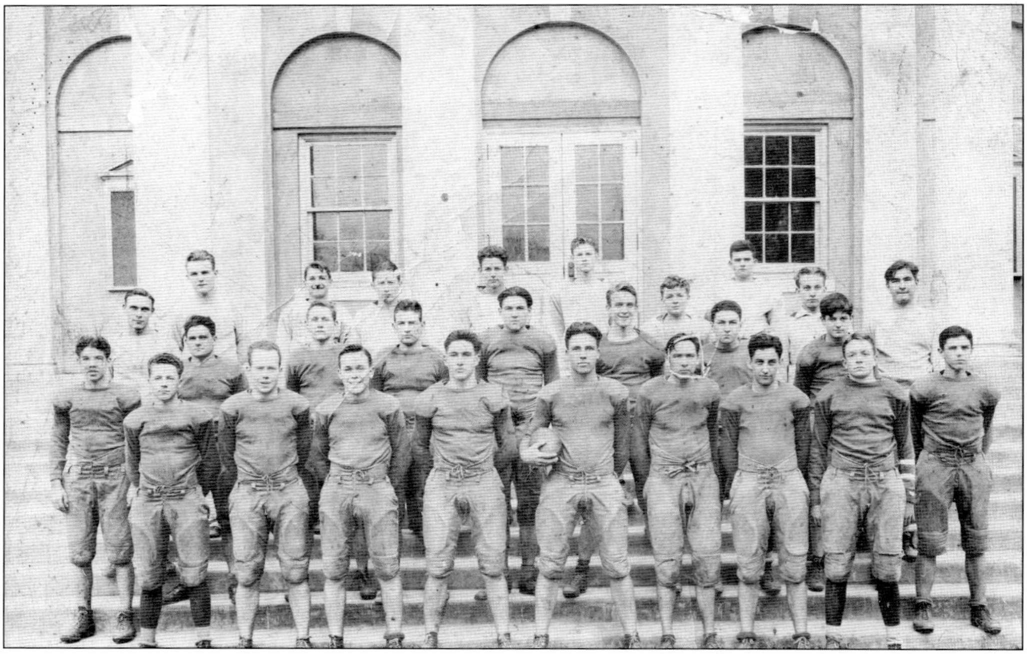

Greenwood High School Sports. It has been said that Greenwood has always been a sports town, and the sport of choice is probably football. No career better displays this love of the game than Julius Wistar "Pinky" Babb, the legendary Greenwood High School football coach who only had two losing seasons in his almost 40-year stay at GHS. Pictured above is the 1930 Greenwood High School football team. Pictured below is the 1917 Greenwood High girls' basketball team. (Both, courtesy of the Greenwood County Library System.)

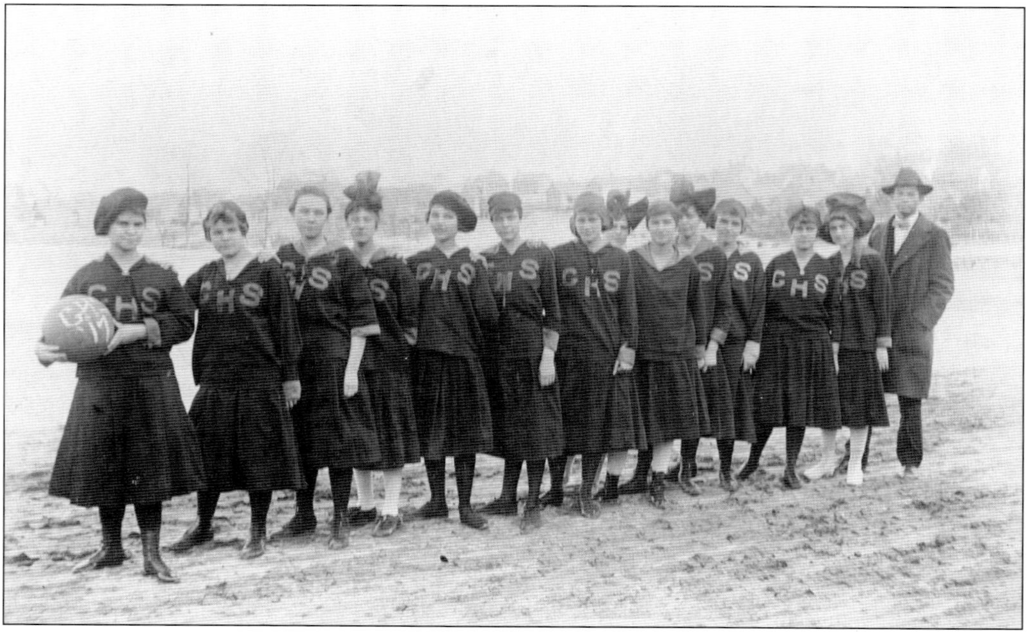

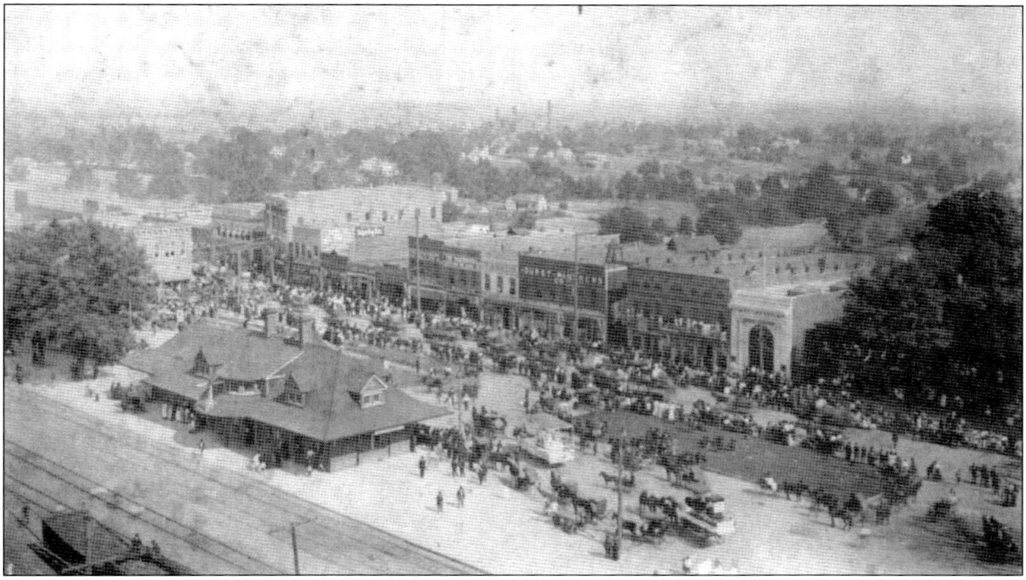

PARADES. Greenwood was, and continues to be, a town that enjoys a good celebration. Parades were held for many different occasions including Christmas, Independence Day, and Founder's Day. There was even an agricultural parade at one time. For these events, homemade floats were created by businesses and organizations. During parades, children enjoyed receiving candy from participating floats.

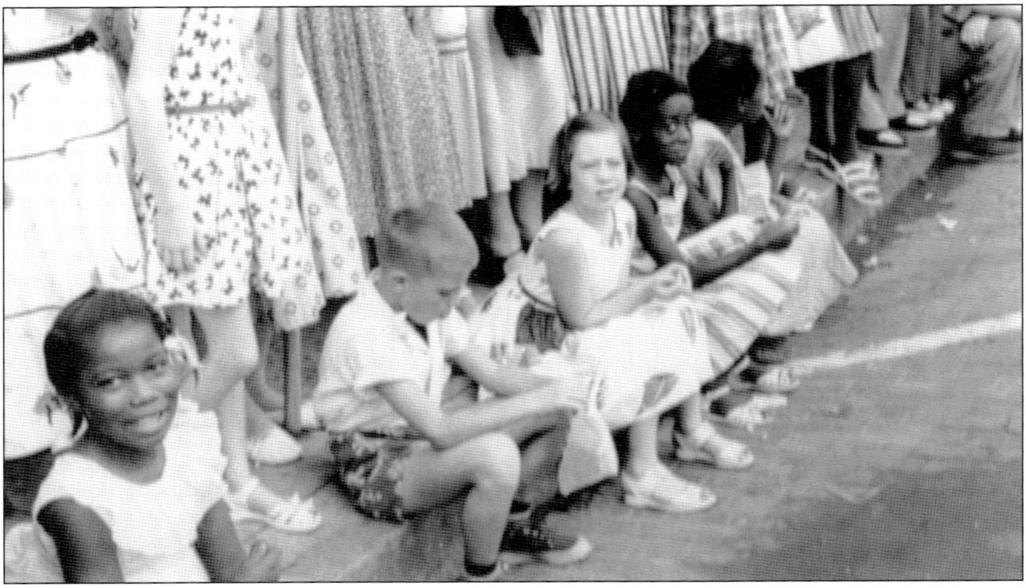

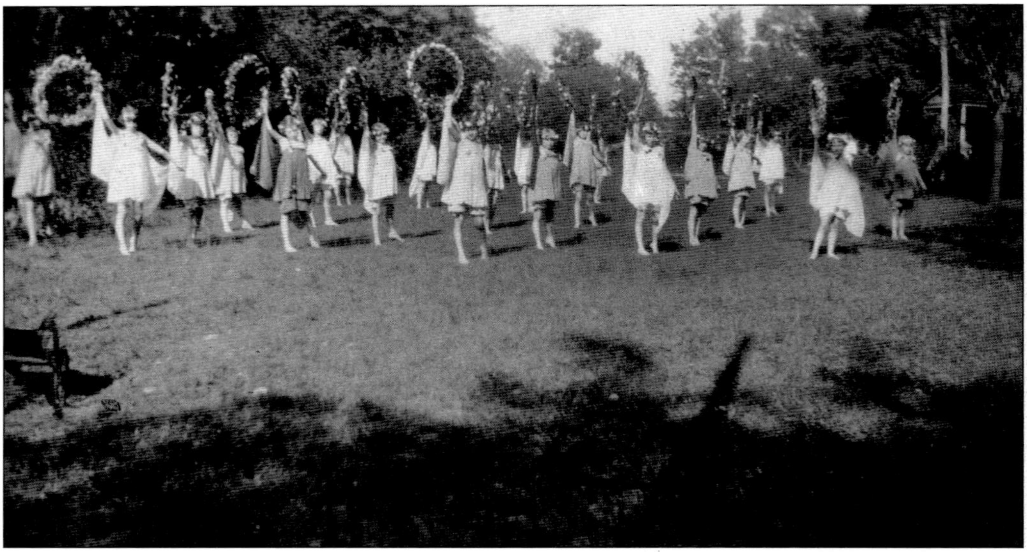

Hoop Dance. A beloved part of many special festivities, hoop dances were often done by the young women of a community. At this particular event, young ladies were taught a hoop dance to perform for a United Daughters of the Confederacy meeting. (Courtesy of the Greenwood County Library System.)

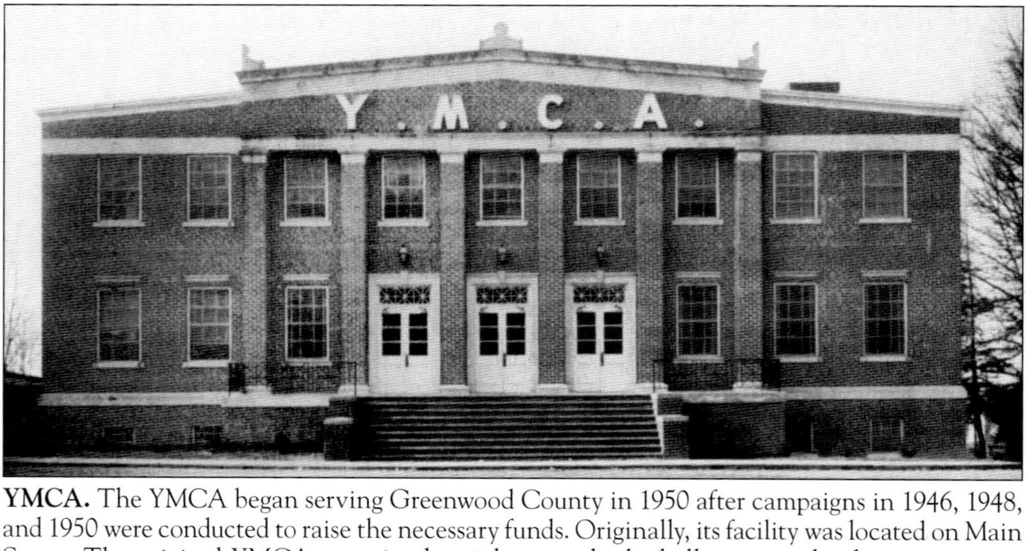

YMCA. The YMCA began serving Greenwood County in 1950 after campaigns in 1946, 1948, and 1950 were conducted to raise the necessary funds. Originally, its facility was located on Main Street. The original YMCA contained social rooms, basketball courts, a kitchen, swimming pool, bowling alley, and even a physical therapy room. (Courtesy of the Greenwood County Library System.)

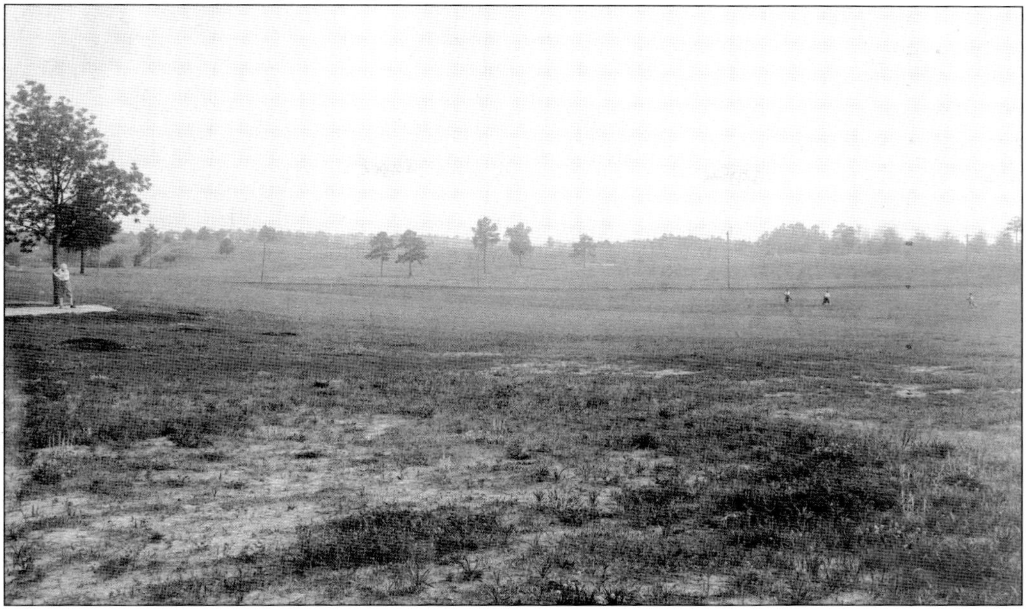

First Golf Course. The Yoe Springs reservoir continued to be used until Greenwood came to rely on Rocky Creek and Coronaca Creek. Ultimately, in the 1950s, Lake Greenwood became the source of Greenwood's water. The original site at Yoe Springs remained significant to Greenwoodians, who renamed it Oak Hill Park and established the first municipal golf course there. (Courtesy of the Greenwood County Library System.)

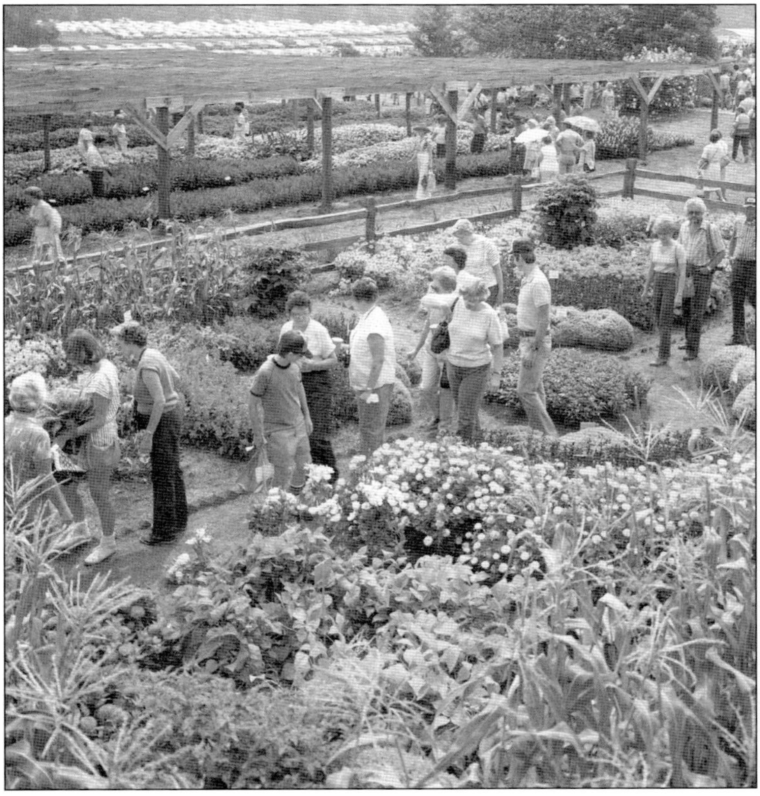

The Festival of Flowers. This famous festival began in 1967 as a tour of local gardens and featured Park Seed Flower Day, pictured here. It has since expanded to include huge topiaries, arts-and-craft shows, demonstrations, and participation from multiple organizations in Greenwood County.

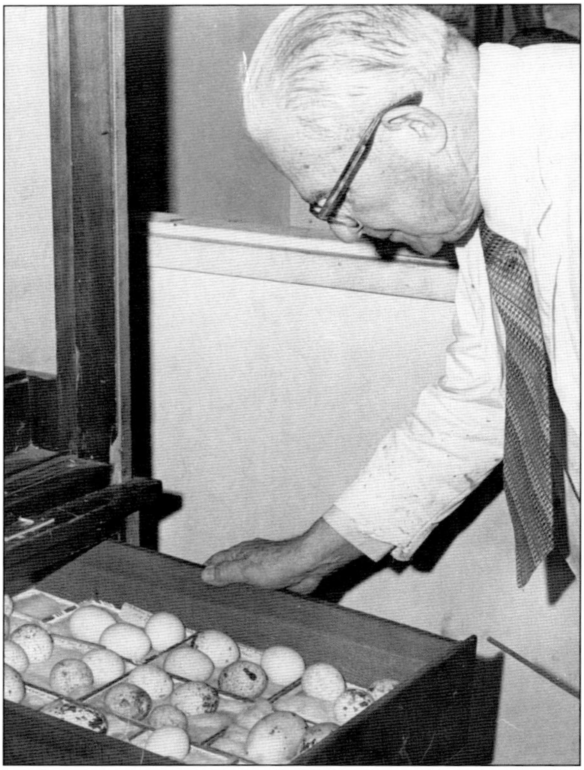

THE MUSEUM. The museum in Greenwood opened on January 25, 1970. The first executive director was James K. Durst who, without being paid, directed the renovation of one of the rooms in the old armory on Phoenix Street. He contributed much of the museum's original collection, with the help of other individuals in the community. The museum remained at this location until 1982, when it moved to Main Street.

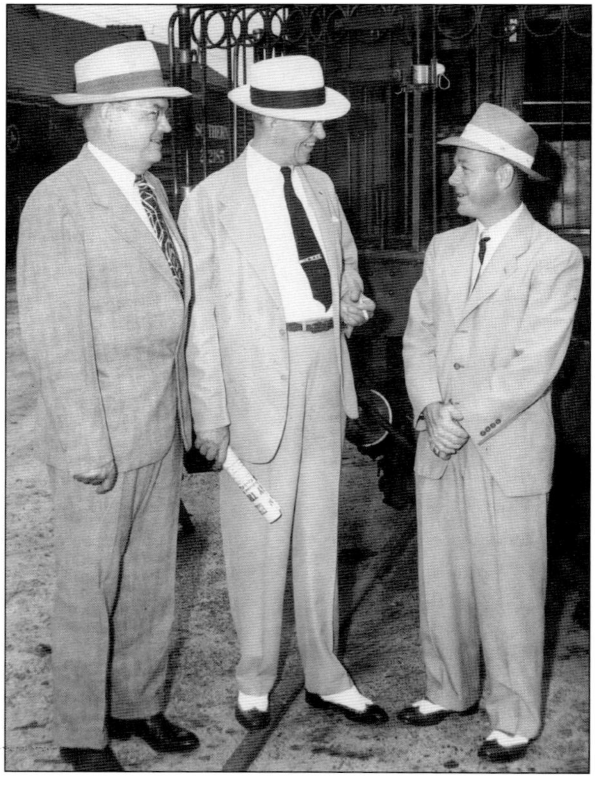

L.B. ADAMS SR. AND JIM SELF. While planning for South Carolina's centennial celebration in 1970, L.B. Adams Sr. (left), Charles Herndon Sr., and Jim Self (right) met to discuss the creation of the Railroad Historical Center. Adams and Self are standing with an unidentified man in front of the office car belonging to the Piedmont & Northern Railway, which was donated for the centennial opening of Greenwood's railroad museum.

Six

DISASTERS

Each city faces its own share of misfortunes. However, for its small size, Greenwood has had to overcome an usual number of obstacles since its establishment. From an 1825 cholera outbreak that shut down the first school in the area to a tornado in 1944 that ripped through the county and killed 38 people, this region has gone through fires, rioting, an explosion, wars, depression, and more, overcoming them all through the strength and unbreakable spirit of its people. With each tragedy, Greenwood discovered what it was made of—neighbors who would come to each other's aid, wealthy community leaders whose generosity would enable their town to recover, and businesses that would rise from the ashes, finding a way to rebuild and restore what had been lost.

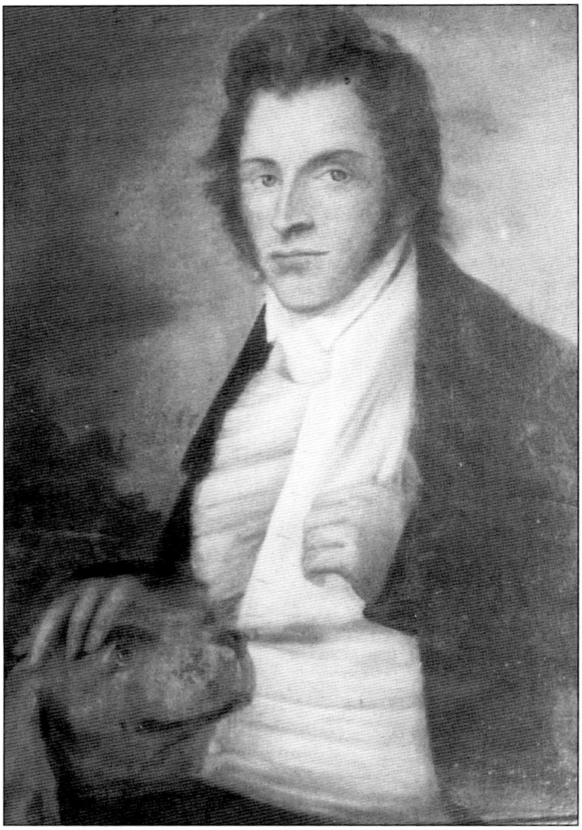

The Revolutionary War in Greenwood County. Brig. Gen. Samuel Mays was born in 1762. During the Revolutionary War, he served under General Sumter in the South Carolina militia and fought at the Battles of Blackstock, Hanging Rock, and Mangrove Mills. In the early 1800s, he continued to serve in the South Carolina militia and, ultimately, was a brigadier general in his own right. Pictured is General Mays, a resident of Greenwood County. (Courtesy of the Greenwood County Library System.)

Star Fort. Located in Ninety-Six, Star Fort was the scene of the longest siege during the Revolutionary War. Patriot Nathanael Greene led a 28-day siege in an attempt to take control of the area from the British. The Patriots were unsuccessful, and the British later burned the village. Pictured are the remnants of the star-shaped siege trenches built by Loyalists. The trenches were 17 feet high and topped with sandbags.

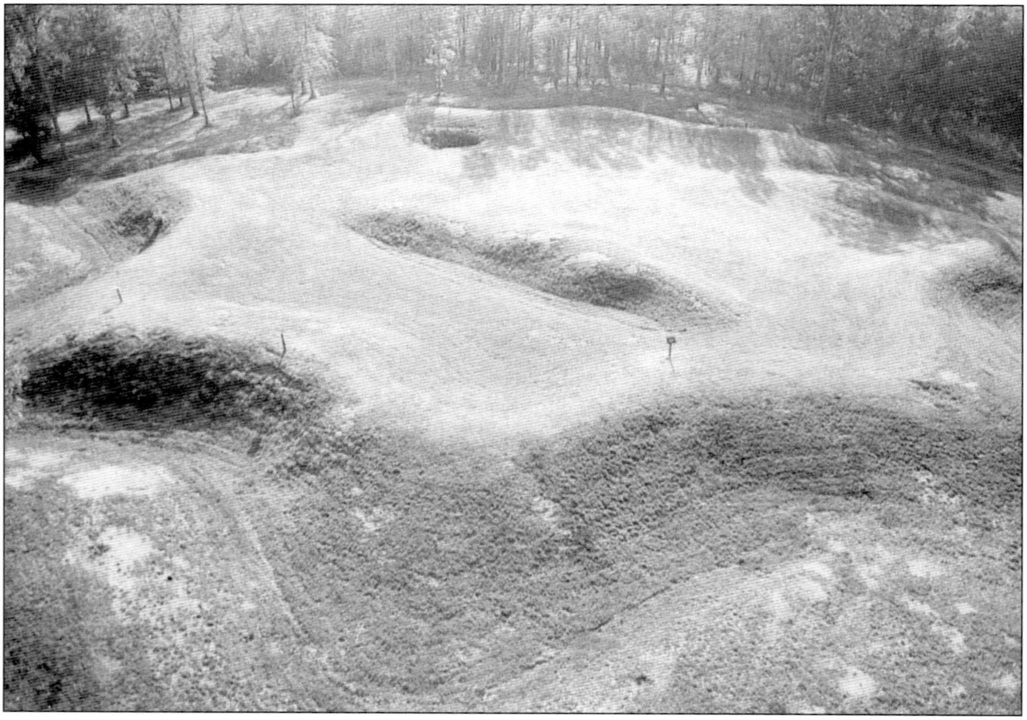

The Civil War in Greenwood. While the War Between the States was devastating to the nation as a whole, its effect was felt intensely in Greenwood. At the start of the war, Greenwood only boasted a population of about 300 people, and 57 of its young men agreed to serve as soldiers. This was 19 percent of the population and a huge loss to Greenwood. The Confederate monument was dedicated in front of the Greenwood County Courthouse in memory of the Greenwood citizens who died in the war.

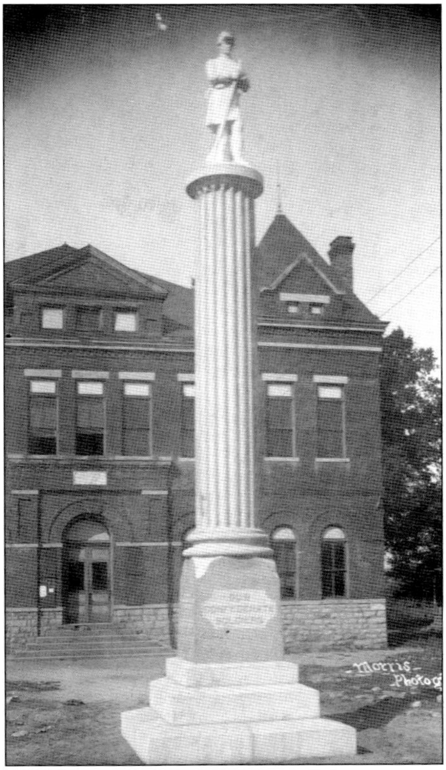

Train Wreck. On February 15, 1893, a total of 13 train cars wrecked as they were arriving at Greenwood Cotton Mill. The freight train derailed, sending one car straight through the side of the mill. The wreckage was recorded in this photograph by B.B. Morris.

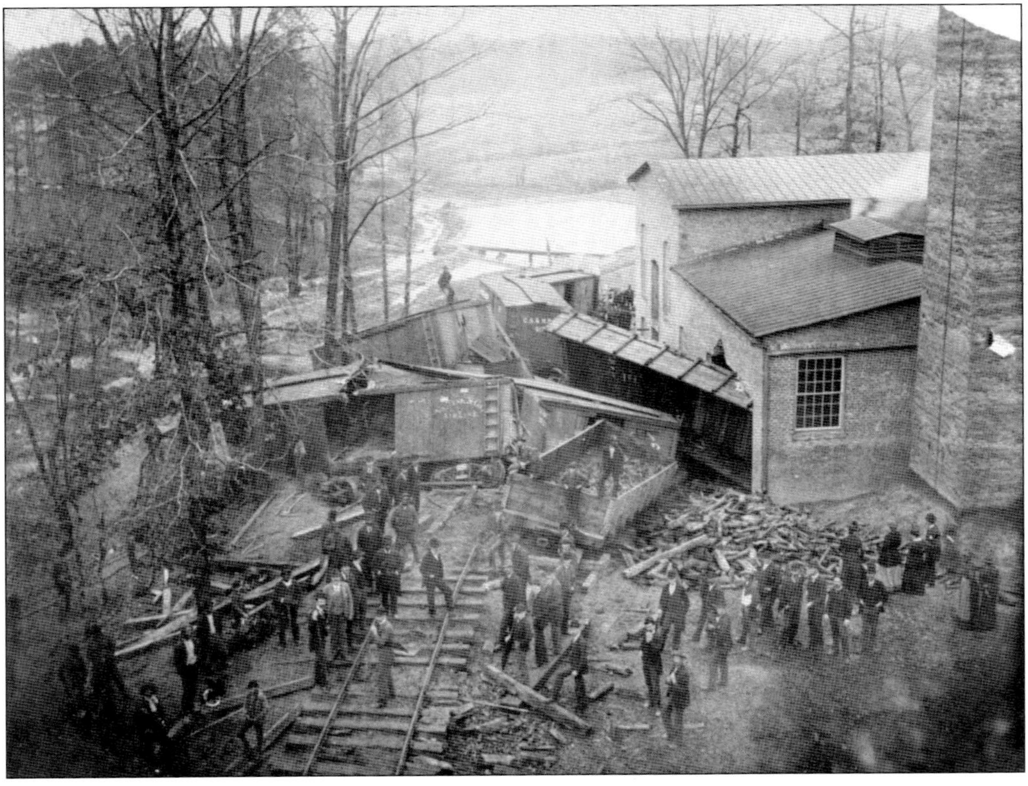

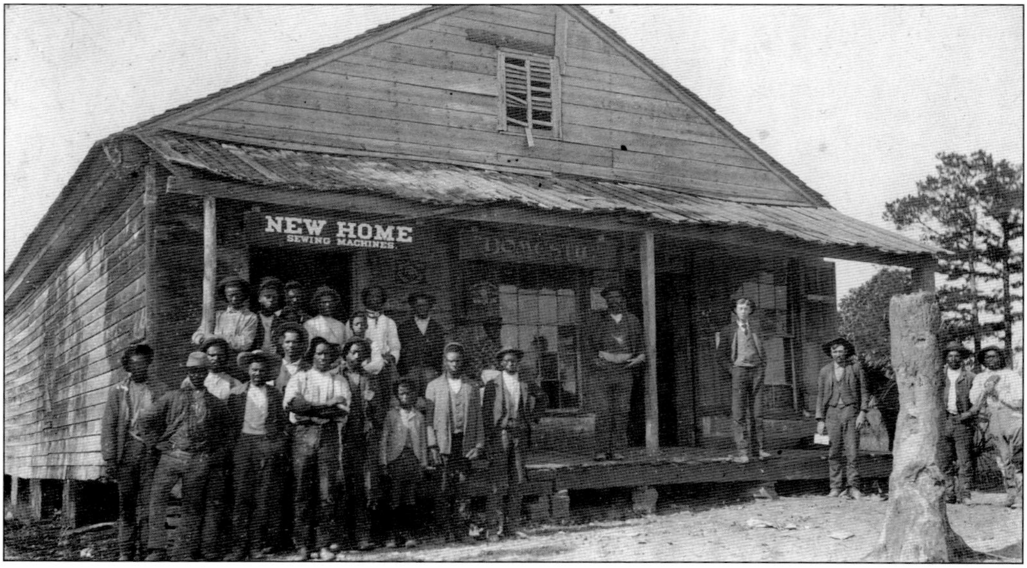

Phoenix Riot. Although African Americans were now free and eligible to vote, many state laws were created to stifle the voting rights of the newly freed slaves. These laws included the implementation of literacy tests, poll taxes, and grandfather clauses. Voting was a very controversial issue in the South, often leading to acts of violence. On November 8, 1898, Thomas Tolbert was registering African Americans to vote at a polling place in the Phoenix community of Greenwood. He had created his own ballot box and told any African Americans turned away from the polls to stop by and see him. After a scuffle with J.G. Etheridge, shots rang out, and Etheridge was killed. In retribution for the death of a white citizen, African Americans and those sympathetic to their cause were targeted, although it was never confirmed who was responsible for Etheridge's death. When the violence ended on November 12, eight men had been murdered. Pictured is a Phoenix store with a group of men standing in front. Below is a photograph of the store's side porch where a tenant living above the store can be seen greeting a friend. (Both, courtesy of the Greenwood County Library System.)

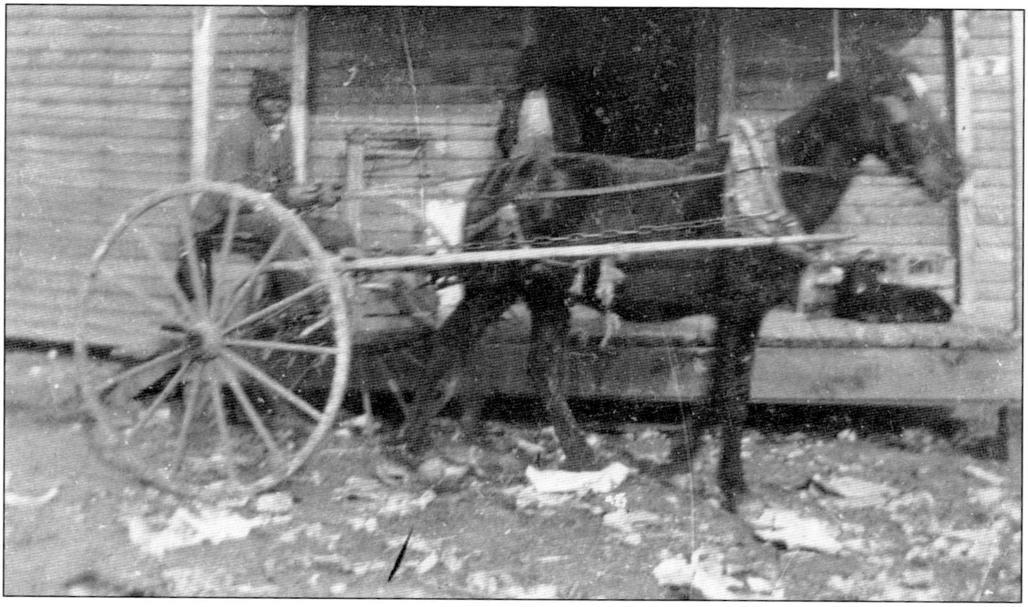

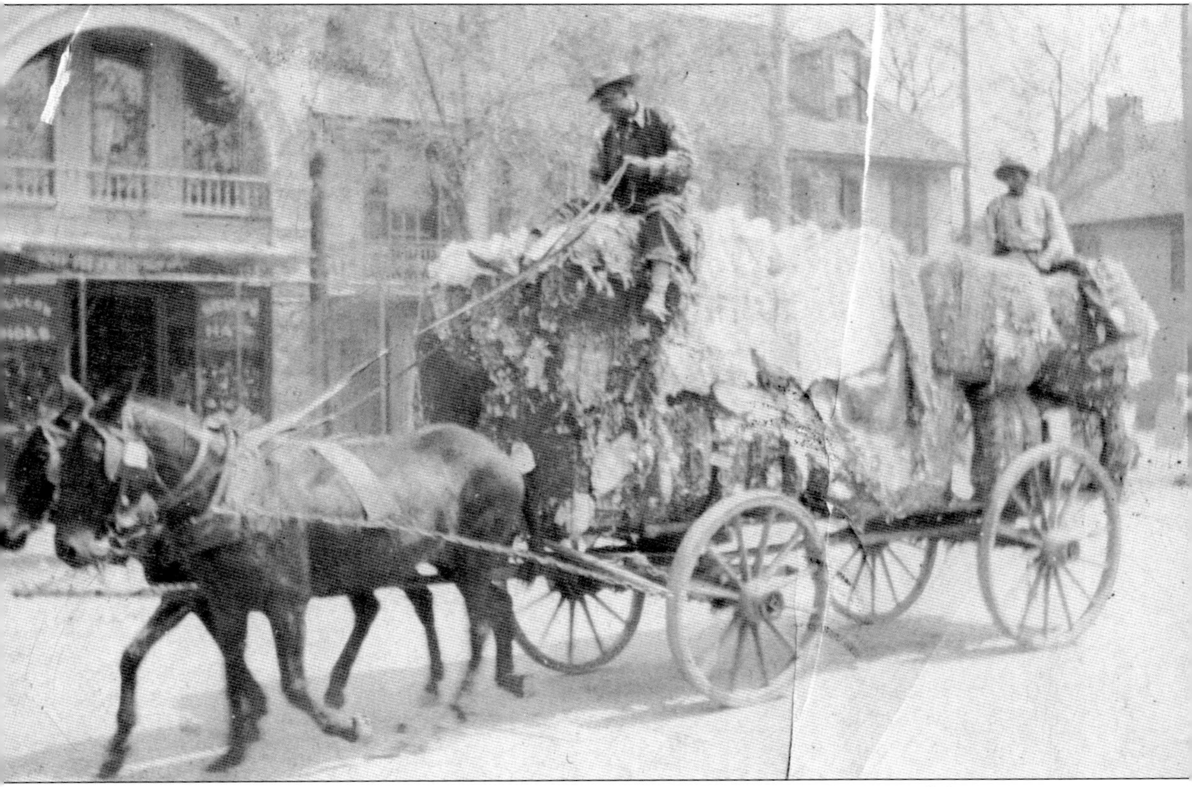

The Boll Weevil and Greenwood Cotton. The boll weevil, a pest imported from Mexico, began attacking cotton crops all over the United States in the early 1900s, ultimately consuming over eight million acres. South Carolina was not exempt from this destruction. However, James C. Self had taken it upon himself to purchase large stores of cotton when prices were at their lowest. While other companies' cotton supplies ran out, Self was able to keep his mills in business. Famers are shown in Greenwood taking cotton from the gin to the storehouse. (Courtesy of the Greenwood County Library System.)

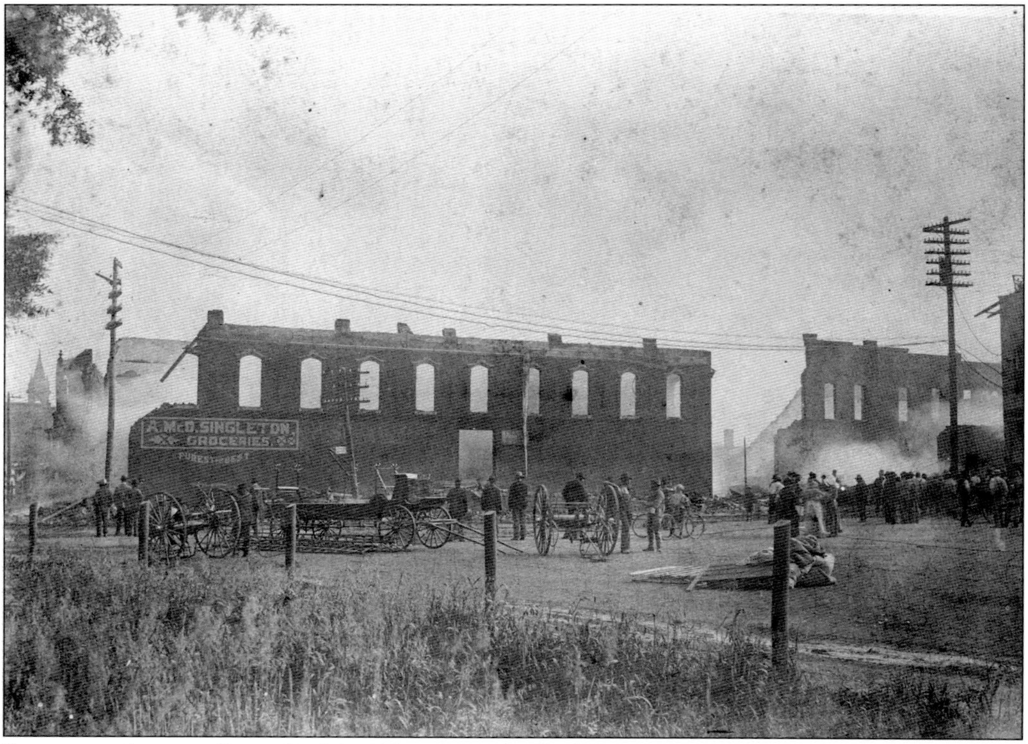

Seaboard Avenue Fire. On May 25, 1904, a fire broke out in Greenwood's business district. It destroyed more than 20 stores and led to the death of one person. The local fire department was still in its early stages of organization, so a man riding a horse and buggy had to go to the water plant and ask that the pumps be turned on in order for the blaze to be fought.

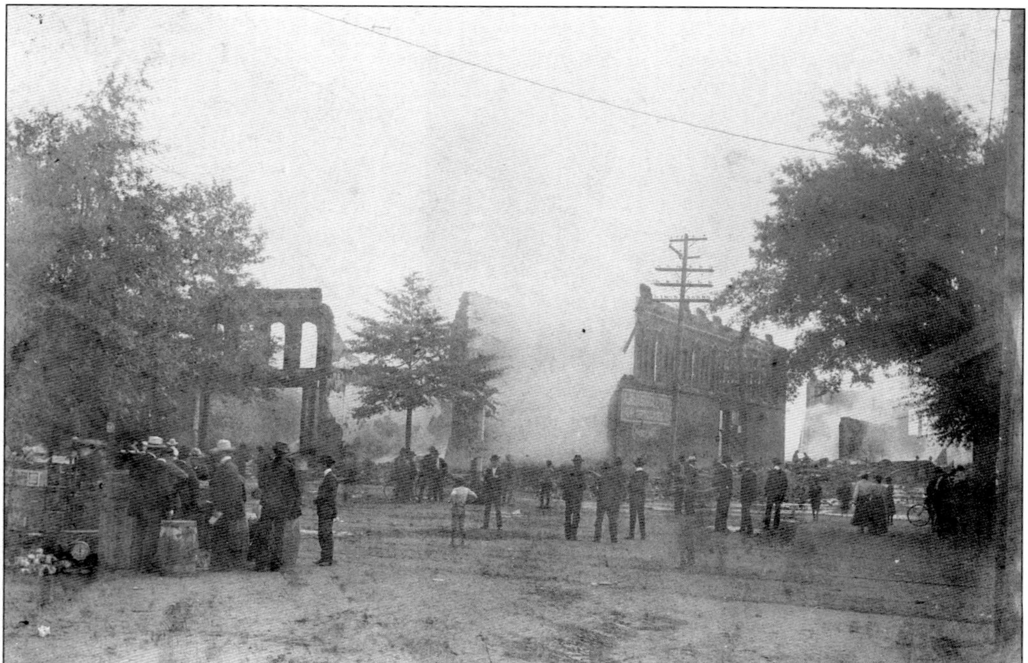

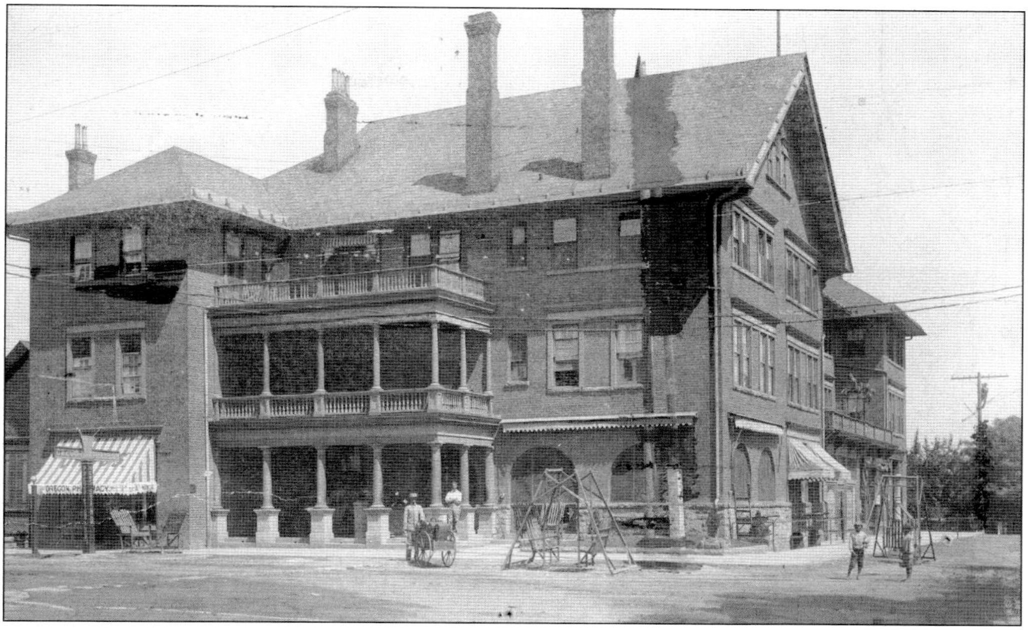

THE OLD OREGON HOTEL. On March 3, 1912, a fire broke out in the hotel and destroyed the entire block. No deaths were reported, but the damage was estimated at $140,000, and many guests lost their personal belongings. The Oregon Hotel was rebuilt and reopened in its new location in 1914. It remained a hotel until 1946.

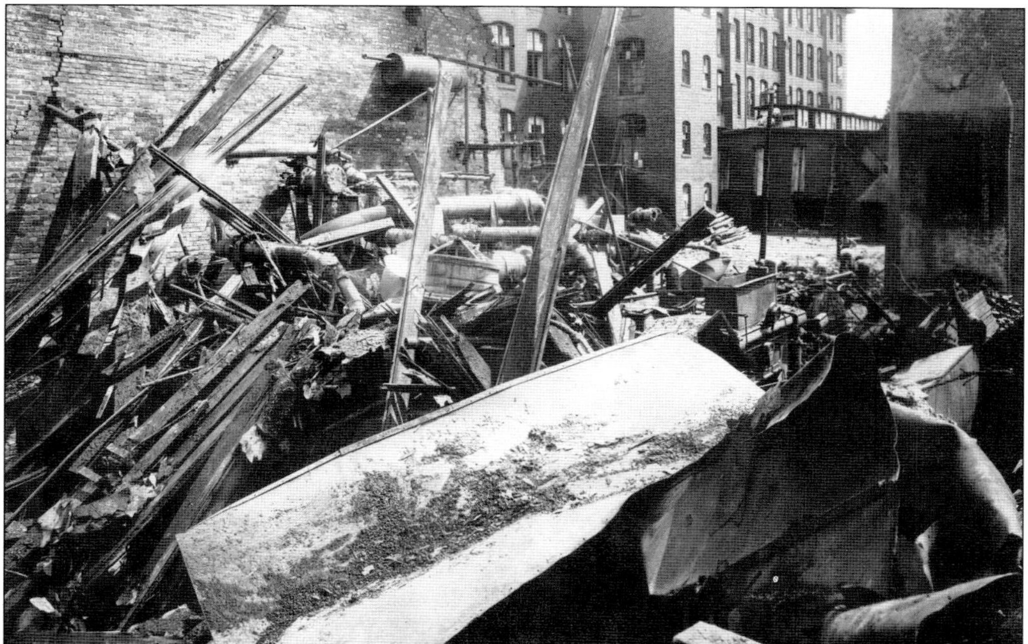

BOILER EXPLOSION. On the evening of May 15, 1923, an explosion rocked Grendel Mills. A boiler, which had been in operation for 27 years and had been inspected that very day, exploded, sending parts of it flying as far as 100 feet away. The boiler room was leveled. Two men were killed, and two were injured in the blast. There was over $50,000 worth of damage done to the buildings and textiles materials at the mill.

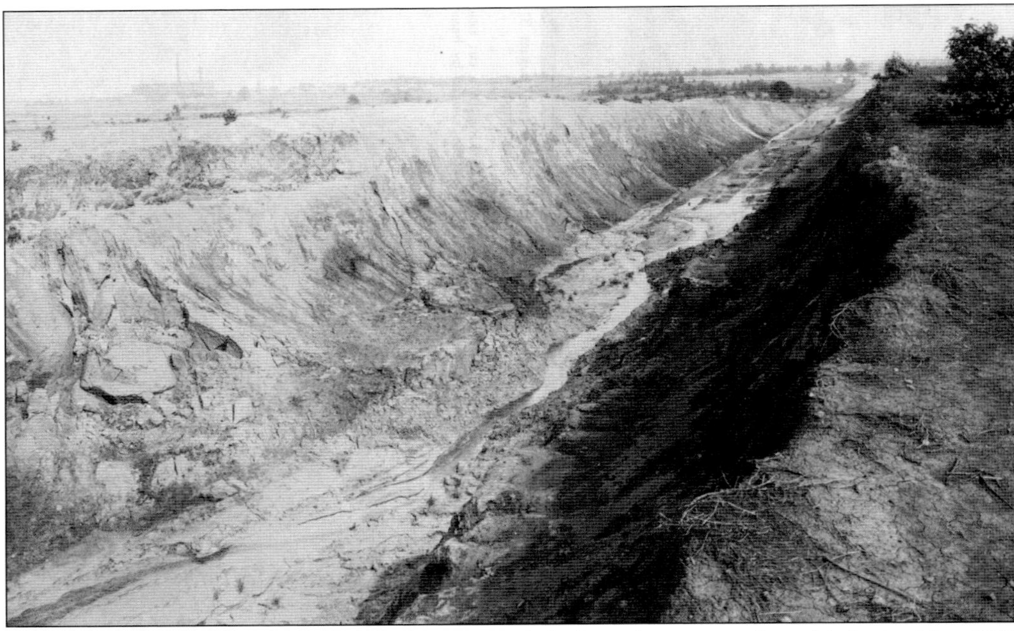

MUD SLIDE. Because of heavy rains, Greenwood dealt with a series of mudslides in May 1928. These slides greatly impacted the railroad industry in town, as one of them covered a newly graded line for the Georgia & Florida Railroad in south Greenwood and another struck in Kirksey, delaying work there.

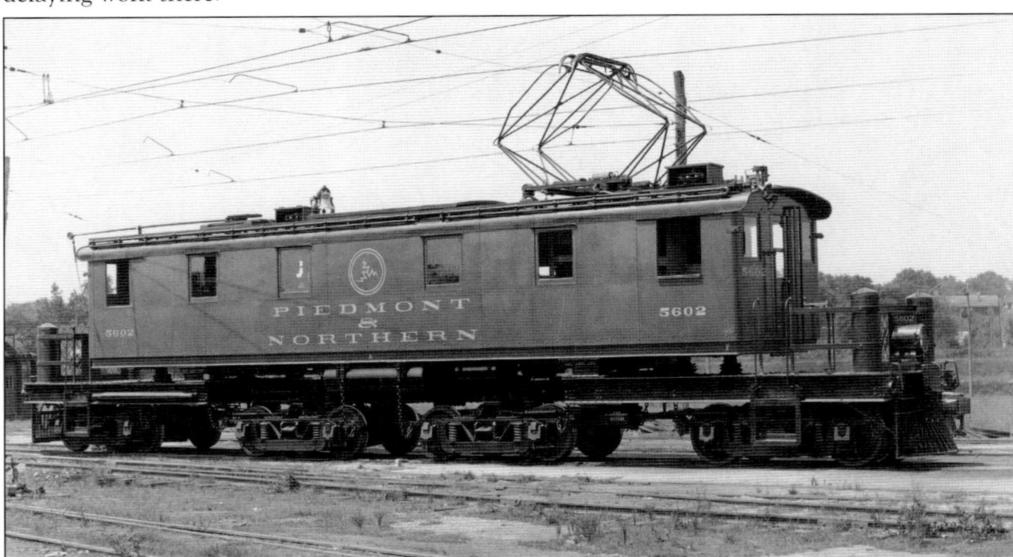

THE GREAT DEPRESSION. A disaster on a national scale, the Great Depression affected Greenwood County in a similar manner to many other towns. Farmers had a hard time providing for their families. Many businesses struggled to remain open. Even the mills struggled to keep production going. Some relief did come in 1933 with the creation of certain New Deal programs in Greenwood. The creation of Lake Greenwood State Park and the Buzzard's Roost project provided employment opportunities for Greenwoodians. During the Depression, citizens began to rely on cheaper modes of transportation, such as the electric Piedmont & Northern Railroad. Pictured is the electric Engine No. 5602 in Greenwood.

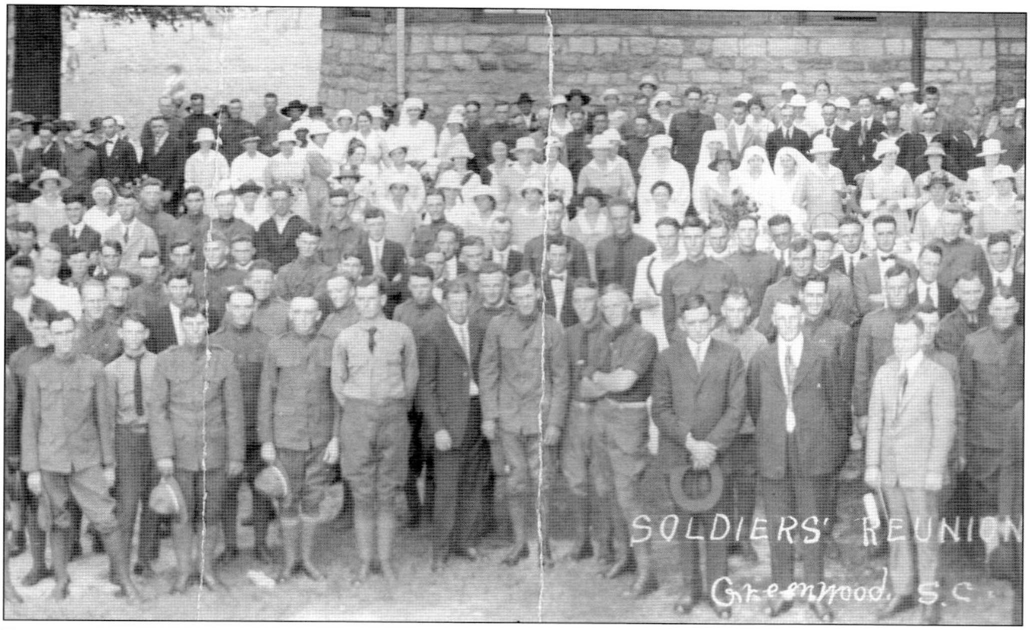

Reunion of Heroes. A little over a year after the Great War, Greenwood's veterans reunited for a barbecue. Beginning on July 28, 1914, and lasting until November 11, 1919, World War I claimed the lives of 117,000 American soldiers, with over 200,000 returning home wounded. American service members found themselves in a variety of countries during this war, including France, Belgium, and Italy.

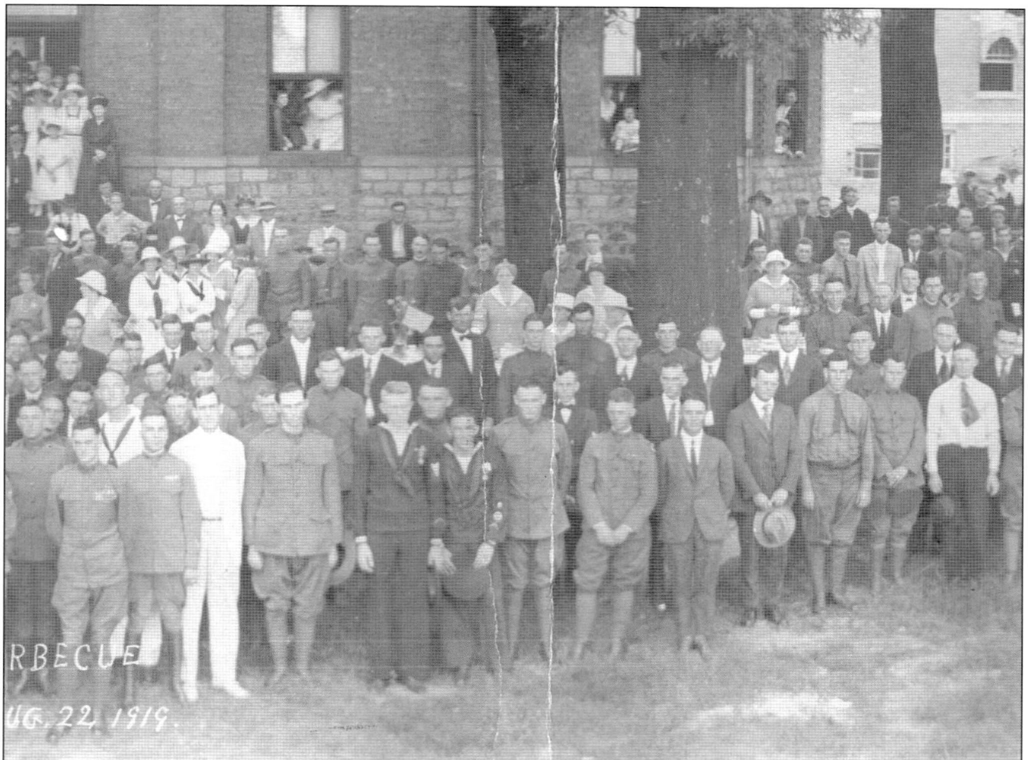

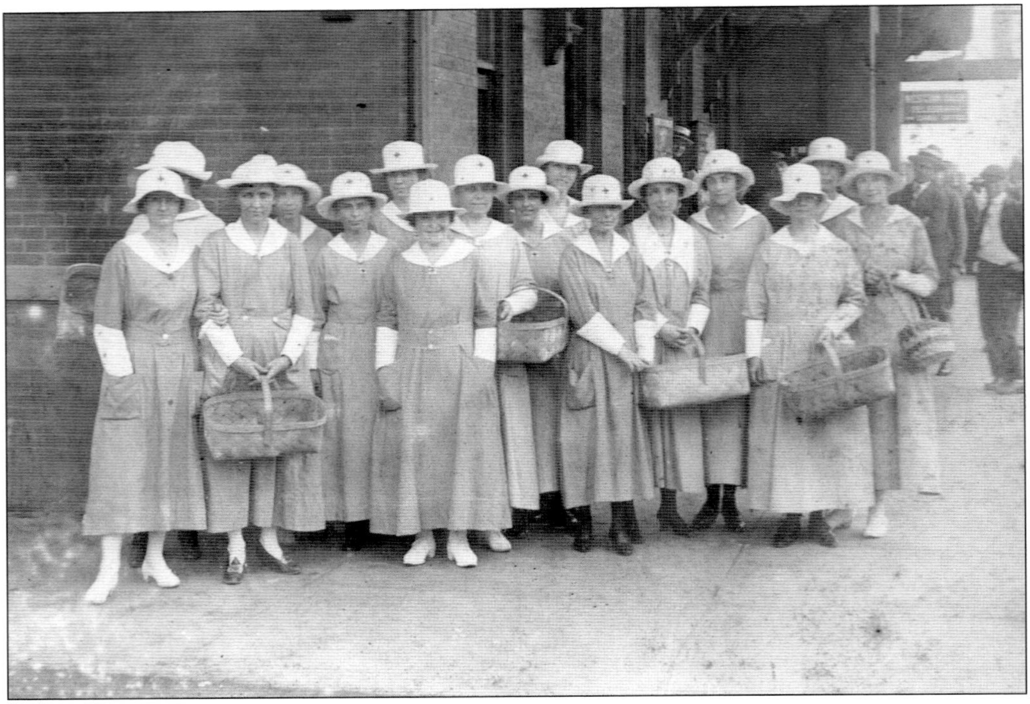

Greenwood Red Cross. During World War I, the Greenwood chapter of the American Red Cross worked hard in this season of conflict. They created, gathered, and shipped items to the Red Cross headquarters, which, in turn, shipped them to soldiers on the battlefront. Items included surgical supplies, knitted items such as socks and sweaters, canned preserves, and "comfort bags." Comfort bags were filled with items such as books of poetry, pencils and paper, cigarettes, chocolate, and even chewing gum. Over four million soldiers from the United States fought in the Great War.

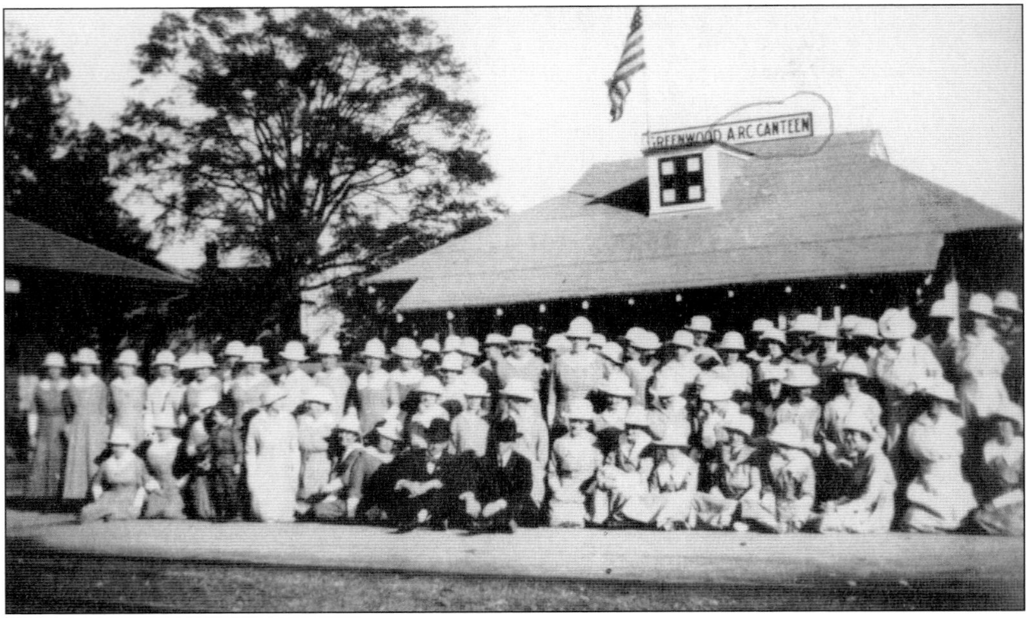

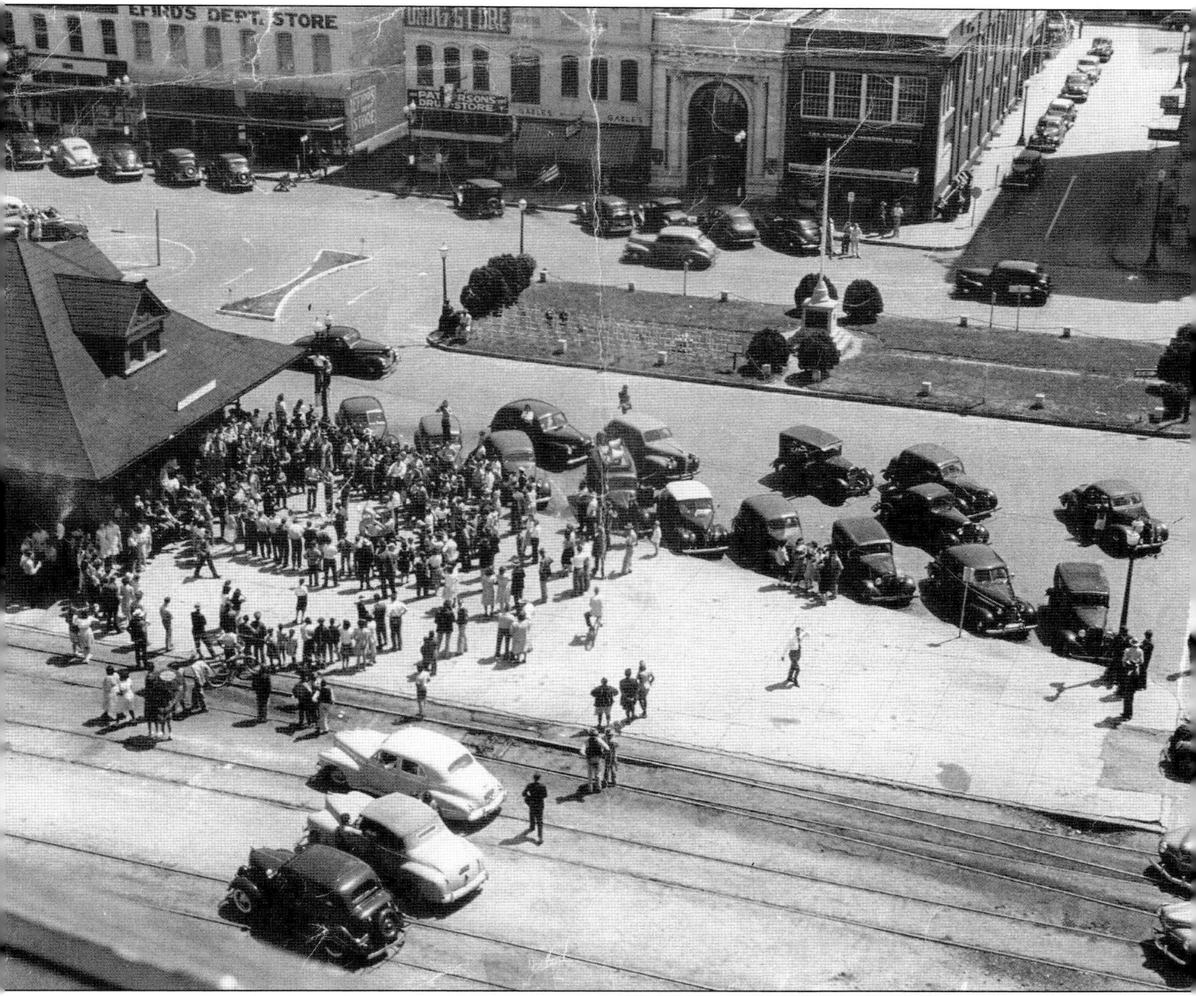

VE Day: May 8, 1945. After the surrender of Germany, communities all across America celebrated VE Day, or Victory in Europe day. This day marked the end of World War II in Europe. Japan signed their surrender in September, finally ending the bloody conflict, which had lasted six years and ended the lives of over 420,000 Americans. This picture captures Greenwoodians gathered for the VE Day festivities.

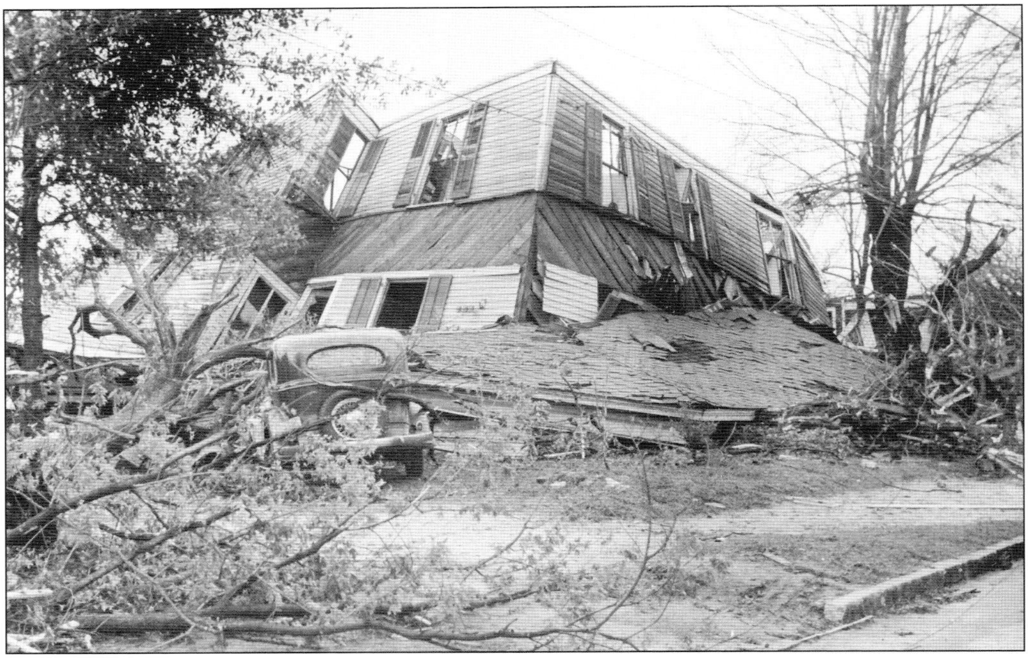

HOME OF MR. AND MRS. R.W. COLE. At about 1:15 on the morning of April 16, 1944, a tornado ripped through Greenwood killing eight people, including a three-year-old girl. 119 buildings were destroyed, with a total of 281 sustaining damage during the storm. The cost of this damage was estimated by the Red Cross to be $250,000–$500,000.

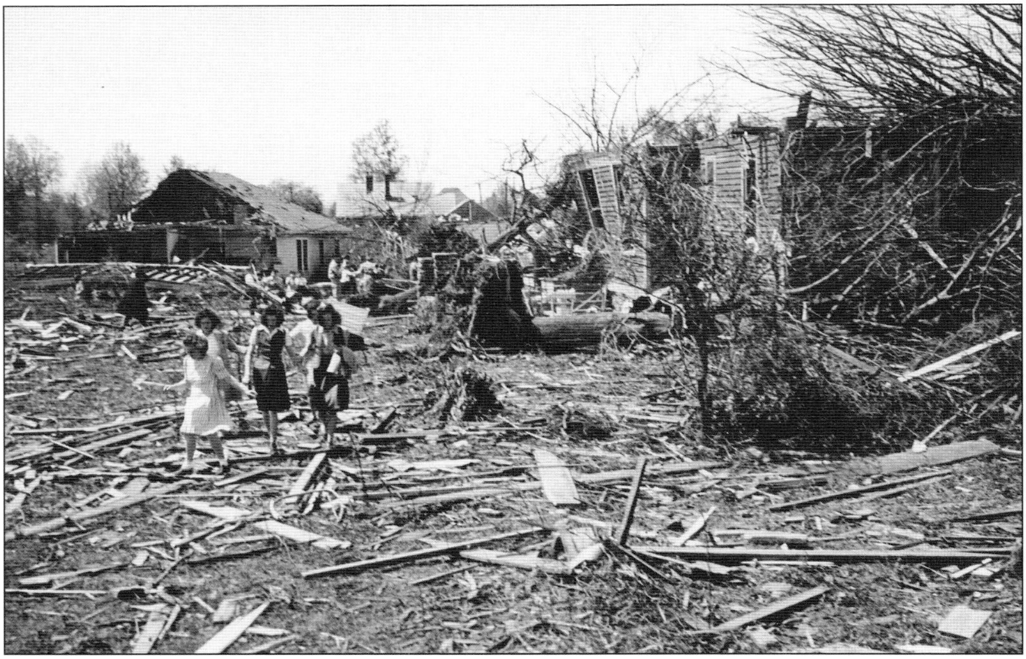

PATH OF DESTRUCTION. Accounts from the 1944 disaster describe barns being lifted up and tossed several yards away, where horses were discovered inside unharmed, or roosters found tied to porch swings in front of decimated homes. Another story involved three passengers whose car was destroyed by the force of the storm. They all survived the ordeal without serious injury.

Seven

Churches

The oldest organized churches in Greenwood began in gardens, local homes, and log cabins. Greenwood citizens of centuries past were so devout in their faith that they showed their dedication through the organization of places of worship. The hard work, dedication, and perseverance of founding church members created a legacy of Christian worship in Greenwood. Baptist, Methodist, and Presbyterian services planted the seeds that resulted in the huge churches that flank Greenwood's Main Street today. During Reconstruction, many new churches in Greenwood were founded by former slaves. The growth and pride of all of Greenwood's churches resulted in a strong emphasis on family and faith throughout the city.

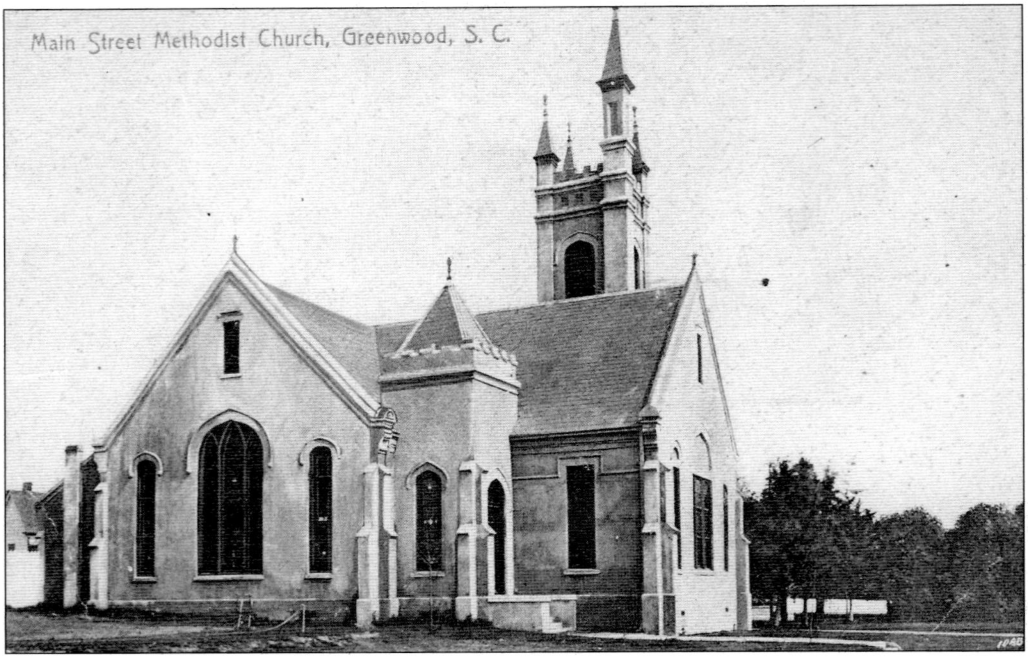

MAIN STREET UNITED METHODIST CHURCH. The Methodist tradition in Greenwood began when the Tranquil Methodist Church was built in the early 1800s. Tabernacle Methodist Episcopal Church followed and was established four miles north of Greenwood in 1858. In 1889, Tabernacle became what is now Main Street United Methodist Church, located on Main Street. The photograph above shows the church soon after it was built. Pictured below is the Methodist children's choir in the 1950s.

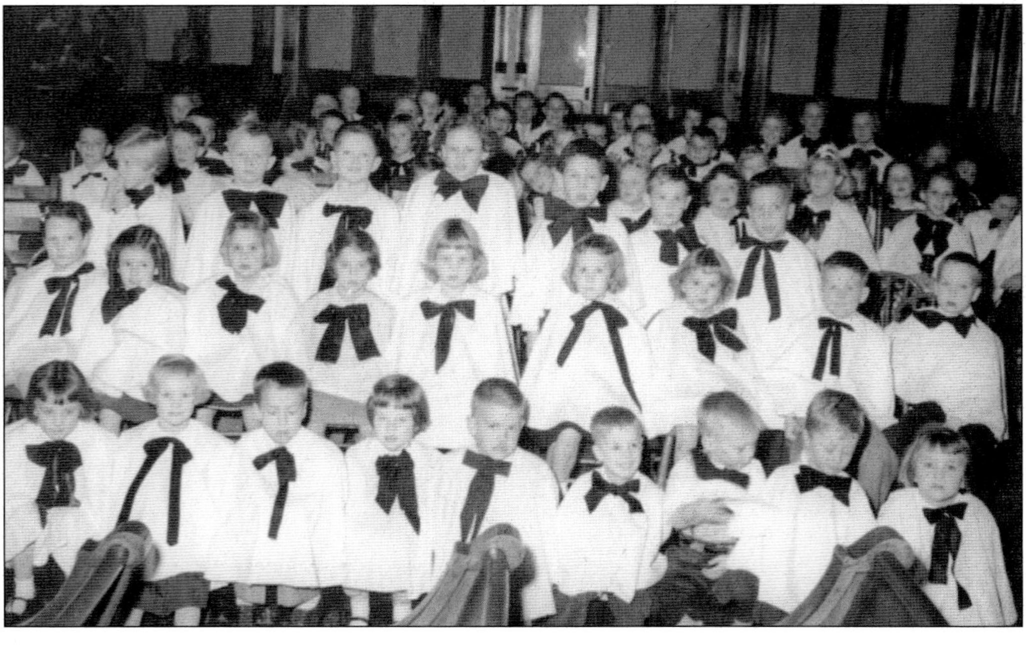

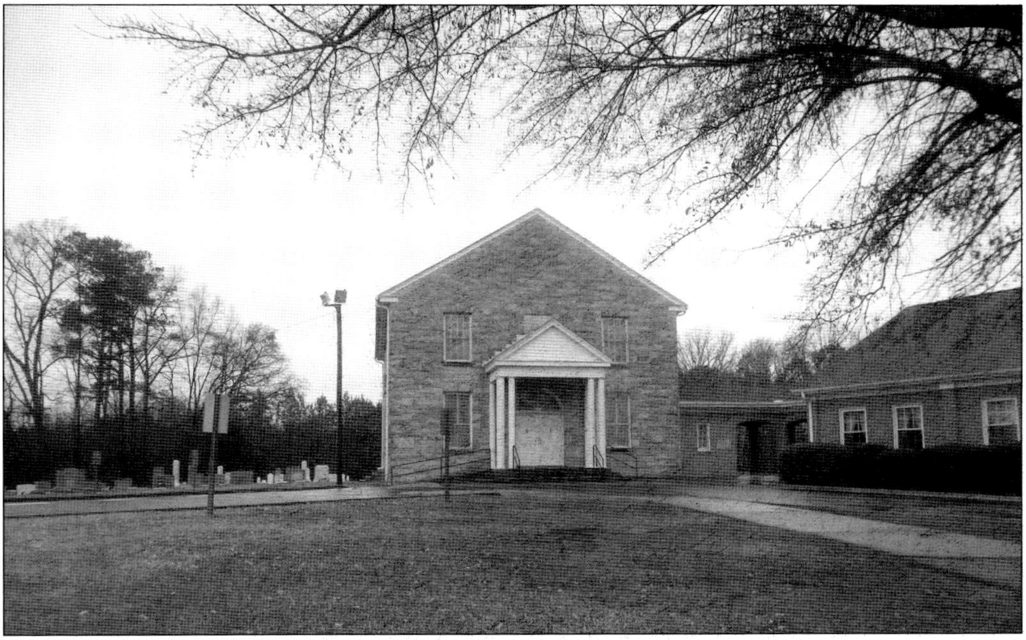

First Mount Moriah Baptist Church. Established in 1810 and opened in 1812, First Mount Moriah Baptist Church was founded by 51 congregants. They met to worship in a small wooden structure called Mount Moriah Meetinghouse. In 1826, the meetinghouse burned to the ground and was not rebuilt until 1834. (Courtesy of Bill Cervenka.)

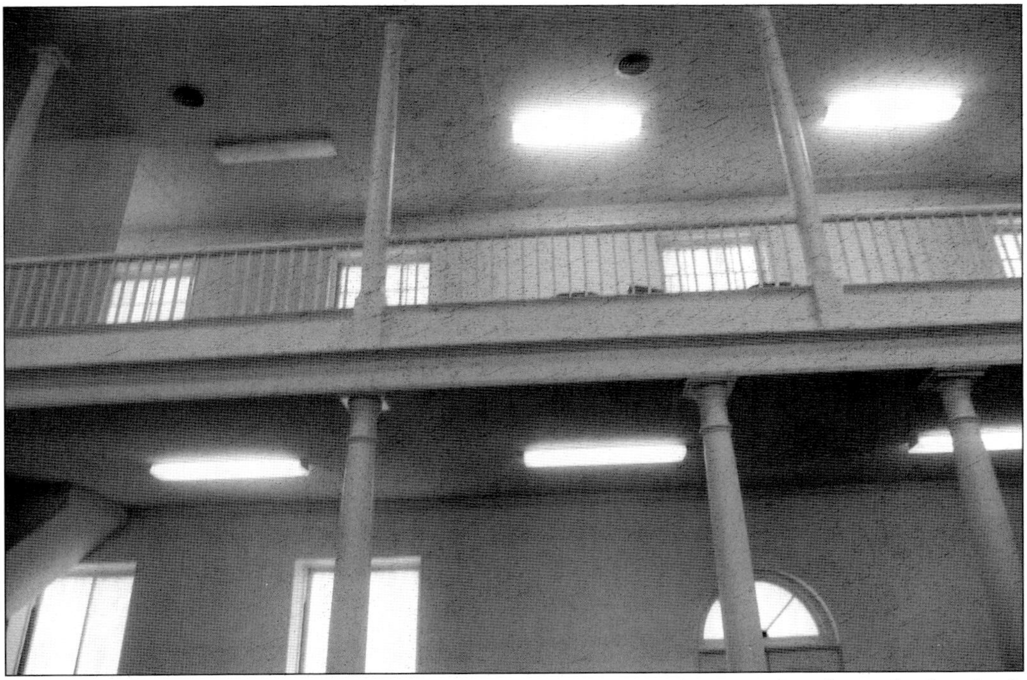

Balcony of First Mount Moriah Baptist Church. In 1835, a new church was built, which included a balcony where slaves were chained during worship services. After the Civil War, Reconstruction led to the creation of Mount Moriah Baptist Church, where former slaves could worship freely. (Courtesy of Bill Cervenka.)

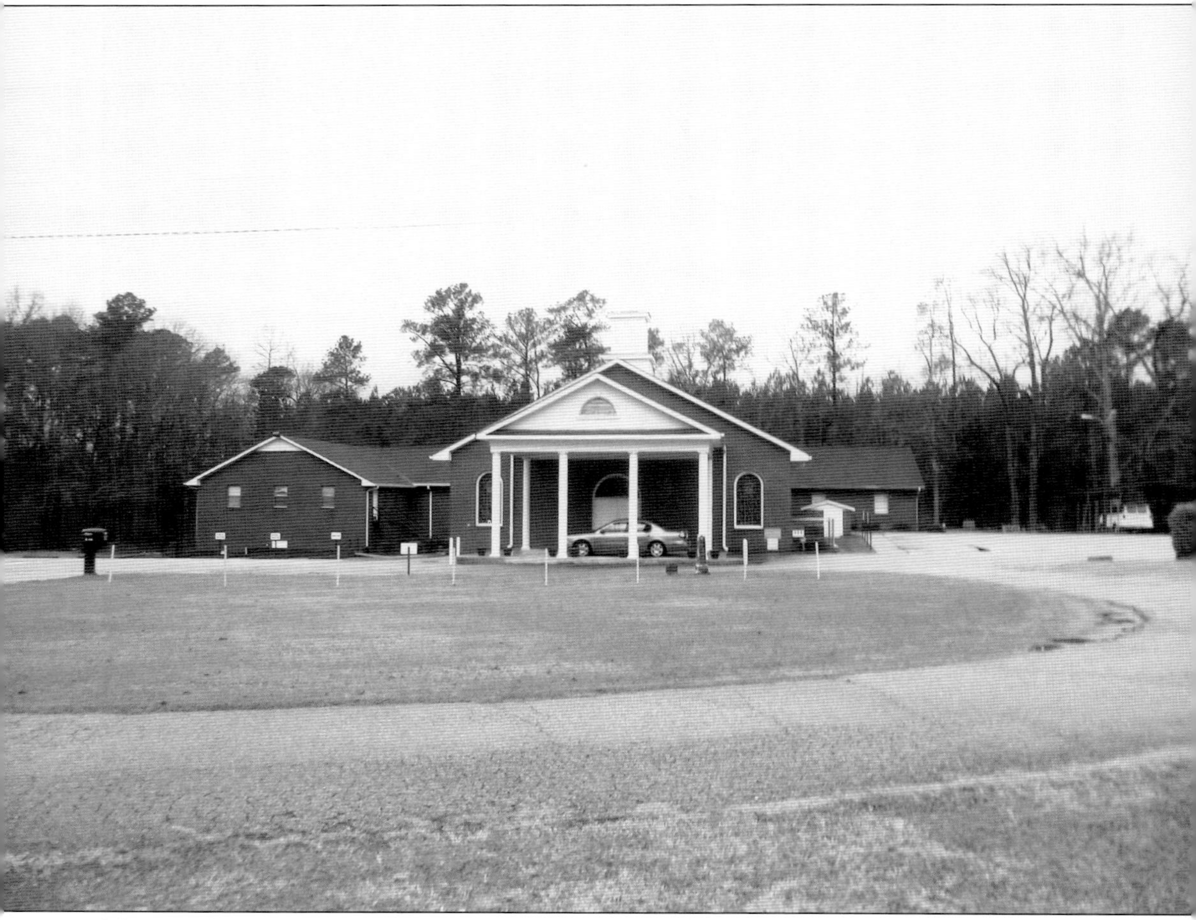

MOUNT MORIAH BAPTIST CHURCH. Services were held in a grass hut, and then a log cabin, before the construction of the first church building in 1919. First Mount Moriah Baptist Church gave the members of the new Mount Moriah Baptist Church land for their structure. In March 1967, a new church was built. (Courtesy of Bill Cervenka.)

First Presbyterian Church. In 1850, Rock Presbyterian Church purchased the Presbyterian High School building so that church members living in the town could meet at a location closer to their homes. This facility was called the chapel, and the pastor, Rev. John McLees, dedicated his time to both congregations. As the railroads moved in and the center of town shifted, over half of the Rock Presbyterian members had homes in town. Eventually the chapel was sold, and a new building was constructed. First Presbyterian Church, or the Greenwood Presbyterian Church, was dedicated on October 17, 1875. Pictured at right is the original church facade, and below is the original sanctuary. (Both, courtesy of First Presbyterian Church.)

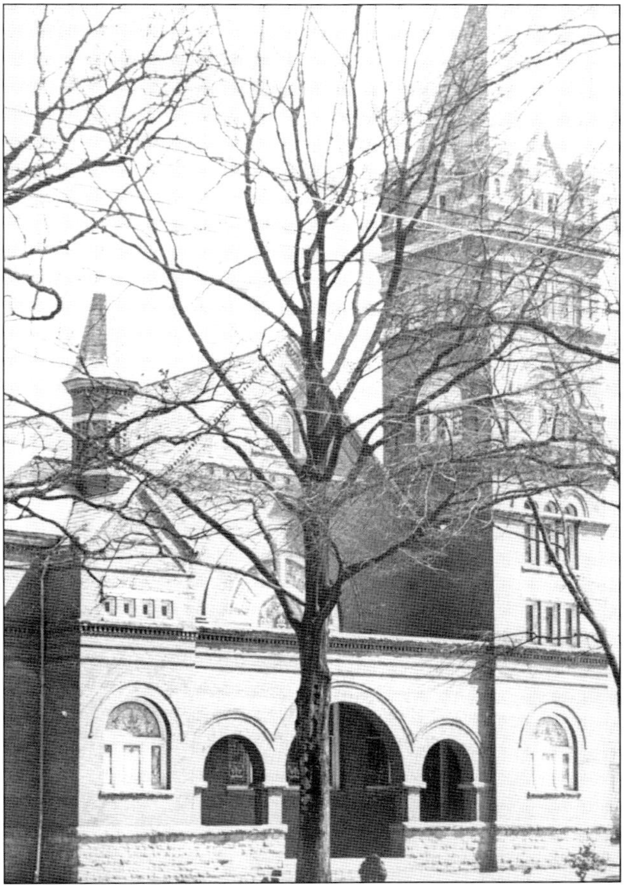

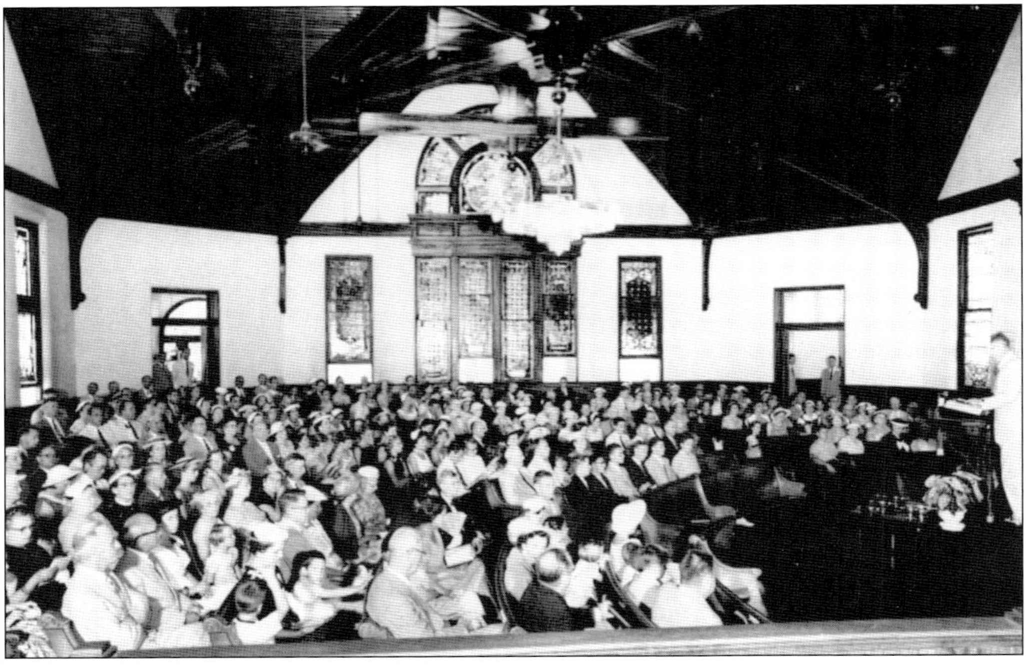

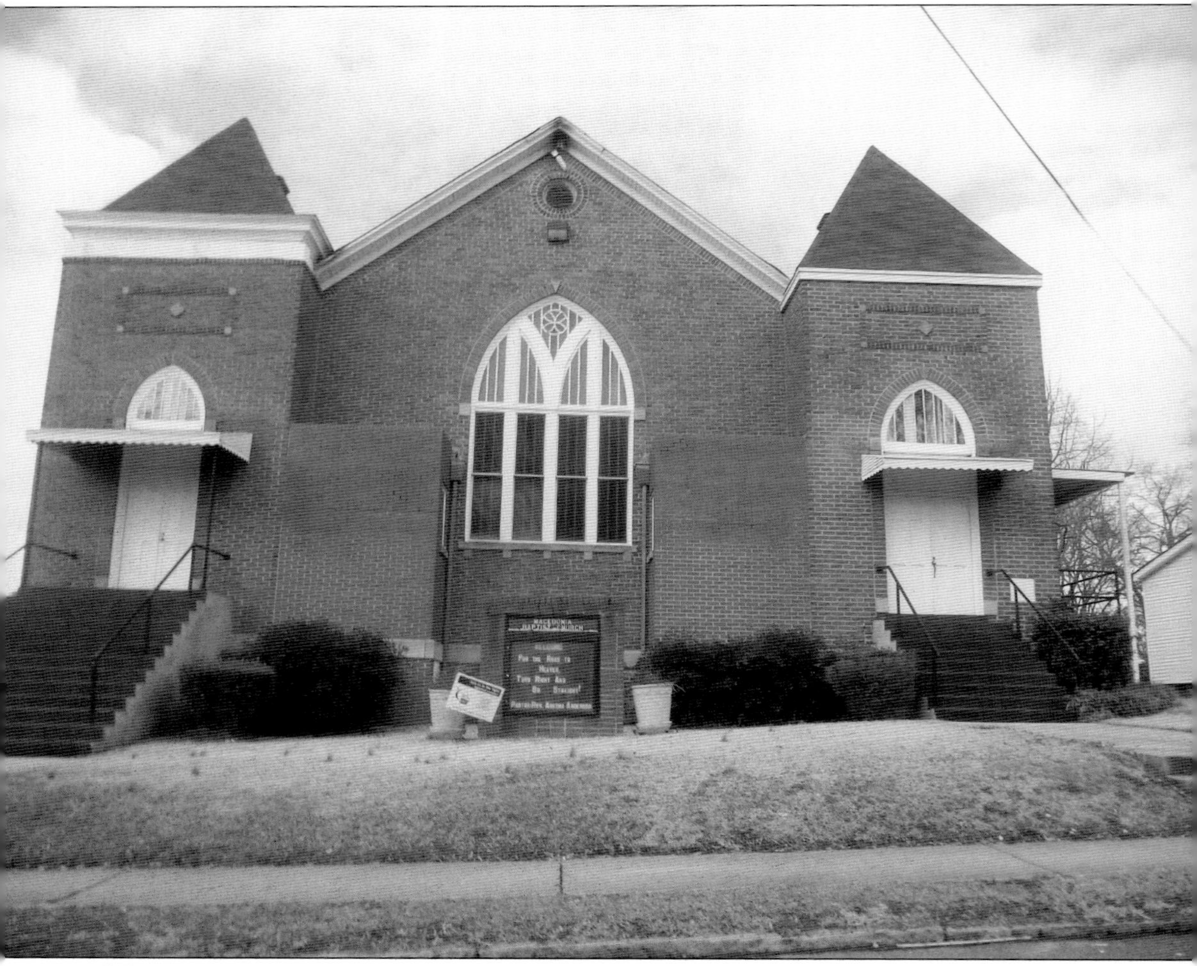

MACEDONIA MISSIONARY BAPTIST CHURCH. Named by Emma Cook in 1882, Macedonia Church was organized when services were moved from a brush arbor to a home on Marion Avenue. In 1901, the church moved to its present location and was able to open a community center in 1977. (Courtesy of Bill Cervenka.)

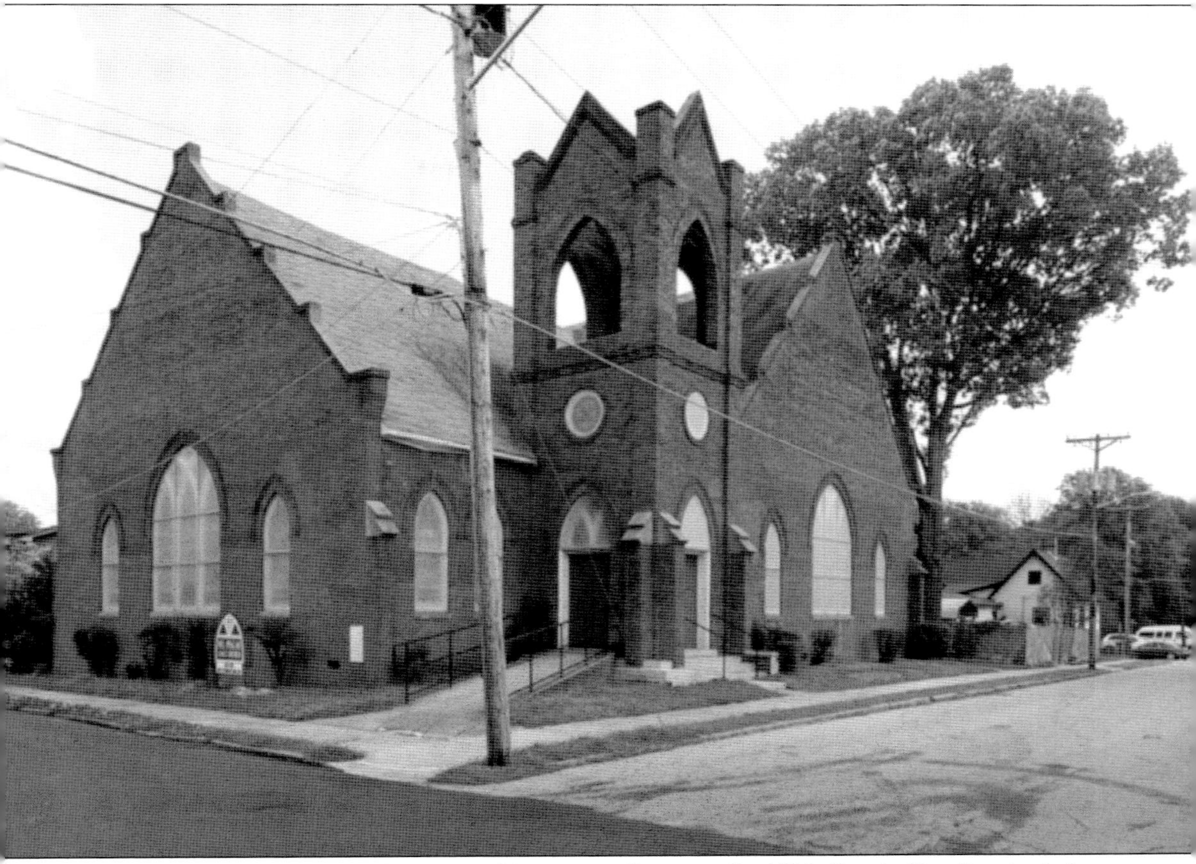

Mount Pisgah African Methodist Episcopal Church. In 1890, South Carolina had the largest African Methodist Episcopal (AME) membership of any state in the country. In 1908, Mount Pisgah AME church was established when members of Weston Chapel Congregation decided to seek a more centralized location. The church was listed in the National Register of Historic Places in 1979.

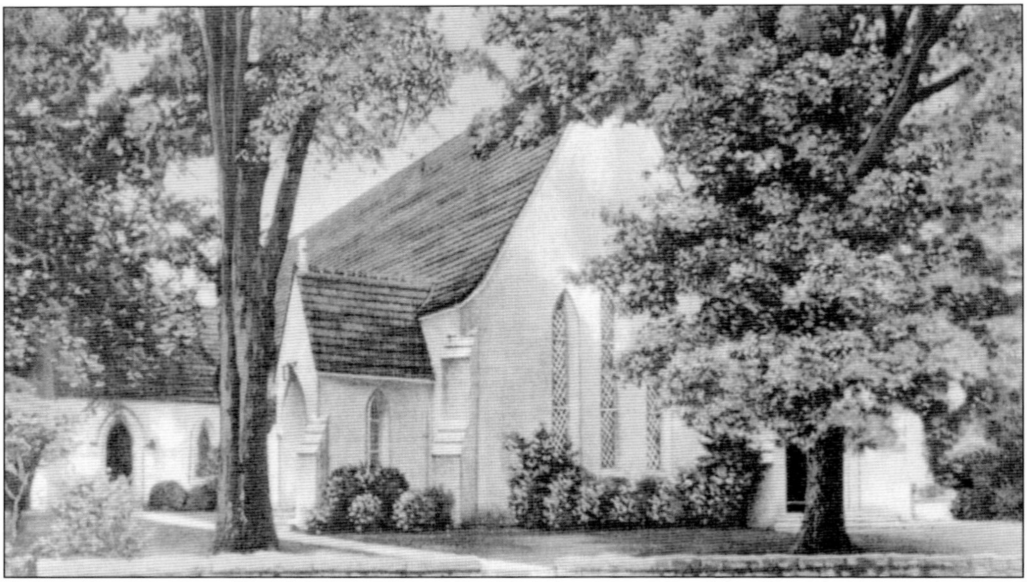

Church of the Resurrection. Believing that Greenwood would be an excellent location for their church, an Episcopal convention was held in February 1892. Plans were made to purchase a lot on Court Street, and until their church was built in 1896, the congregation met at the Methodist church. The chapel was consecrated, and services began, on April 26, 1896. The church moved to its current location in 1934. Pictured below is a postcard showing the original church. The photograph above shows the church in its current location.

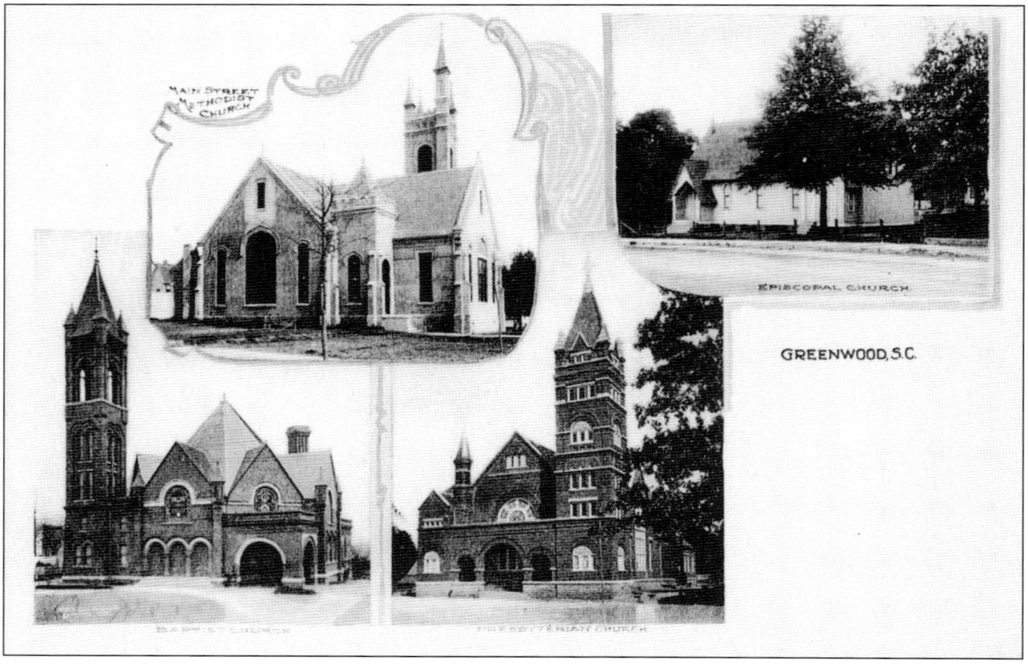

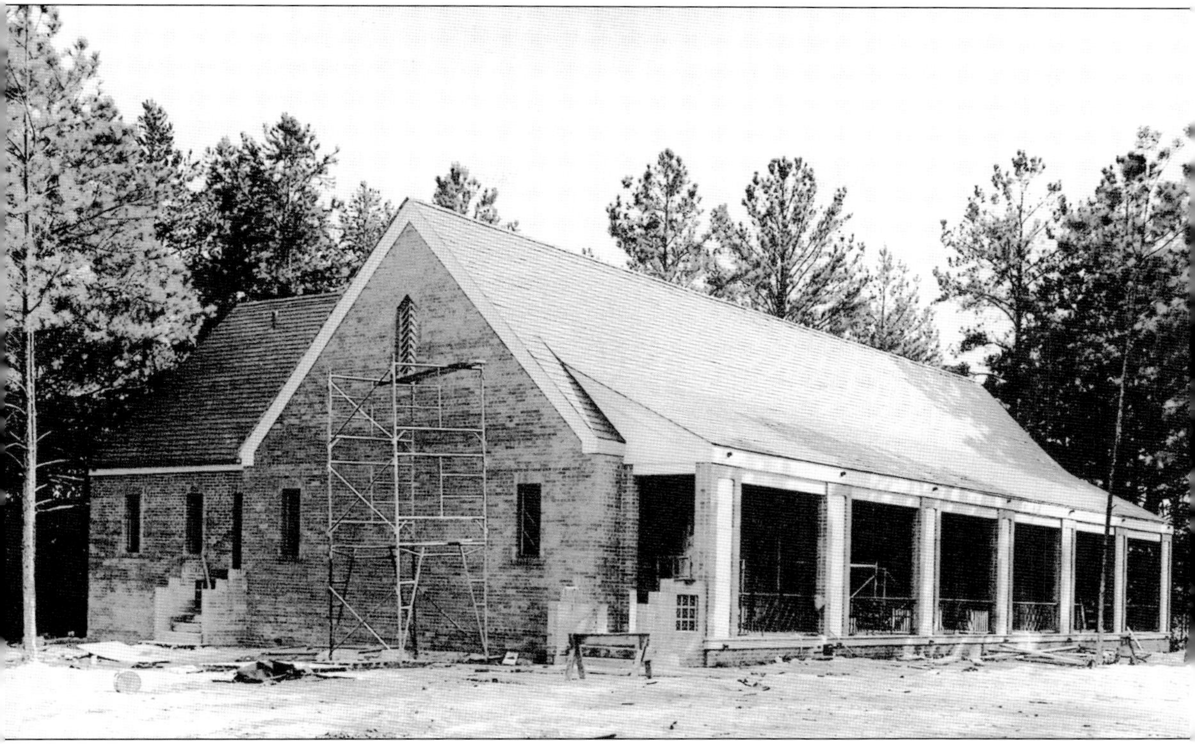

Our Lady of Lourdes Catholic Church. In 1913, Catholic Mass became available to the growing Greenwood population at the home of Mr. and Mrs. W.H. Turner. Traveling priests served the community in a Quonset-style hut, given by the Knights of Columbus in 1920 and dedicated as Our Lady of Perpetual Help. It was not until 1926, when a new building was dedicated, that the church changed its name. (Courtesy of Our Lady of Lourdes Catholic Church.)

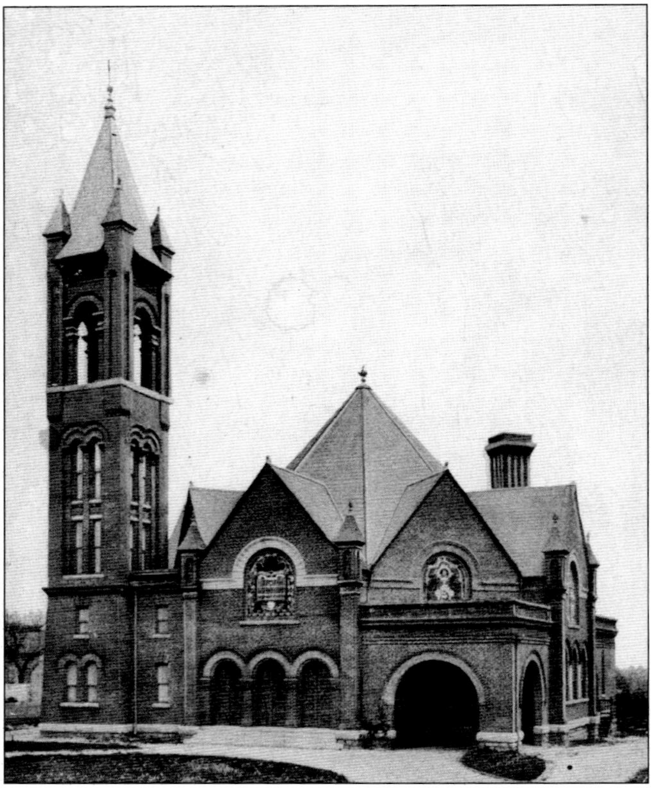

Greenwood Baptist Church. On September 20, 1870, the first Baptist Church was established in Greenwood with 23 founding members. A wooden structure referred to as Waller Hall, located on the East side of Waller Avenue, was the site of the first services. The church moved to a new building on East Cambridge Street in 1872. In November 1897, the church members dedicated a new building, the Greenwood Baptist Church, located on Main Street.

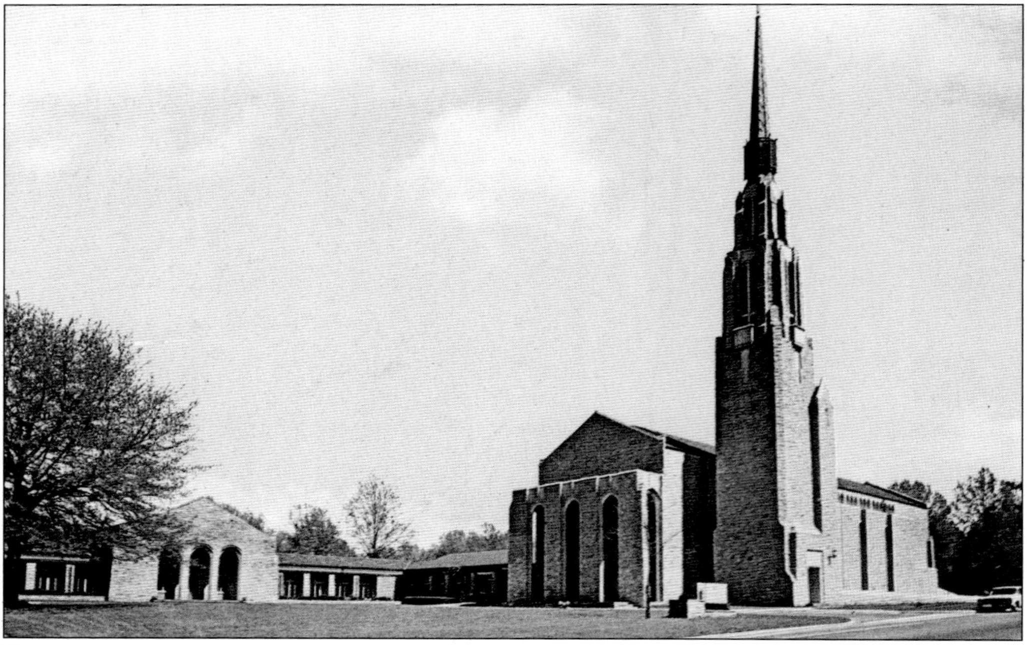

First Baptist Church. On August 5, 1956, Greenwood Baptist Church on Main Street relocated to a stone structure on Grace Street. The church became known as First Baptist Church. Church members considered themselves mission minded and have offered equality to women and men since establishment in 1870.

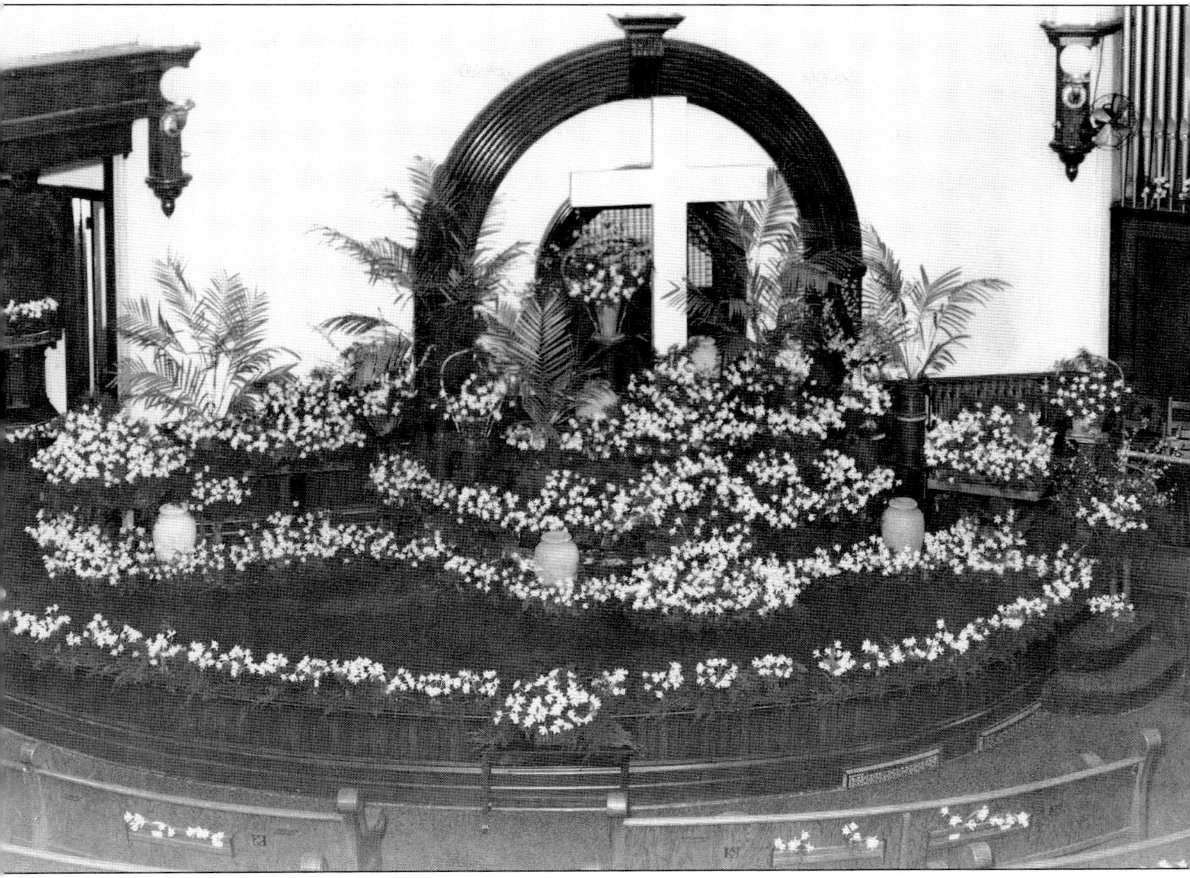

DAFFODIL DAY. At First Baptist Church's Daffodil Day in 1941, over 40,000 daffodils surrounded the altar of this historic church. The beautiful flowers were later given to the elderly and the shut-ins of the community. (Courtesy of the Greenwood County Library System.)

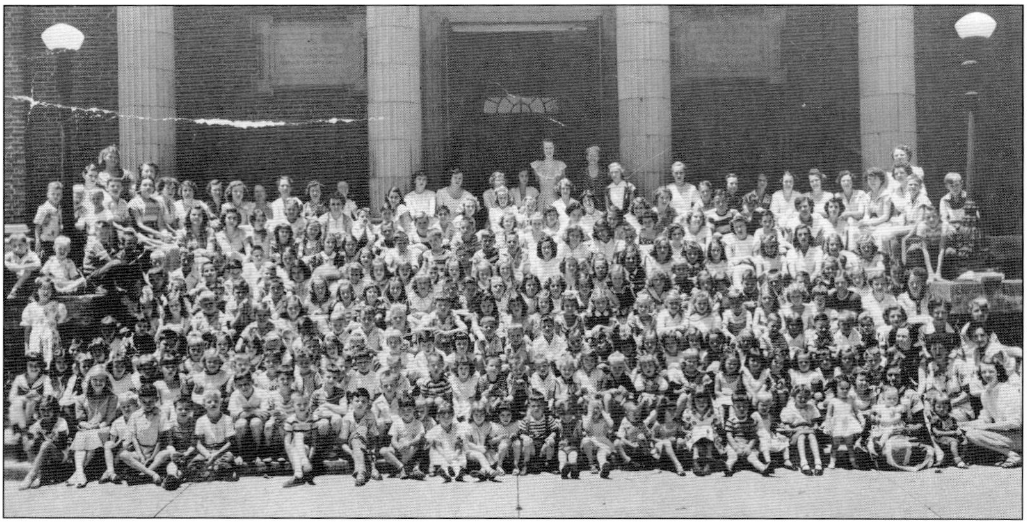

South Main Street Baptist Church. In 1910, a group of Greenwood Baptist Church members decided to establish a place of worship south of the city center. They met at Magnolia School and the Greenwood County Courthouse before moving into their new church building on June 2, 1912. Pictured is the vacation Bible school classes of 1951. (Both, courtesy of South Main Street Baptist Church.)

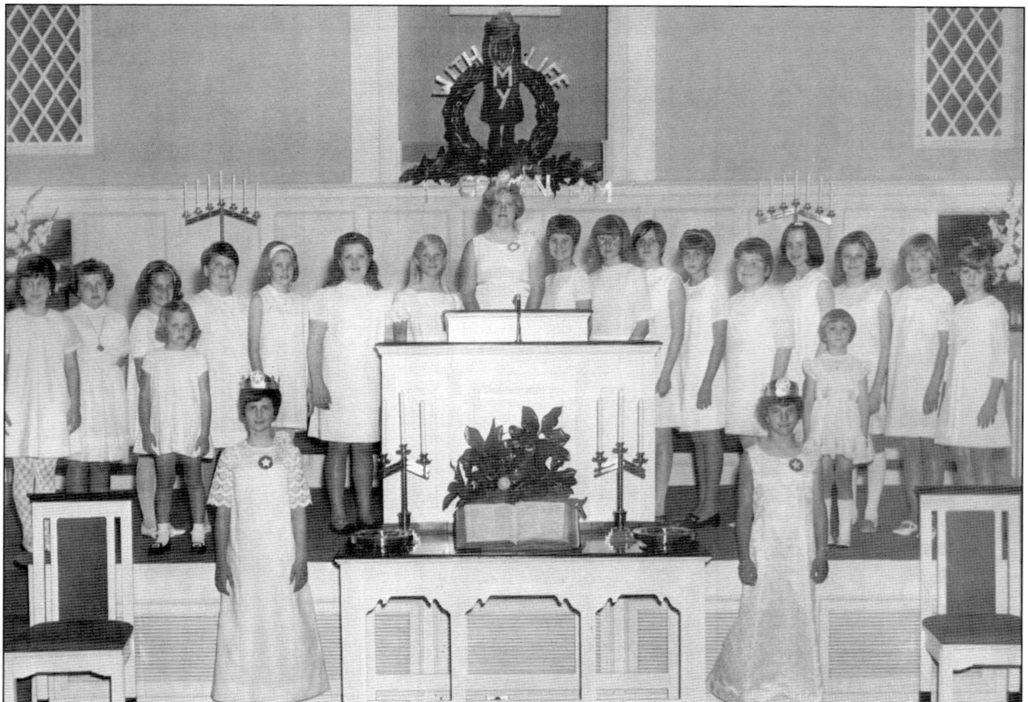

Eight

Education

When looking back at this region of the state, one can trace a heritage of education that extends well beyond Greenwood. Schools and colleges were established all over the upstate, including in cities such as Anderson, Greenville, Clemson, and Spartanburg, to educate young people regardless of race or gender. Greenwood was one of many cities to contribute to this educational revolution, establishing a school for African Americans (Brewer Normal School) and a college for young women (Lander College) very early in its history. Both institutions were quite radical for this time, as were instructors such as Samuel Lander, who believed that the education of young women should go further than mere finishing school lessons. Indeed, Greenwood should be proud of this legacy. As a community, Greenwood placed a high value on the minds of its young people, taking steps to ensure they had the very best and most modern school buildings and technologies.

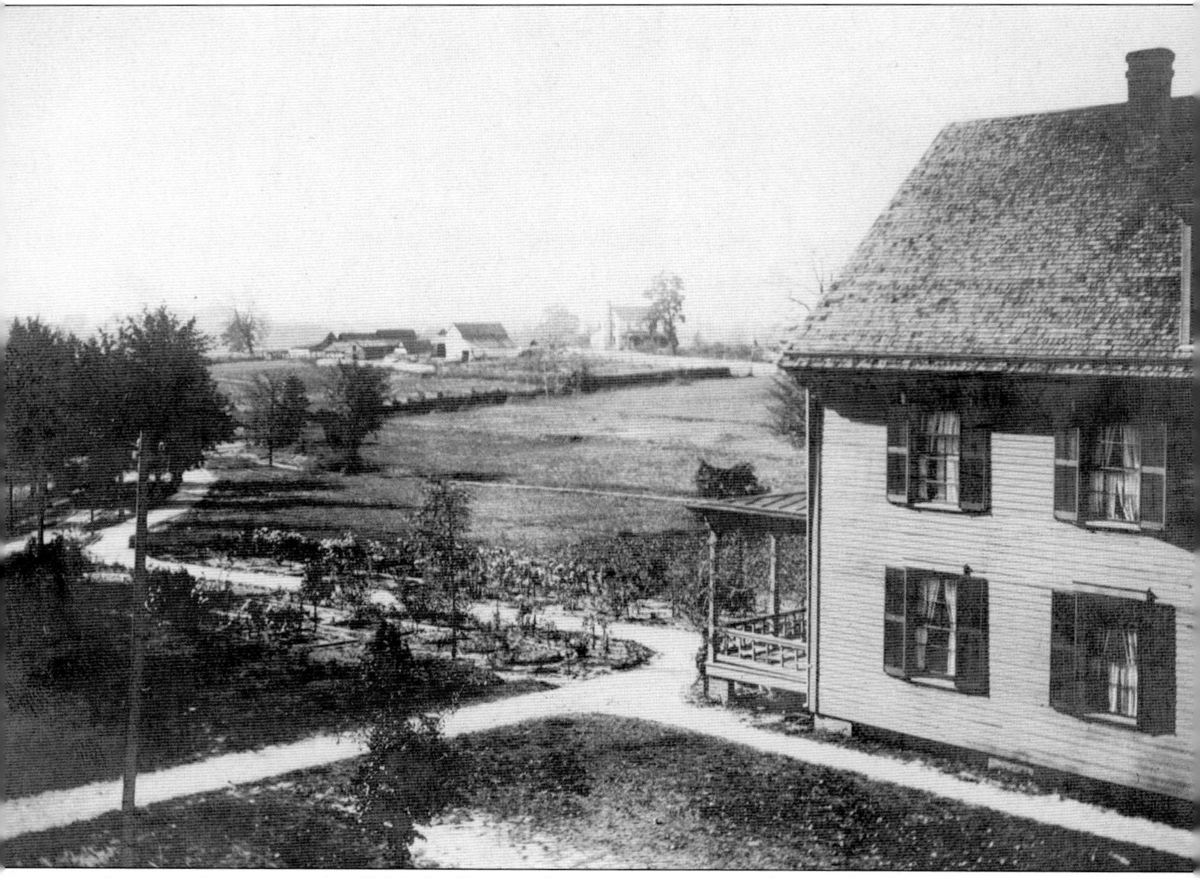

HODGES INSTITUTE. In 1847, the Baptist denomination opened two schools in Greenwood. The Hodges Institute, named for Rev. Nicholas Ware Hodges, was the school for boys. This institution ran for less than 20 years. The property was ultimately sold to the Congregational Church and was later used as the site for Brewer Normal School. Also, in 1941, the school housed Greenwood's African American library.

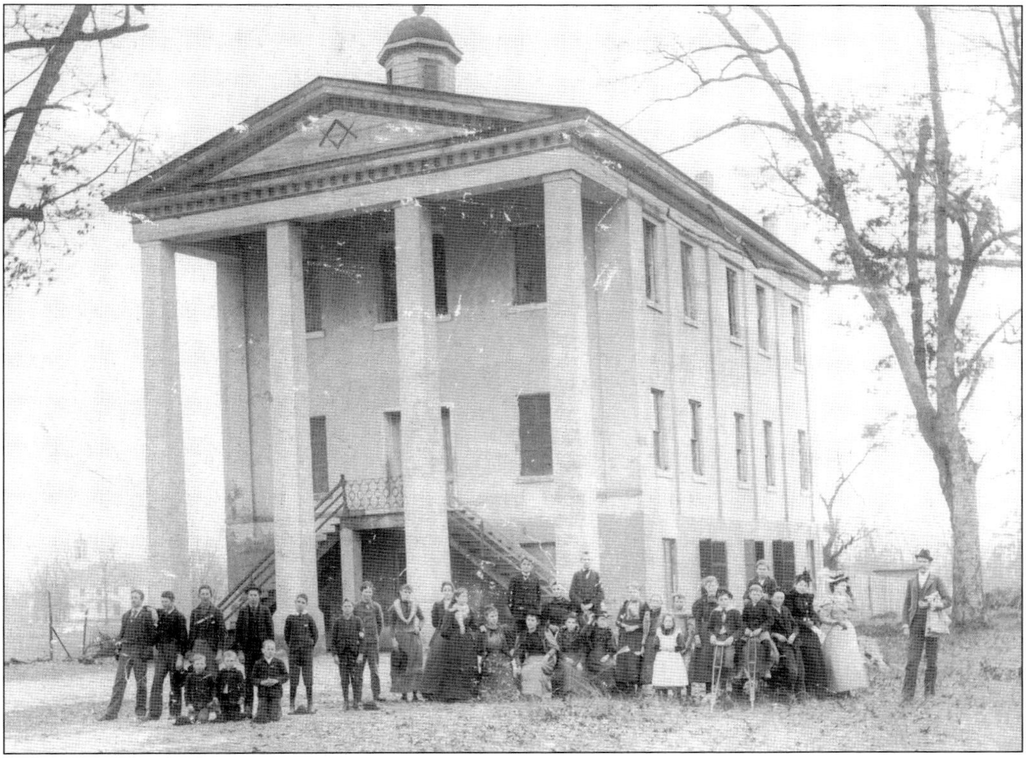

Cokesbury College. Located in the Cokesbury community of Greenwood County, which was named after two Methodist ministers, Cokesbury College was built in 1854 as the Masonic Female College of South Carolina. This school operated under the control of Bascomb Lodge No. 80 until 1878. From this point until 1954, this facility served as the Cokesbury Conference School, a boys' school, co-educational school, and finally, a public school facility. Above is the college at the turn of the 20th century. At right is Cokesbury's one-room schoolhouse during the same era.

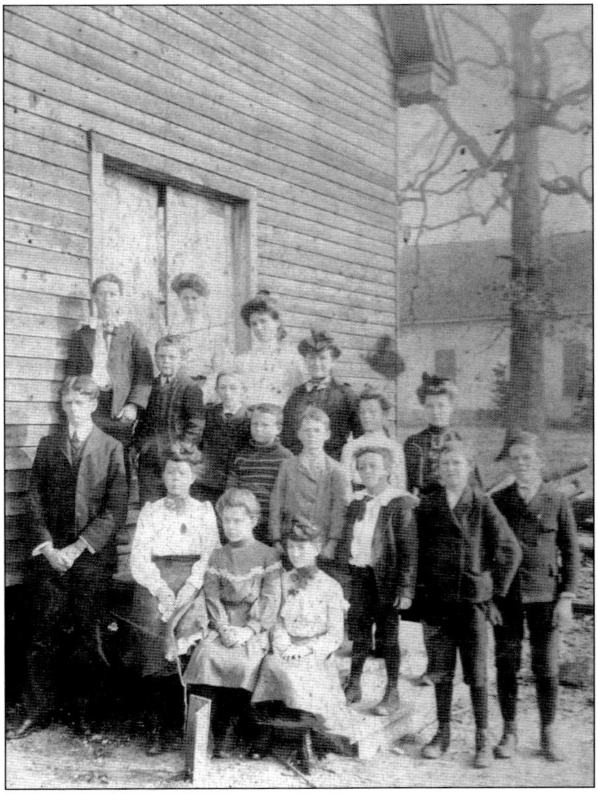

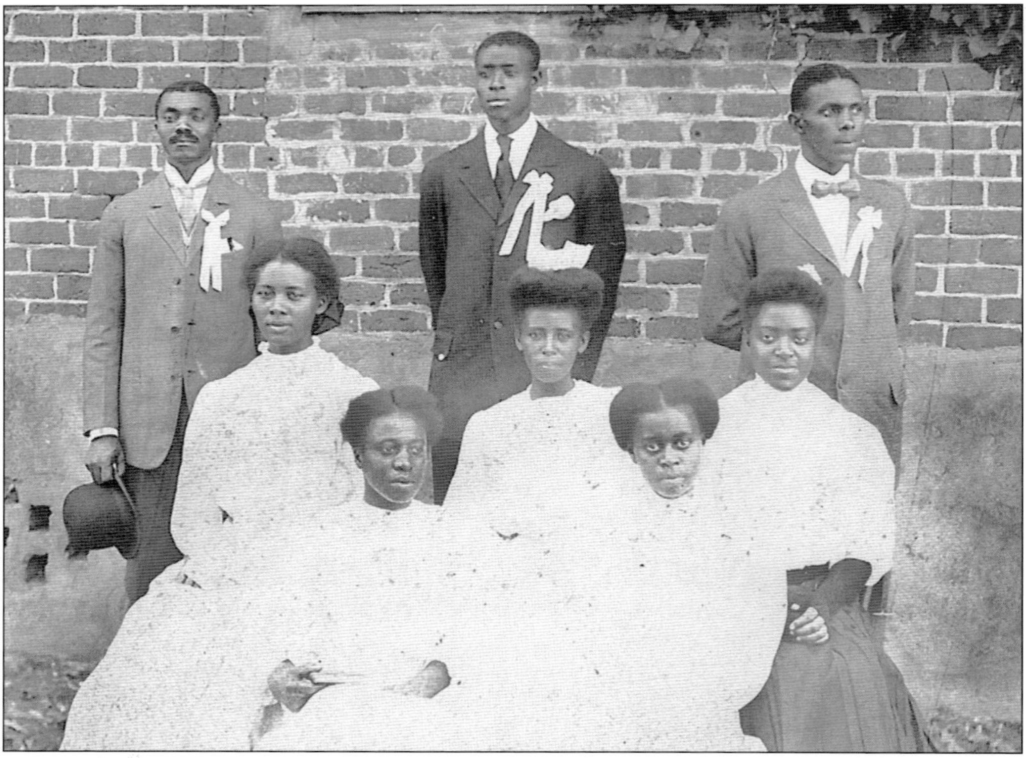

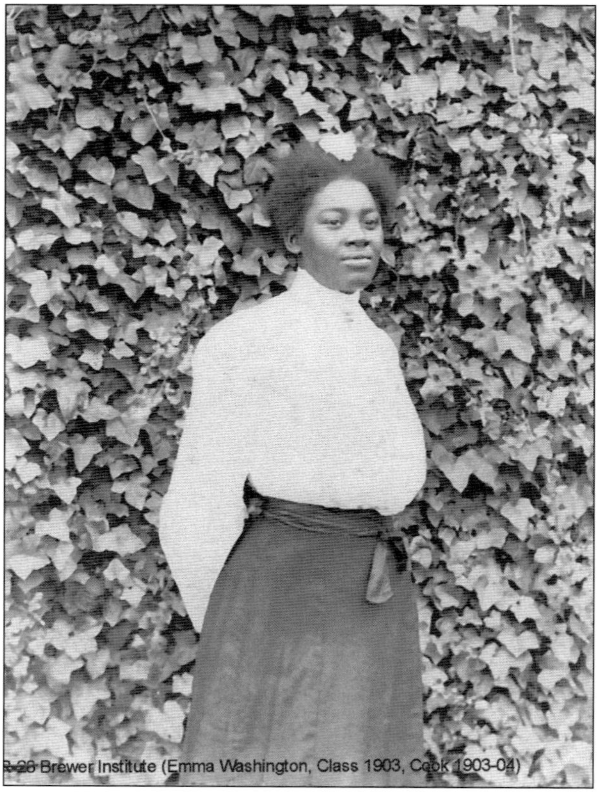

The Brewer Institute. Named after Rev. Josiah Brewer, a missionary, the Brewer Institute was the first school for African American children in Greenwood. Established in 1872, the school's name was soon changed to Brewer Normal School, and by 1897, the school had 7 teachers and 280 students, 78 of whom lived on campus. The class of 1908 is pictured above, and at left is Emma Washington after she graduated in 1903.

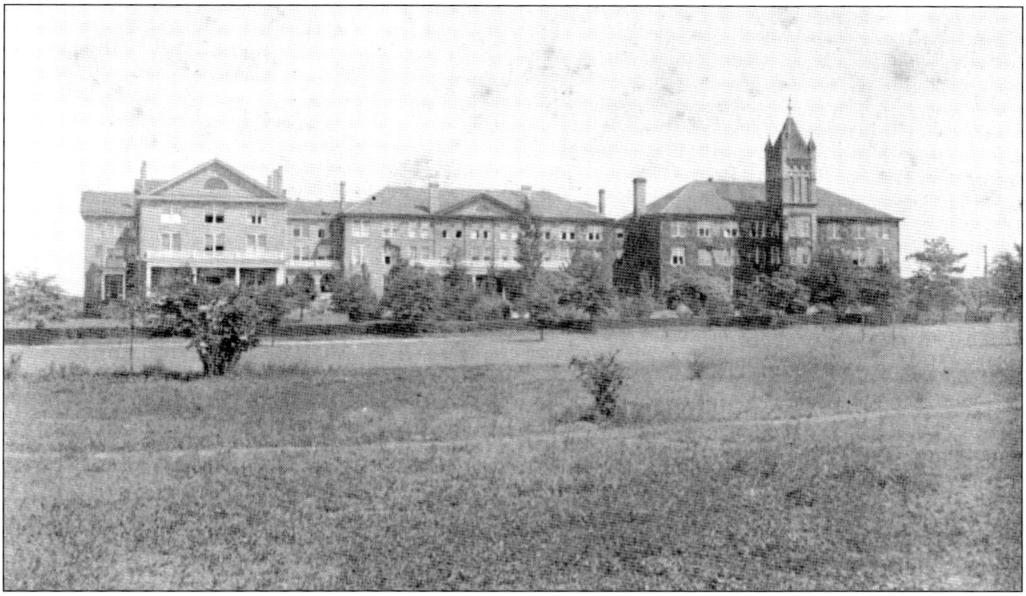

Lander College. Lander College was originally located in Williamston, South Carolina, and was called Williamston Female College. Established by Methodist minister Samuel Lander in 1872, Williamston's size would not allow for the continued growth of the school, so Lander negotiated a fair price with Greenwood officials and began building. The school was named in his honor, but he was never able to see the project completed. Lander died on July 14, 1904, right before the school opened to students. This photograph was taken in 1915.

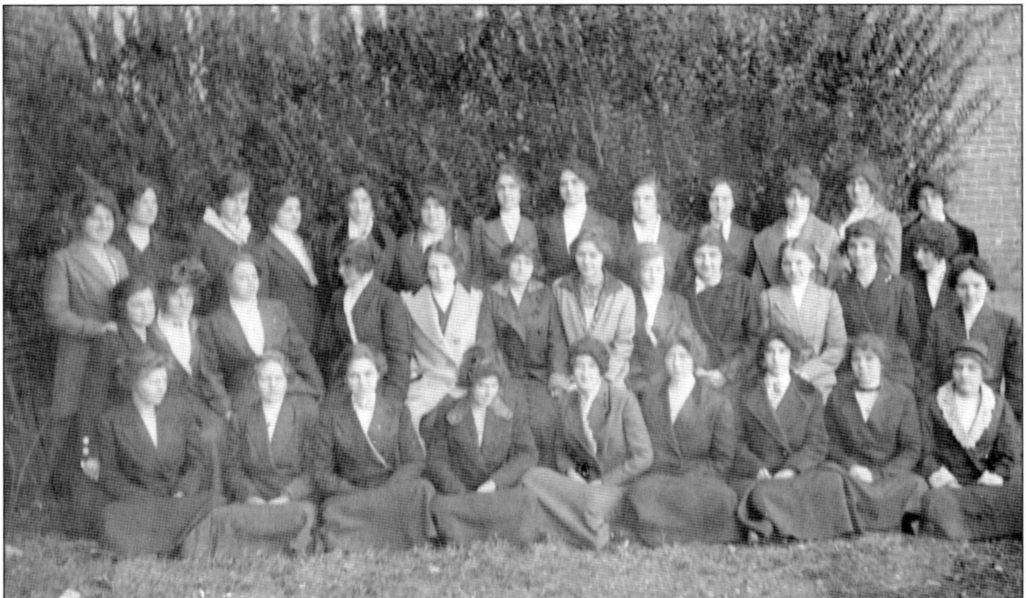

Lander College, Class of 1914. Samuel Lander was very progressive in his opinions about the education of young women. When describing Lander, Dr. Henry Snyder, the president of Wofford College, said: "superficial show, shallow shams, bedizened and bedecked pretense . . . [these] have been too often the glaring characteristics of what the so-called female college stands for. If his gentle nature hated anything, it was these things—[the] sham and show of educational pretence."

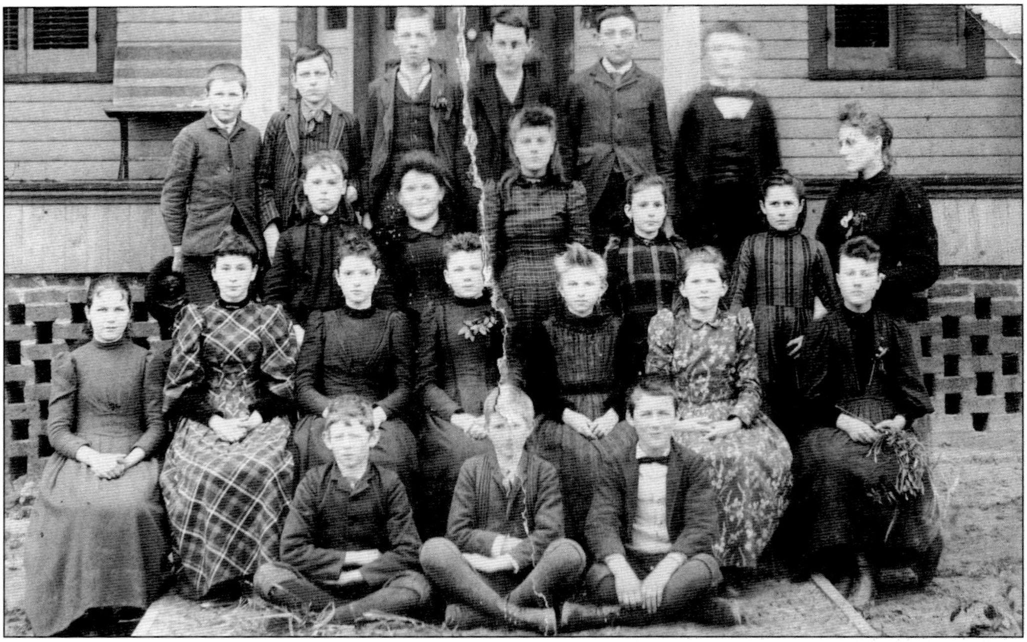

Greenwood Graded School. In the late 1800s, Greenwood contained two schools, Greenwood Male High School and Greenwood Female College. In 1891, these two institutions merged to form the first public graded school in Greenwood, called Greenwood Graded School. Pictured above is the 1891–1892 sixth-grade class. Shown below is the graduating class of 1901. (Courtesy of the Greenwood County Library System.)

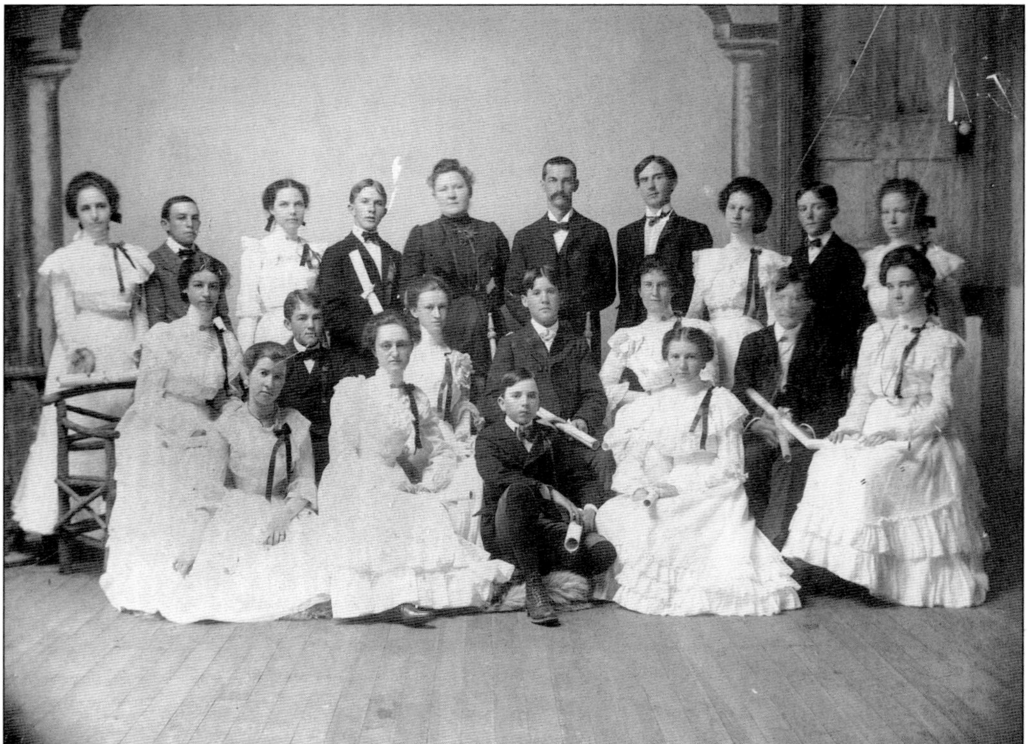

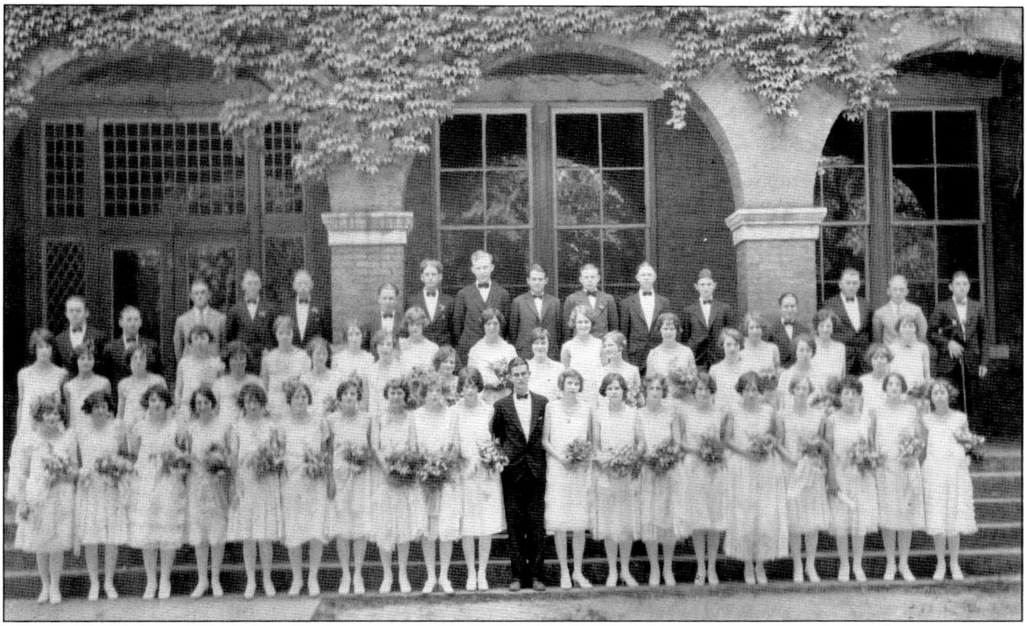

Magnolia Street School. When Greenwood's first graded public school burned down in 1903, famed Chattanooga designer R.H. Hunt was hired to design the new school. Greenwood's students had enjoyed opportunities that were not always afforded to those learning in a one-room schoolhouse setting; therefore, the town wasted no time in building the new school. Magnolia School was built in 1904 and welcomed 11 teachers and 492 students in grades one through nine. By 1914, the 10th and 11th grades had been added. Shown above is a graduating class from the 1920s. Pictured below is Miss Leslie's fourth-grade class in the 1950s.

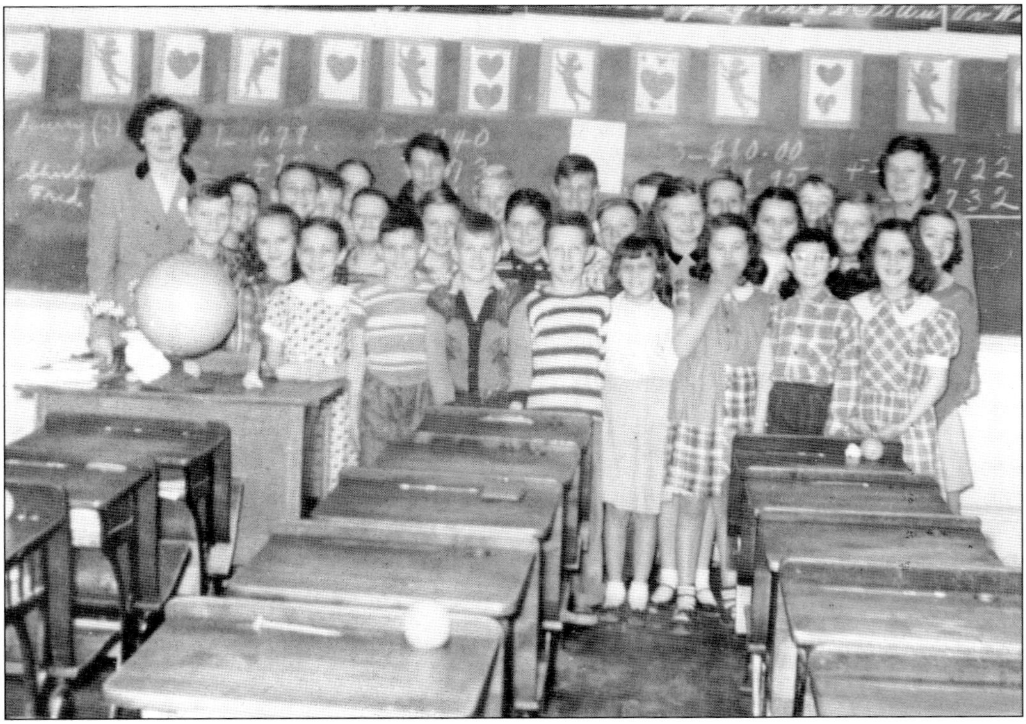

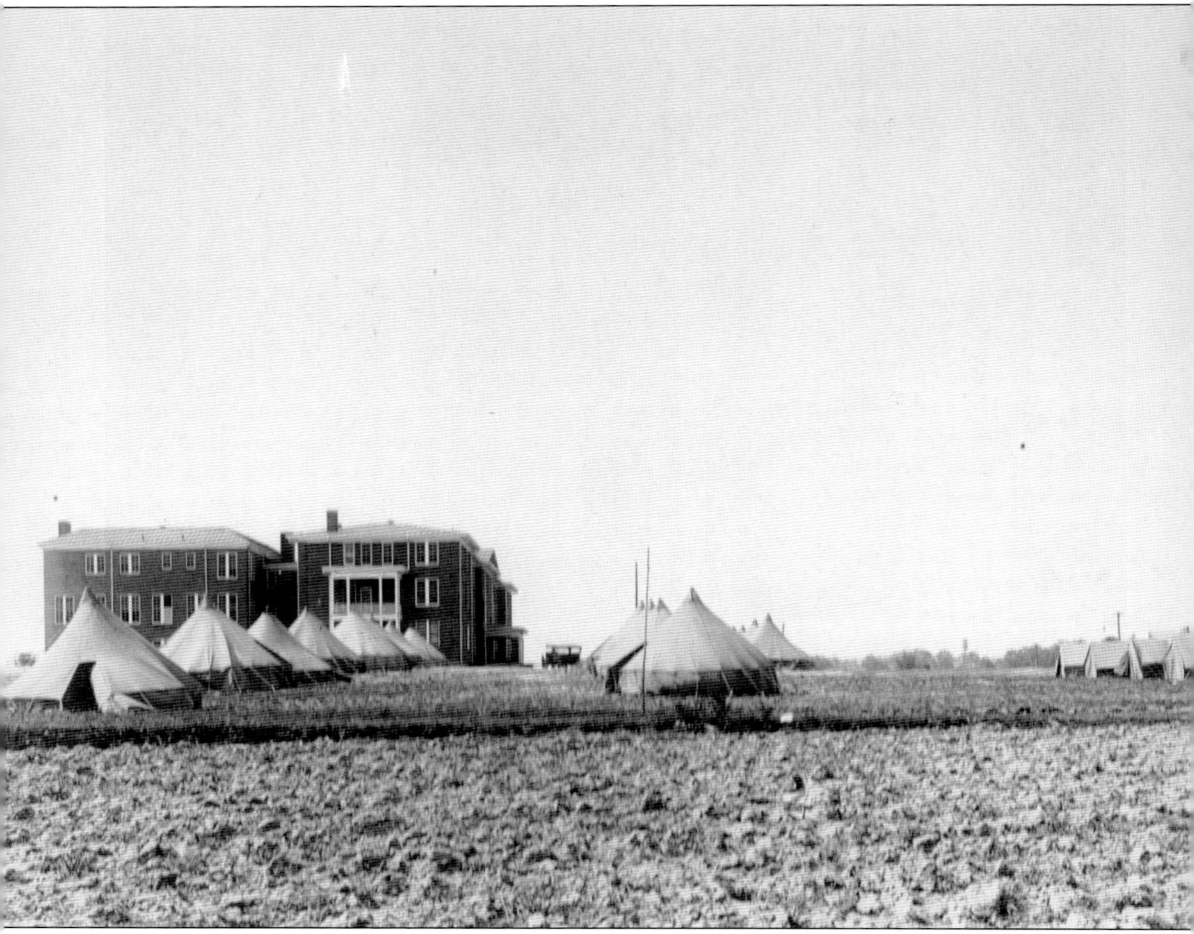

Bailey Military Institute. This preparatory school for boys ran from 1913 through 1936. Established by Franklin Newton Kierulf Bailey, this school used a military setup in order to instill discipline in the young men of Greenwood. While all staff members were given rankings, including Colonel Bailey, many of them had never served in the military. This photograph was taken in 1913. (Courtesy of the Greenwood County Library System.)

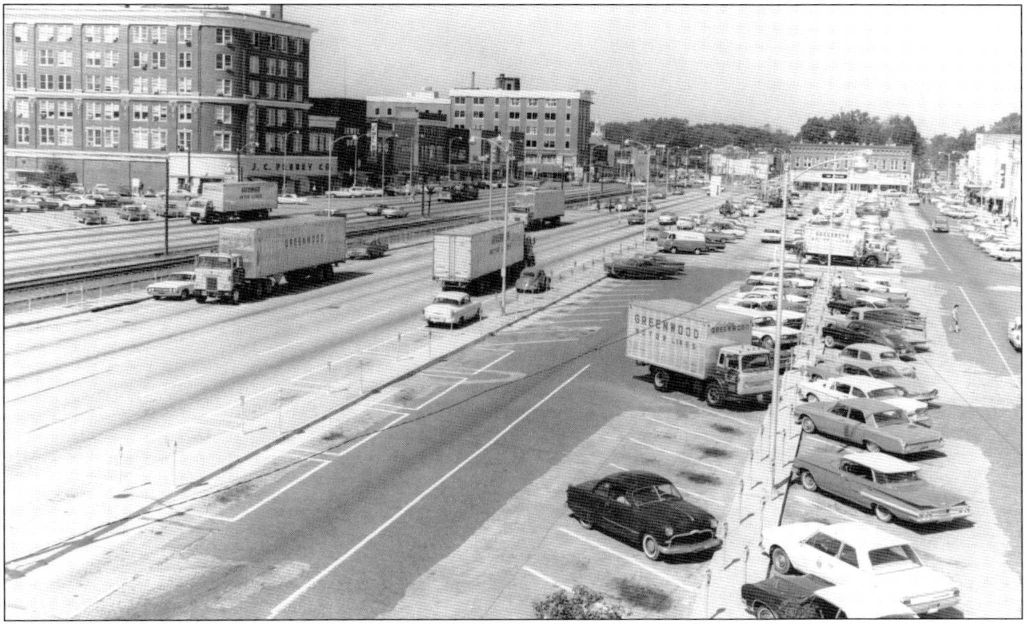

Greenwood College of Commerce. Originally named Peterson Business College when it opened in the Textile Building (at left) in 1917, this school produced more than 2,000 alumni before it closed its doors in 1969. Graduates from this excellent program opened their own businesses, worked for local organizations, and even filled government positions during World War II.

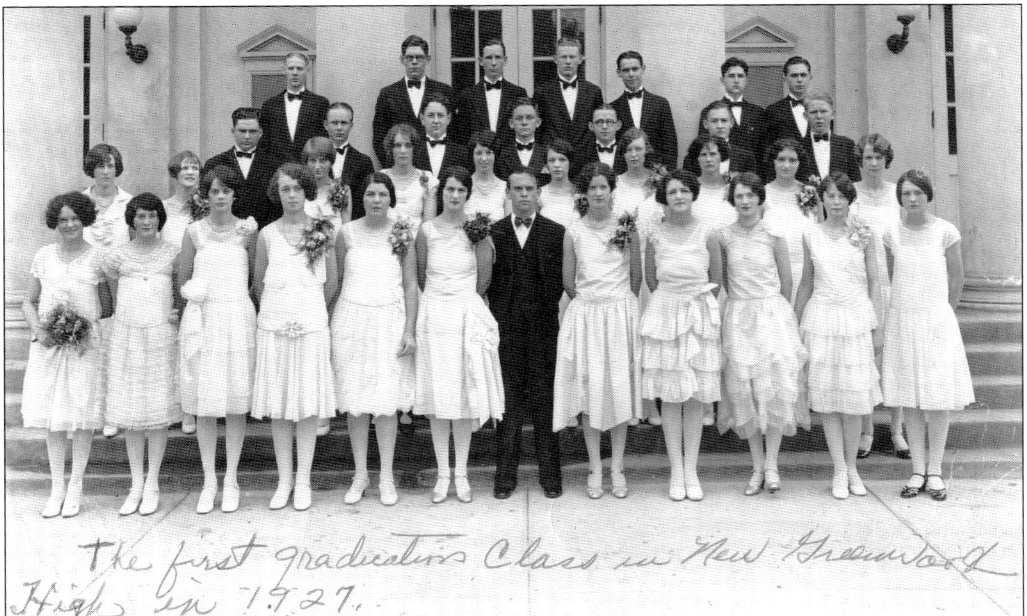

Greenwood High School. Due to overcrowding, Greenwood officials began to work toward the construction of a new, modern high school. When the new school was formally dedicated on January 21, 1927, it contained 27 new classrooms, laboratories, domestic science rooms, and all the latest technologies. This original building was used until 1969. It was sold in 1984 and converted into apartments. Pictured here is the first graduating class of Greenwood High School, the class of 1927.

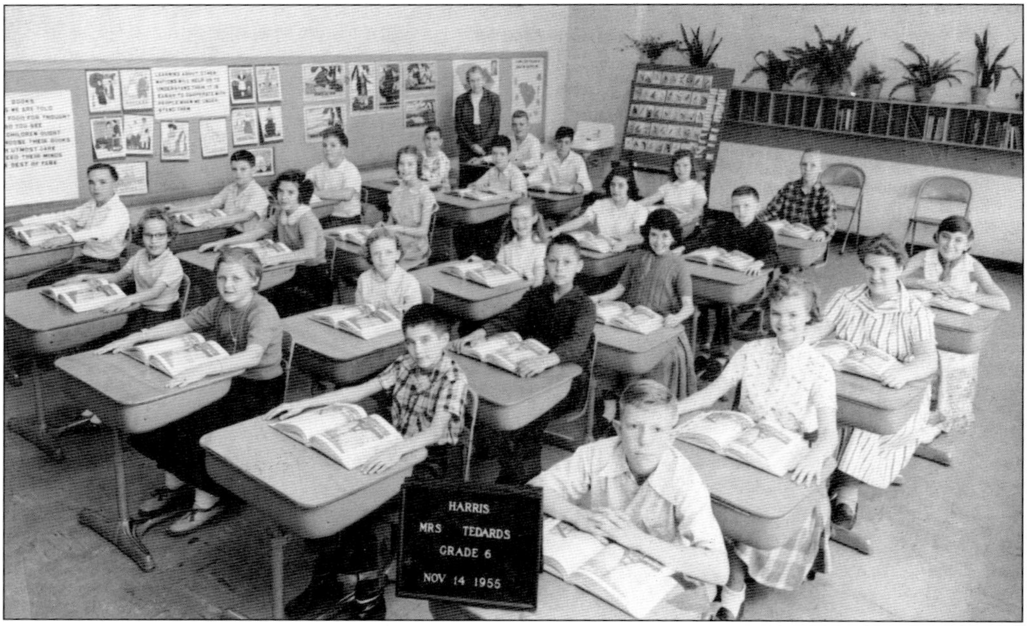

Harris School. This institution is one of numerous examples of schools created by the local textile mills. Greenwood Mills created the school in 1950 in order to serve the children of Harris Plant; students began attending regular Greenwood County schools in 1964. The legacy of Harris School lives on today, as it became the site of Cambridge Academy. Pictured is the sixth-grade class on November 14, 1955.

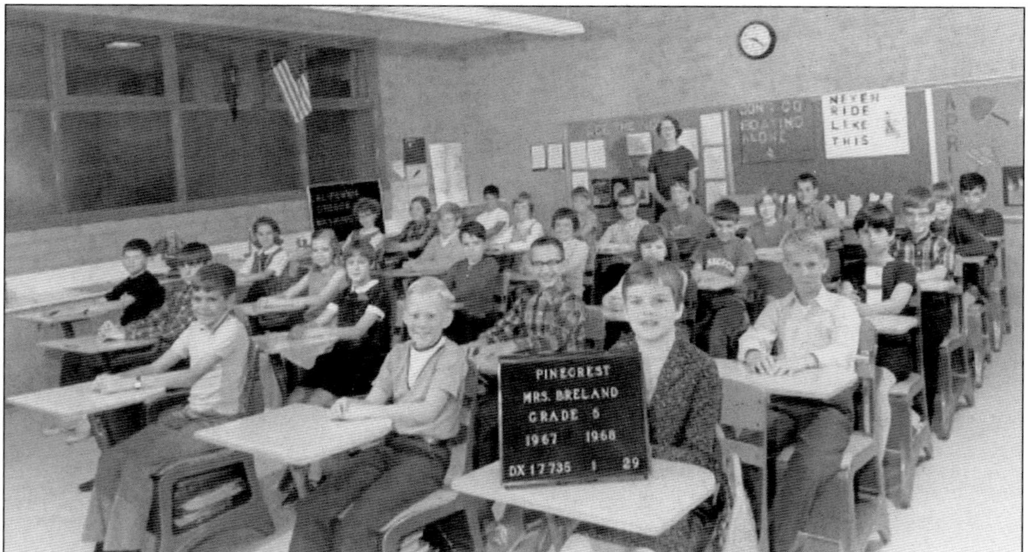

Greenwood County School Districts. Originally, there were 48 different school districts in Greenwood County alone. Most schools were one-room schoolhouses and only had one to two teachers to serve the student population. However, in 1952, two official educational districts were created: District No. 50, which included Greenwood and Ninety-Six, and District No. 51, which contained the schools in Ware Shoals. Three years later, District No. 50 was split, and Ninety-Six schools were placed in District No. 52. The 1967 fifth-grade class of Pinecrest School, which is now a part of District No. 50, is seen here.

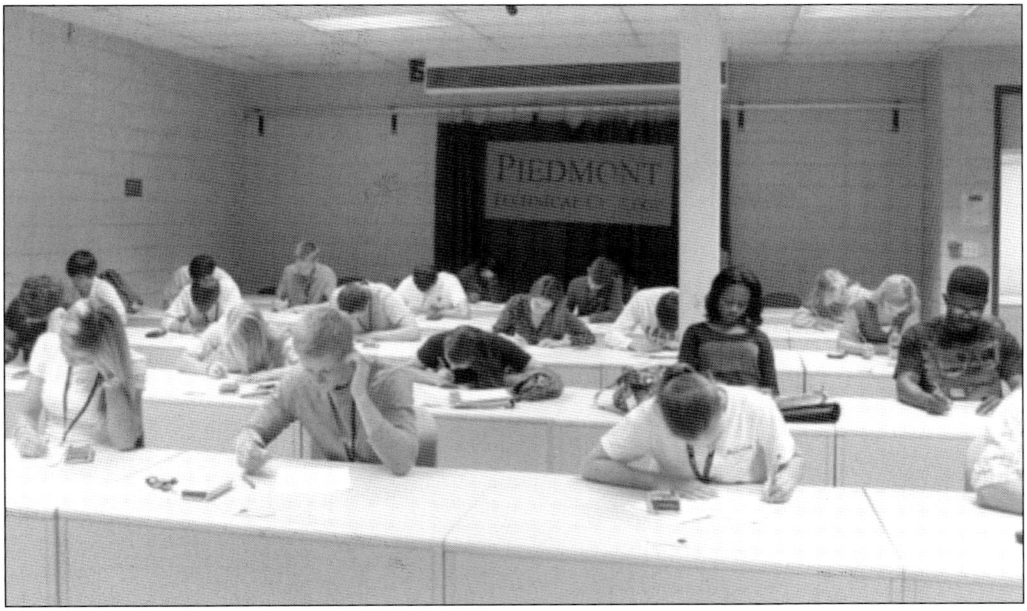

PIEDMONT TECHNICAL COLLEGE. In 1961, the South Carolina General Assembly passed mandates that created a system of technical education centers in the state. The Piedmont Technical Education Center opened in 1966, and its name was shortened to Piedmont Technical College in 1974. Technical schools in the state sought to create a better-informed workforce that could meet the changing demands of industry.

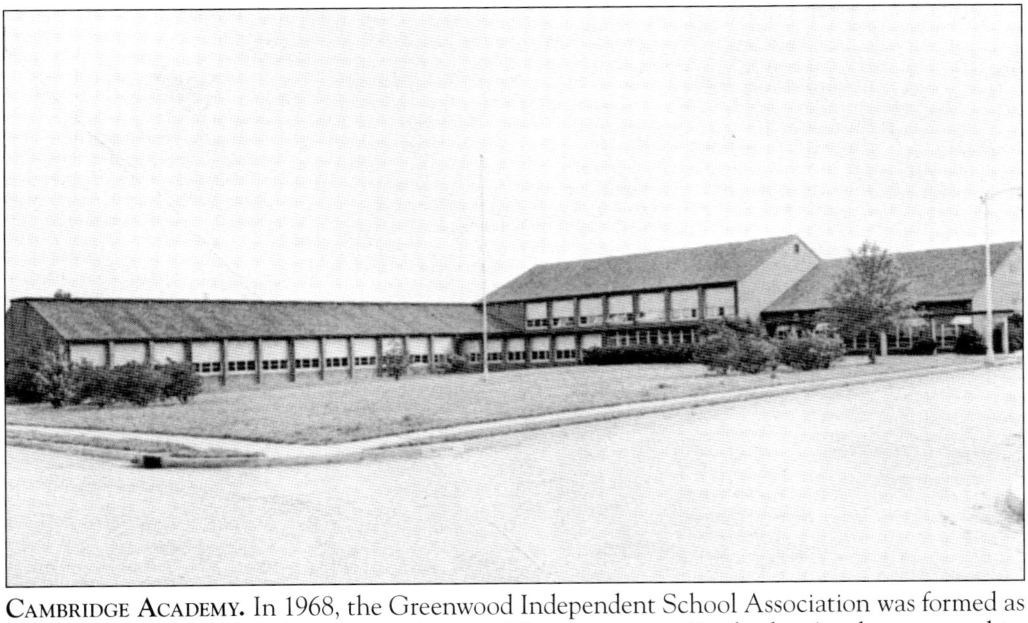

CAMBRIDGE ACADEMY. In 1968, the Greenwood Independent School Association was formed as an alternative to public education in the area. This same year, Cambridge Academy opened its doors to 72 students in first through sixth grades. Cambridge Academy is still the only private school in Greenwood not associated with another institution.

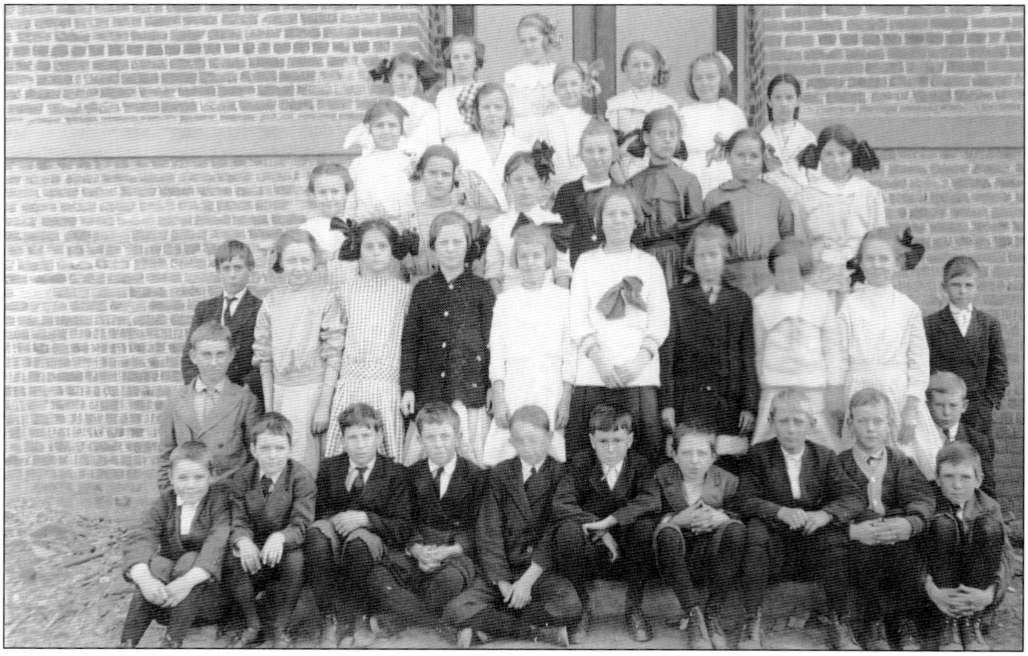

Learning in Greenwood. There are not enough pages to write about all the schools that have served Greenwood County students before 1980. These schools include but are not limited to the following: College of Cambridge (1785), Woodville Academy (1858), Phoenix High School (1897), Leslie School (1913), Blake School (1916), Matthews (1951), Northside Junior High School (1956), West Hodges Elementary (1957), Southside Junior High School (1958), Woodfields (1958), Merrywood (1961), and Ninety-Six Elementary and High School (1955). Pictured above is Leslie School's 1912–1913 fifth-grade class; seen below is a celebratory conga line at a Greenwood school in the 1950s.

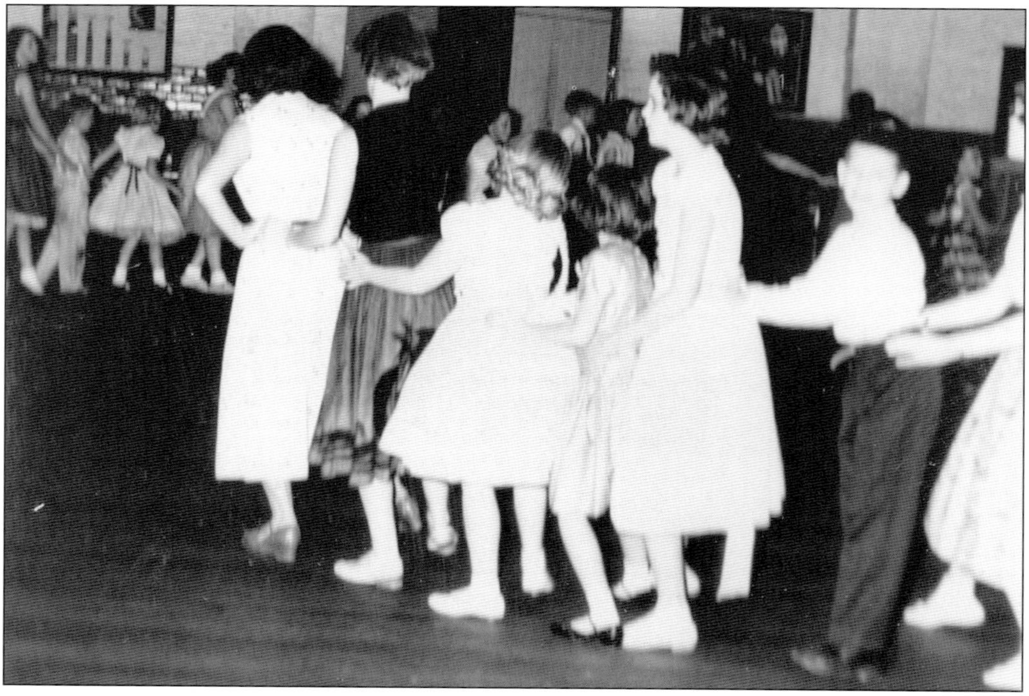

About the Organization

The Museum and Railroad Historical Center
Saving, Sharing, and Celebrating Greenwood's History
Since 1970

The Museum and Railroad Historical Center
The Museum—106 Main Street
The Railroad Historical Center—908 South Main Street
PO Box 3131
Greenwood, SC 29648
864-229-7093
www.greenwoodmuseum.org
www.greenwoodhistoryproject.org

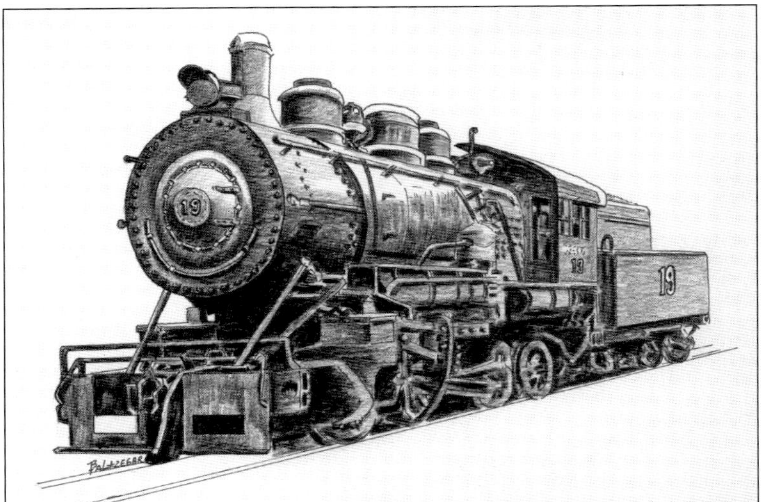

(Courtesy of Mack Baltzegar.)